NAMING THE BIRDS AT A GLANCE

A Guide to the Eastern Land Birds
from South Carolina west to the
Rocky Mountains and north to the Arctic

BY *Lou Blachly & Randolph Jenks*

GUIDE DRAWINGS BY *Sheridan Oman*

BONANZA BOOKS
New York

Based on *Land Birds of the Northeast* by the same authors, first published in an entirely different format.

Copyright © MCMLIX, MCMLXIII by Lou Blachly and Randolph Jenks

This 1989 edition is published by Bonanza Books, distributed by Crown Publishers, Inc., 225 Park Avenue South, New York, New York 10003, by arrangement with Alfred A. Knopf, Inc.

Printed and Bound in the United States of America

Library of Congress Cataloging-in-Publication Data

Blachly, Lou.
    Naming the birds at a glance : a guide to the eastern land birds from South Carolina west to the Rocky Mountains and north to the Arctic / by Lou Blachly & Randolph Jenks : guide drawings by Sheridan Oman.
        p.   cm.
    Reprint. Originally published : New York : Knopf, 1974, c1963.
    Includes index.
    ISBN 0-517-67954-X
    1. Birds—United States—Identification.   2. Birds—Canada—Identification.   I. Jenks, Randolph.   II. Title.
QL681.B63   1989   88-37318
598.297—dc19   CIP
h g f e d c b a

Acknowledgments

ALTHOUGH this guide is the result of four decades of bird study, it would have been impossible to assemble it without reference to most of the published books on ornithology, notably Roger Tory Peterson's and Richard Pough's authoritative bird guides. The analysis of bird songs has been aided by reference to Aretas Saunders's *A Guide to Bird Songs* and with the assistance of Geoffrey Carlton.

Indispensable help has been received from Dean Amadon, Eugene Eisenmann, Charles O'Neill, and Helen Hays, of the American Museum of Natural History; Allen H. Morgan, Director, and Mrs. Ruth Emery, of the Massachusetts Audubon Society; Dr. Joe T. Marshall, of the University of Arizona; J. T. Carithers, of the Department of the Interior, Washington, D.C.; J. C. Greenway and Dr. R. A. Paynter, of Harvard; Lewis Wayne Walker and William Woodin, of the Arizona-Sonora Desert Museum; and John Terres, until recently editor of the *Audubon Magazine;* Florence Thornburg; and David Stejskol.

All descriptions were written and drawings made from skins supplied to the authors and artist by the American Museum of Natural History and the Smithsonian Institution. To the Ornithology Departments of these great institutions we are profoundly grateful.

Last, we must mention Angus Cameron, editor for our publisher, whose knowledge of the subject, patience, and fortitude passeth understanding.

LOU BLACHLY
RANDOLPH JENKS

Introduction

WHAT is the justification for a new kind of bird guide? Perhaps the following will answer this question.

In the spring of 1958 the senior author, while on an Audubon bird hike near Tucson, Arizona, was confronted with an indignant comment by Annette Richards Parent, western author: "I wish to heaven someone would write a bird guide so I wouldn't have to thumb through two hundred pages to find a bird."

Shortly thereafter the senior author, then studying the bird life at the Southwest Research Station of the American Museum of Natural History, did write a bird guide for the Southwest on a wholly new principle. It was typed and circulated by the National Parks Service. It worked!

Later, in San Diego, he wrote a similar guide for land birds of the Pacific Coast. Then, since he had done his basic work in ornithology at the University of Wisconsin and had spent much of his life in the East studying birds, he wrote and copyrighted a guide for land birds of the Northeast.

Not long after, he became associated with Randolph Jenks, who had done advanced work in ornithology at Princeton and the University of California and who possesses one of the largest private collections of bird literature in the country. Together, with artist Sheridan Oman, they published privately a pocket guide to land birds of the Northeast. This guide had a wide favorable response throughout the East.

The present guide is an outgrowth of that book and three seasons of extensive field use throughout the Northeast by a great number of observers.

Of course, a bird guide is possible only because of the labors of generations of scientists who have worked out— generally, in the last analysis, from detailed laboratory study—a scientific classification and nomenclature for birds. However, this very scientific classification, which is based to a great extent upon the birds' anatomy and skeletal structure—the birds' *insides*—appeared to be the greatest stumbling block to bird identification in the field, where only the *outsides* are visible. Therefore, in this guide a wholly new principle for grouping has been adopted.

Because of this, it is our hope, and belief, that bird enthusiasts will consider this guide "something new under the sun." The users of the booklet edition (*Land Birds of the Northeast*, 1959) seemed to think so. Indeed the authors are indebted to those who experimented with our first effort to present this new system of bird identification, for they gave us much useful advice for improving the method; and their enthusiasm was an inspiration which encouraged us to seek this more permanent and useful form. Briefly, *Birds at a Glance* teaches you how to observe the obvious and then how to use that first, often fleeting observation to lead you to an identification of a new bird.

Most people are not able to classify a bird—that is, as a Finch, Sparrow, Warbler, etc.—when they catch that first look at an unfamiliar specimen. Rather they see a "small brownish bird" or a "mostly blue bird" whose *other* distinguishing characteristics they have forgotten by the time they have thumbed through their field book. This book offers instantly an array of patterns and color characteristics, available at a flip of the finger to The Color Pattern Guide. Listed there, in easily usable form, are not technical classifications, but rather a key to the obvious markings ("black cap" or "white rump" or "yellow crown") which the user has seen but will not retain beyond that first moment. Handily organized under overall color categories, the user will find those *additional* markings which will refer him to the page of picture and description of that particular bird. These marking notations will guide the user to his bird *no matter which one of several characteristics he may have noticed first!* Although the system is, we believe, self-teaching, we have presented below (1) lessons in the use of the sight system and (2) further helpful hints. We hope it will lead a new generation of bird enthusiasts to a long Life List with a minimum of frustration.

Designating Relative Size

IN this guide the size of the birds is not indicated in inches or centimeters since most people do not success-fully visualize size this way. Rather we have placed three relative-size bars alongside the drawing of each bird. The top bar represents the relative length of the House Sparrow, the middle bar that of the American Robin, the bottom bar that of the American Crow—all common birds whose sizes are generally familiar. The vertical cross line represents the length of the bird in question in relationship to either the Sparrow, Robin, or Crow, as the size may dictate. Users of the earlier edition of this guide found that relative length indicated in this manner is quickly grasped by all bird watchers, inexperienced as well as experienced.

—— HOUSE SPARROW
———— AMERICAN ROBIN
—————— AMERICAN CROW

A Note on Field Glasses

FIELD GLASSES are well-nigh indispensable for identifying the smaller birds—such as the Warblers, Sparrows, and Vireos—and are a useful tool for identifying any bird. Fortunately, there are now a number of binoculars, of both domestic and foreign manufacture, which can be had at a reasonable price. Ideally, 7x50 binoculars should be used for bird identification; 8x40's, however, will do almost as well.

If possible, you should buy binoculars that have individual as well as dual adjustment. After a little practice focusing the binoculars on various objects, you will be able to adjust your binoculars at any distance in a fraction of a second. This kind of practice is invaluable, because quite often a bird will not give you much more than a second or two. After you have completely familiarized yourself with your glasses, practice first on birds that are both common and reasonably unwary. The trick, of course, is to focus on the area where your quarry generally sits—a particular crotch or special limb or leaf formation. It is often helpful to focus on a subject in the immediate vicinity of the bird before focusing on the bird itself. Get into the habit of checking your focus on a piece of bark or twig or leaves near the bird. This is the quickest and surest way to be sure your focus is exact.

When you see a bird fly into a tree and are not able to spot it immediately, focus on the tree itself. Then if the bird appears, you've got him without losing the split second needed to turn the adjustment screw.

Last, but not the least important advice, always carry your binoculars around your neck.

Parts of the Bird

THE terms used in the Color Pattern Guide (see endpapers), on the drawings, and in the descriptive sections for each bird are illustrated in the sketch below. The meaning of two additional terms—"upperparts" and "underparts"—is generally clear from the context. "Upperparts" generally includes only the bird's back, but sometimes the rump, nape, and head as well. Similarly, "underparts" may include belly, breast, and even throat. The entries of the Color Pattern Guide (the key) have subheadings which usually make the use of these two general terms clear in the context of each identification. Where they do not, the notations on the drawings and in the text will eliminate any confusion.

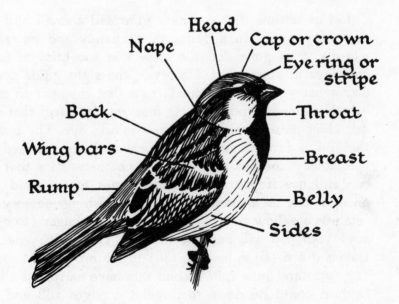

FIRST, let us make clear that the sight system has three chief advantages:

(1) It will lead to identification no matter which characteristic of a bird you may notice first.

(2) It will refer you to a picture of *your* bird (with text conveniently at hand) on the *same page* (or near it) as the other species with which you might confuse it, thus making identification by *elimination* a part of the system.

(3) The system thus ends for all time the always frustrating and often unsuccessful method of "thumbing through" after the bird has flown and as your mental picture rapidly escapes you.

One example will serve to demonstrate these advantages in practice.

A FIRST LESSON *"A yellow rump was all I saw."*

Let us assume that you have glimpsed a small bird in a new May wood. In a flash, unfortunately and characteristically, it is gone and the view was too brief to fix its markings in your mind. However, the sight guide system uses what you *have* retained from that moment to make identification still possible. At first you may feel that only one chief pattern remains in your mind's eye. The truth is that for a few moments you have actually retained unconsciously another two or three characteristics that you can still use if your field guide comes to your aid soon enough. Let us assume that the one flashing memory you retain is a yellow rump. With a flip of the finger (to either key) your eye will find the heading YELLOW; your eye travels down (from head to tail) to "Rump yellow," pages 188–191, and in a split second you have narrowed all the birds it could be down to three! On pages 188 and 190 are three excellent drawings (with descriptions on the facing pages). Those three drawings are reproduced here.

You may say at once: "Yellow-rumped Warbler!" and all is

settled. But if you have a doubt it will be only momentary, for you still invariably retain a bit more than you thought. You might think: "Or could it be a Magnolia...?" But right there before you is the Magnolia drawing, and you say: "No, mine had no tail bars." Just as likely you may exclaim: "No, mine had a yellow cap." It *was* a Yellow-rumped Warbler!

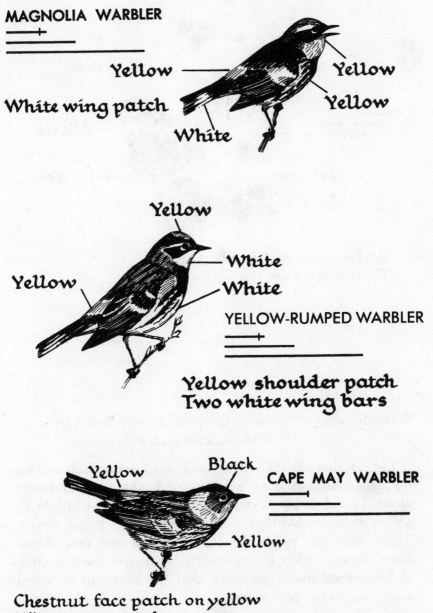

MAGNOLIA WARBLER

Yellow

Yellow

Yellow

White wing patch

White

Yellow

Yellow

White

White

YELLOW-RUMPED WARBLER

Yellow shoulder patch
Two white wing bars

Yellow

Black

CAPE MAY WARBLER

Yellow

Chestnut face patch on yellow
White wing patch

Let us assume, however, that you saw that same small bird and *did not* see the yellow rump; all you saw was a yellow cap. A flip to the key to YELLOW; a swift look at "Cap or face yellowish," pages 178–183. Seven birds to pick from. Six eliminate themselves! With drawing and text in front of you it is obviously:

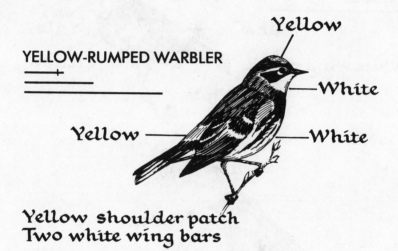

YELLOW-RUMPED WARBLER

Yellow

White

Yellow

White

Yellow shoulder patch
Two white wing bars

A THIRD LESSON   *"Bluish? Grayish? Maybe, but I know he had black through his eye."*

Let us glimpse that same small bird a third time. This time the only mark we are *sure* of is that the little bird wears a black mask. A quick turn in either key to BLACK, and from there swiftly to "Eye mask black," pages 12–19. There on eight pages are the drawings and text of ten birds. Again, either by sight memory or quick elimination of the wrong traits you know that the bird you glimpsed a few moments before was:

YELLOW-RUMPED WARBLER

Yellow

White

Yellow

White

Yellow shoulder patch
Two white wing bars

IF YOU HAVE FOUND HAWK IDENTIFICATION DIFFICULT, TURN TO THE HAWK KEYS ON PAGES 267–269 AND 295–297 FOR A SIMILAR LESSON IN IDENTIFYING, PERCHED OR IN FLIGHT, USING THE SIGHT GUIDE SYSTEM.

FURTHER HINTS TO THE USE OF THE BOOK

BIRDS are most easily identified by color and song in spring and early summer. That is the time to observe them, and, in general, this guide will be *most* useful then. Major color classifications in the guide are based upon the color of the male (see *Female* birds below). Rare, unusual, and immature birds and birds in changed fall or winter plumage are not included. Almost all birds whose plumage changes in the fall go south in winter and so are of no concern to people in the Northeast. A few common winter visitors are included.

Female birds. Although in many cases the female and the male are identical in appearance, there are instances where the differences might make for difficulty. In *every* bird description there is a category entitled "Sexes," which will guide the user of this book to female identification. The sexes are usually paired off in spring and summer, however, making identification of the female by association fairly simple.

Immature birds, for a short period, often differ considerably from mature birds. Young American Robins, for example, resemble the old birds in size and shape but their underparts are heavily spotted.

The size of the small birds in each instance is compared, by means of a black bar, with one of three well-known birds: House Sparrow, American Robin, or American Crow. In every group birds are arranged from smallest to largest. If yours is a little bird, look at the beginning of the group; if big, at the end.

Birds, like humans, have distinctive habitats, places where they build nests and raise a family; and about three fourths of them take winter vacations. The male is the dandy and dresses up. The mother on her nest usually has inconspicuous, protective colors. All these factors are listed and help you identify your bird.

Voice or Song. Most varieties have their own "theme" song, with occasional variations. When the user has once learned the song characteristic of each species, that song or call not only will aid in identification, but will greatly increase the pleasures of bird study itself. This guide offers, wherever possible, descriptive and illustrative material on such songs and calls.

Where the bird is seen is often an effective help toward identification, although birds in migration may often be found outside their normal habitat. It will be noted that certain kinds of birds, such as Woodpeckers, Hawks, and Owls, are grouped separately. There are many other natural groupings, such as Flycatchers and Warblers. As you advance in your knowledge of birds you will want to check further in one of the larger guides, such as Peterson's *Field Guide to the Birds* or Pough's *Audubon Bird Guide —Eastern Land Birds*.

Area covered. This guide covers all common land birds from South Carolina west to the Rockies and north to the Arctic, except a few which occur regularly from the Rockies out into the Great Plains.

Names used are those found in the 1983 edition of the *American Ornithologists' Union Check-List of North American Birds*. The American Ornithologists' Union has officially adopted the name *House Sparrow* in place of the often criticized *English Sparrow;* this revised terminology is used throughout this guide. The common names of birds differ, of course, in every country and in every language, although in many cases the birds may be identical or similar. There has, therefore, been developed by generations of scientists throughout the world a uniform designation based upon Latin or Greek names, and in turn upon minute differences, often determined only by exacting laboratory observation. The classification of birds in this system is based upon the fact that some birds, such as water birds, are very simple in structure, while others, such as sparrows, are very complex.

Although such a classification is essential for scientific purposes, it is quite unnecessary in bird *identification* and is most confusing until one has advanced far into bird study. When that time comes, and when mere identification is no longer your chief concern, you will naturally turn to more advanced works on ornithology. In order that you may gradually become acquainted with this scientific classification, all the birds in this guide are so arranged just preceding the index, where both the common name and the scientific classification are given.

In any large community you will find a local Audubon Society. Join it. It can furnish you with a check list of local birds.

PART I

Picture Guide to the Birds

Based on Color and Pattern

ORCHARD ORIOLE

Chestnut —

Chestnut

White wing bar

NORTHERN ORIOLE

Orange —

Bright orange

Orange

White wing bar

ROSE-BREASTED GROSBEAK

White

Rose-red patch

White

White rump

Head Black

ORCHARD ORIOLE
(1) *Chestnut underparts and rump.*
(2) *Black head, extending down back, black tail and wings.*

White wing bar and feather edgings.
FEMALE: Olive above, yellow below, no black markings. Immature males resemble females, but have black throats.
VOICE: Long, high, sweet warble, Robin-like but of much finer quality, almost like Purple Finch.
NESTS: South-central Canada to North Dakota, east to central New York, and south to Gulf.
WINTERS: Central and South America.

NORTHERN ORIOLE*
(1) *Brilliant orange underparts, rump, and outer tail tips.*
(2) *Black head, back, wings, and tail center.*

White wing bar, wing feathers white-edged.
FEMALE: Olive-brown above, yellow below, spotted throat. Top of head and back often blackish.
VOICE: (1) Several rich rolling whistles very distinctive in quality. (2) A rounded chatter.
NESTS: Central Canada to Gulf States.
WINTERS: Mostly Mexico to Colombia.

ROSE-BREASTED GROSBEAK*
(1) *Brilliant red throat patch.*
(2) *Black head, back, wings, and tail.*

Large stubby bill. White wing bars, rump, and belly.
FEMALE: Brownish-striped, white line above eye and on top of head.
VOICE: A beautiful full-toned warble, notes running into each other similar to that of the American Robin.

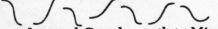

NESTS: Northern and central Canada, south to Missouri, and east to northern Georgia.
WINTERS: Southern Mexico to South America.

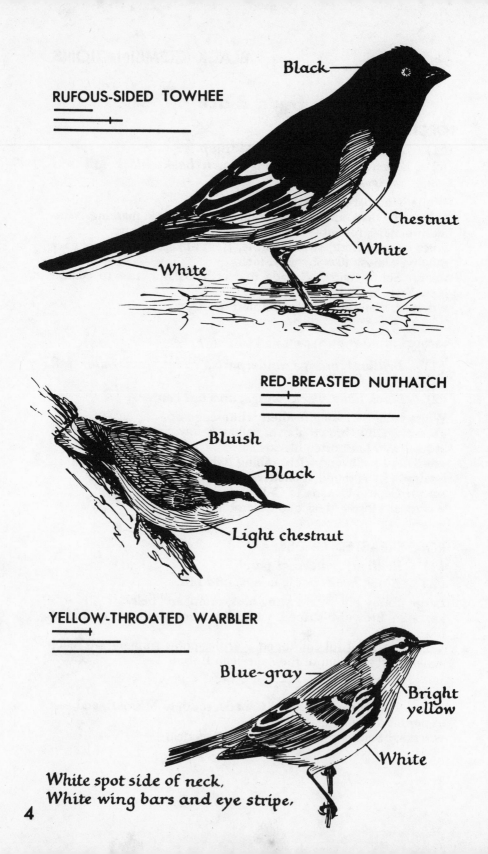

RUFOUS-SIDED TOWHEE

Black

Chestnut

White

White

RED-BREASTED NUTHATCH

Bluish

Black

Light chestnut

YELLOW-THROATED WARBLER

Blue-gray

Bright yellow

White

White spot side of neck,
White wing bars and eye stripe,

4

Head Black

RUFOUS-SIDED TOWHEE*

(1)   *Chestnut sides.*
(2)   *Black head, back, wings, and tail.*

Wings and outer tips of tail white-edged. White belly. Commonly seen, and heard, scratching around on ground in low shrubbery.

FEMALE: Brown replaces black markings.

VOICE: (1) *tow hee.* (2) *drink your teeee.* Last note high and wavering.

NESTS: Southeastern Canada to Gulf States.

WINTERS: Mostly in Southern States.

Cap Black

RED-BREASTED NUTHATCH

(1)   *Black cap, black eye line surmounted by white. White throat.*
(2)   *Light chestnut underparts.*

Outer tail feathers white. Bluish above. "Upside-down" bird. Usually seen in evergreens.

FEMALE: Generally lighter.

VOICE: A sharp, high, nasal *ank-ank.*

NESTS OR RESIDENT: Alaska, Canada, northern edge of Great Lakes States, and in mountains to North Carolina.

YELLOW-THROATED WARBLER

(1)   *Bright yellow throat, white belly.*
(2)   *Black on forehead, below and behind eye, and in stripes on sides. White stripe above eye and white patch on side of neck.*

Two wing bars. Upperparts blue-gray. Underparts whitish.

SEXES: Similar.

VOICE: Series of clear notes, slurred and dropping in pitch. Last note higher.

NESTS: Southern Ohio to central New Jersey (rare) and south to Gulf.

WINTERS: Southern States southward into Central America.

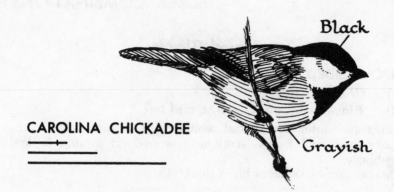

Black

Grayish

CAROLINA CHICKADEE

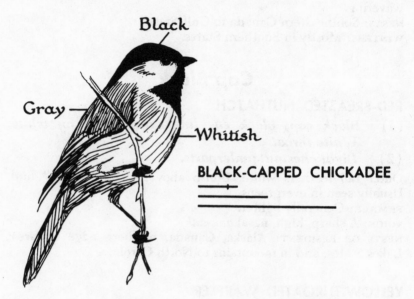

Black

Gray

Whitish

BLACK-CAPPED CHICKADEE

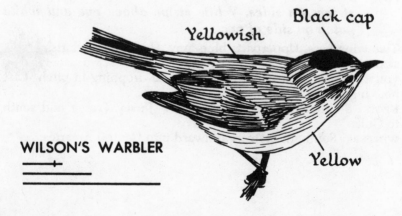

Yellowish

Black cap

Yellow

WILSON'S WARBLER

BLACK COMBINATIONS

Cap Black

CAROLINA CHICKADEE

(1)   *Top of head and throat black.*
(2)   *White face.*
Underparts whitish to grayish, faintly buffy sides. Smaller than Black-capped Chickadee.
SEXES: Alike.
VOICE: (1) *chickadee* very fast and high. (2) Gentle, high, delightful

see me, see me, higher and faster than northern species.
RESIDENT: Central Illinois to central New Jersey and south to Gulf.

BLACK-CAPPED CHICKADEE*

(1)   *Black cap and throat.*
(2)   *White face.*
Upperparts gray. Breast white, rest of underparts tinged with buff. Often seen upside down. Resembles Carolina Chickadee but larger.
SEXES: Alike.
VOICE: (1) Often-repeated *chickadee-dee-dee.* (2) Delightful,

melodious languid *see me.*
RESIDENT: Alaska and Canada to central Illinois, east to northern New Jersey, and in mountains to Tennessee.

WILSON'S WARBLER*

(1)   *Head and underparts pure yellow.*
(2)   *Black cap.*
Yellowish above. No wing bars. Beady black eye.
FEMALE: Black cap less sharply defined.
VOICE: High, thin, chattery, dropping at end.
NESTS: Labrador to Alaska, south to northern Minnesota in West and Maine in East.
WINTERS: Central America.

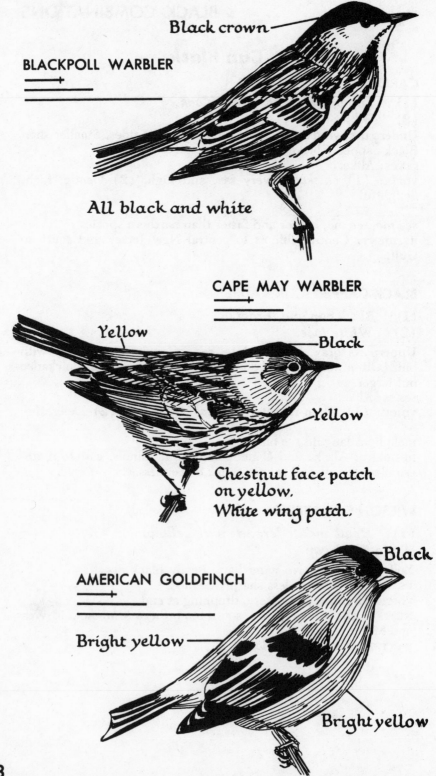

Black crown

BLACKPOLL WARBLER

All black and white

CAPE MAY WARBLER

Yellow

Black

Yellow

Chestnut face patch
on yellow.
White wing patch.

AMERICAN GOLDFINCH

Black

Bright yellow

Bright yellow

Cap Black

BLACKPOLL WARBLER

(1)   *Large black cap.*
(2)   *Lower face white.*

Upperparts gray, yellowish-tinged, and black-striped. Underparts white, black-striped. Two wing bars. Black-and-white Warbler, which is similar, does not have solid-black crown.
FEMALE: Lower face gray, no black cap. Streaked with olive above. White below, lightly streaked.
VOICE: Thin, regular, high-pitched *zi-zi-zi-zi-zi-zi-zi*.
NESTS: Labrador to northern Alaska, south to Maine and high mountains of New York and New England.
WINTERS: South America.

CAPE MAY WARBLER

(1)   *Black cap. Chestnut patch on yellow face.*
(2)   *Yellow below, heavily striped.*

White wing patch. Yellow rump.
FEMALE: Lighter-striped below, no chestnut cheek patch, yellowish rump. Yellow spot on side of head. Olive above, streaked with black.
VOICE: Hurried, wiry, and irregular.
NESTS: Central Canada to northern edge of Great Lakes States east to southern Maine.
WINTERS: West Indies.

AMERICAN GOLDFINCH*

(1)   *Striking yellow body.*
(2)   *Black forehead, wings, and tail.*

Wing feathers white-tipped. Winter males resemble summer females.
FEMALE: Olive-yellow; wing bars, no black forehead patch.
VOICE: (1) Canary-like call, with rising inflection. Also in undulating flight a musical *per chickery*. (2) Long, varied, sweet warble.
NESTS OR RESIDENT: Nebraska and Minnesota to Nova Scotia and south to Gulf States.

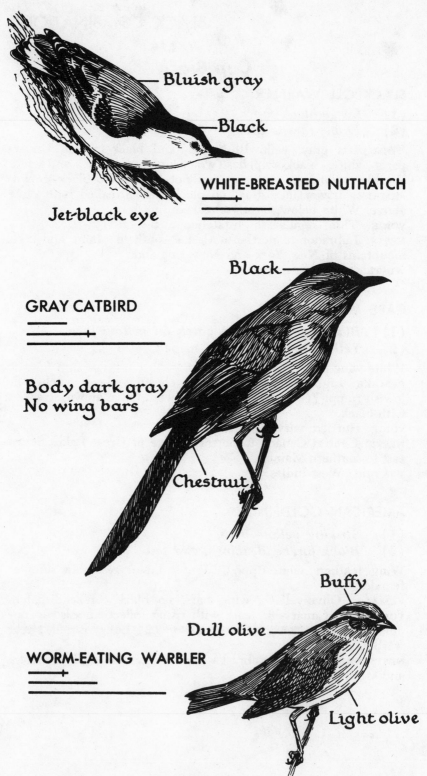

Bluish gray

Black

WHITE-BREASTED NUTHATCH

Jet-black eye

Black

GRAY CATBIRD

Body dark gray
No wing bars

Chestnut

Buffy

Dull olive

WORM-EATING WARBLER

Light olive

Cap Black

WHITE-BREASTED NUTHATCH*

(1) *Black crown.*
(2) *Jet-black eye in white face.*

Upperparts bluish gray. Underparts white. Usually works head down. Climbs along limbs and tree trunks.
FEMALE: Top of head lighter.
VOICE: (1) A pleasant, rather musical, rapid *onk onk onk onk onk*. (2) A nasal *yank yank yank yank*. Both often repeated.
RESIDENT: South-central and southern Canada to Gulf.

GRAY CATBIRD*

(1) *Solid dark gray throughout.*
(2) *Black cap.*

No white marking. Rusty under long tail. Commonly seen in low bushes or shrubbery.
SEXES: Alike.
VOICE: (1) A catlike *mayow*, slurred downward. (2) Great variety of whistles, frequently harsh. Often resembles that of the Northern Mockingbird.
NESTS: Nova Scotia to southern British Columbia and south to Gulf States.
WINTERS: Usually in southern United States to Central America; few in Northeast.

Head Stripes Black and Buff

WORM-EATING WARBLER

(1) *Prominent black stripes on buffy head.*
(2) *Dull olive above, lighter below.*

No other stripes or markings of any kind. Usually found on wooded hillsides.
SEXES: Alike.
VOICE: Thin *buzz* almost like an insect, resembling song of Chipping Sparrow.
NESTS: Northeastern Kansas to southern Connecticut and south to northern Georgia.
WINTERS: Florida, West Indies, and Central America.

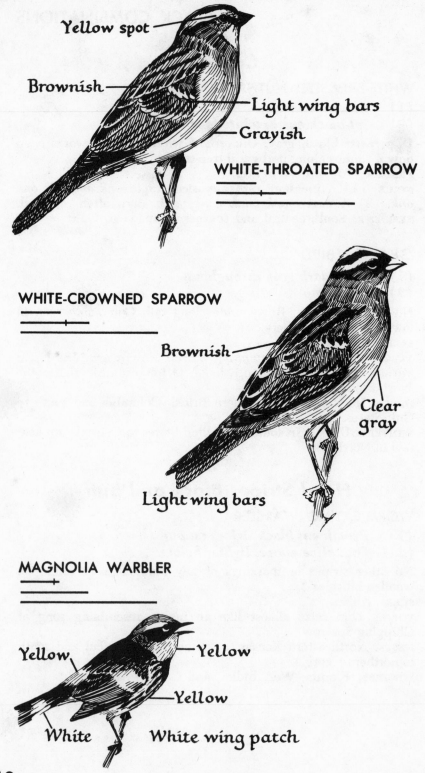

Yellow spot

Brownish

Light wing bars

Grayish

WHITE-THROATED SPARROW

WHITE-CROWNED SPARROW

Brownish

Clear gray

Light wing bars

MAGNOLIA WARBLER

Yellow

Yellow

Yellow

White

White wing patch

Head Stripes Black and White

WHITE-THROATED SPARROW*

(1) *Crown white, bordered by black stripes.*
(2) *White throat, yellow spot behind bill.*

Upperparts brownish-striped; two light wing bars; underparts grayish. (In immature, white lines are buffy and black lines are chestnut.)
FEMALE: Usually duller.
VOICE: Lovely plaintive whistle in minor key and long-drawn-out. ___ ___ ___ ___   ___ ___ ___ ___
___   ___

NESTS: Alaska and northern Canada to central Minnesota and east to Massachusetts.
WINTERS: Mostly Southern States to Mexico.

WHITE-CROWNED SPARROW*

(1) *White crown, bordered by heavy black stripes.*
(2) *White line over eye and thin black line behind eye.*

Upperparts brownish-striped. Light wing bars. Underparts clear grayish, no stripes. (Immature: White head stripes are buffy and black stripes reddish brown, giving chestnut-crown effect.)
FEMALE: Usually duller.
VOICE: Clear plaintive whistle followed by husky trilled whistle.
NESTS: Labrador to northern Alaska and south to southeastern Quebec.
WINTERS: Southern States to Mexico.

Mask Through Eye Black

MAGNOLIA WARBLER*

(1) *Yellow underparts heavily black-striped.*
(2) *Yellow rump. White patches on wings and white bar on tail.*

White line above black mask. Upperparts gray and black.
FEMALE: Lighter striping and mask.
VOICE: Warbling *weeta-weeta-weetee*, rising or falling on last note.
NESTS: Northern Canada to northeastern Minnesota, east to Massachusetts, and in mountains to Virginia.
WINTERS: Central America.

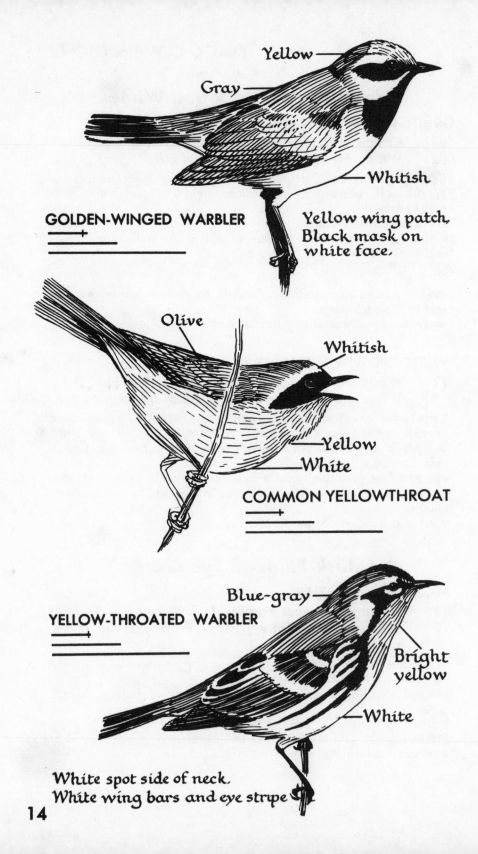

Yellow

Gray

Whitish

GOLDEN-WINGED WARBLER

Yellow wing patch,
Black mask on
white face.

Olive

Whitish

Yellow

White

COMMON YELLOWTHROAT

Blue-gray

YELLOW-THROATED WARBLER

Bright
yellow

White

White spot side of neck.
White wing bars and eye stripe

14

Mask Through Eye Black

GOLDEN-WINGED WARBLER

(1)   *Yellow wing patch and cap.*
(2)   *Black throat and black eye patch against white.*

Upperparts gray, underparts whitish.
FEMALE: Black replaced by gray.
VOICE: Four or five buzzy notes.
NESTS: Southern Ontario to southeastern Manitoba; south to southeastern Iowa, east to southern Connecticut, and in mountains to Georgia.
WINTERS: Central America and northern South America.

COMMON YELLOWTHROAT*

(1)   *Black mask bounded above and behind by white.*
(2)   *Yellow throat. White belly.*

Uniform olive above. No wing bars. Usually found in low shrubs in moist places.
FEMALE: Grayish mask. Brownish above, duller below.
VOICE: *witchity-witchity-witchity-witch.*
NESTS: Newfoundland to southern Alaska and south to Gulf.
WINTERS: Southern States.

YELLOW-THROATED WARBLER

(1)   *Bright yellow throat, white belly.*
(2)   *Black on forehead, below and behind eye, and in stripes on sides. White stripe above eye and white patch on side of neck.*

Two wing bars. Upperparts blue-gray. Underparts whitish.
SEXES: Similar.
VOICE: Series of clear notes, slurred and dropping in pitch. Last note higher.
NESTS: Southern Ohio to central New Jersey (rare) and south to Gulf.
WINTERS: Southern States southward into Central America.

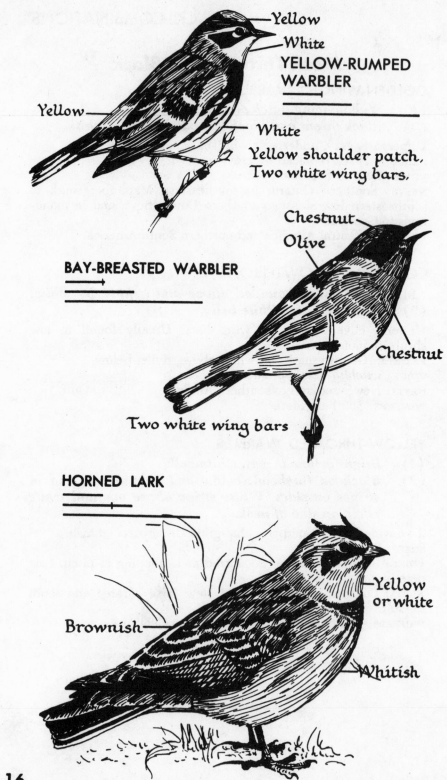

Yellow

White

YELLOW-RUMPED WARBLER

Yellow

White

Yellow shoulder patch,
Two white wing bars.

Chestnut

Olive

BAY-BREASTED WARBLER

Chestnut

Two white wing bars

HORNED LARK

Yellow or white

Brownish

Whitish

16

Mask Through Eye Black

YELLOW-RUMPED WARBLER*

(1)   *Yellow crown spot, rump, and sides of breast.*
(2)   *Black mask, surmounted by short white line.*

White chin. Underparts white with heavy black stripes. Two white wing bars. Above bluish slate-gray, streaked black. White outer tail tips. Magnolia Warbler easily distinguished from Yellow-rumped Warbler by yellow instead of white underparts.
FEMALE: Duller and more brownish above.
VOICE: Clear warble of about eight notes.
NESTS: Labrador to Alaska, south to northern part of Great Lakes States, and east to Maine.
WINTERS: Frequently in Northeast, mostly southern United States to Central America.

BAY-BREASTED WARBLER

(1)   *Chestnut crown, upper breast, and sides.*
(2)   *Prominent white area behind black mask.*

Back olive-streaked. Two white wing bars. Belly whitish.
FEMALE: Similar but markings much paler and less distinct.
VOICE: Commonly short, wiry, high, on one pitch.
NESTS: Central Canada to northeastern Minnesota and east to southern Maine.
WINTERS: Panama and northern South America.

HORNED LARK

(1)   *Black mask and throat patch on yellow or white.*
(2)   *Black patch top of head ending in "horns," often hard to see.*

Brownish-striped above. Usually seen on ground in open country.
FEMALE: Similar but smaller and duller. No black on top of head.
VOICE: Often long, high-pitched, tinkling; frequently in flight.
NESTS: Arctic coast of North America, south to eastern Kansas in West and North Carolina in East.
WINTERS: South to Gulf States.

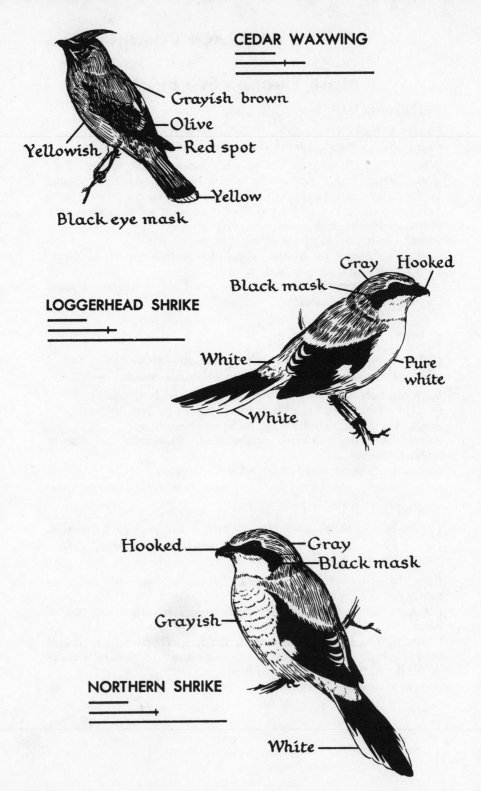

CEDAR WAXWING

Grayish brown

Olive

Red spot

Yellowish

Yellow

Black eye mask

Gray   Hooked

Black mask

LOGGERHEAD SHRIKE

White

Pure
white

White

Hooked   Gray
                          Black mask

Grayish

NORTHERN SHRIKE

White

18

Mask Through Eye Black

CEDAR WAXWING*

(1) *Prominent crest.*
(2) *Black eye mask and chin.*

Other upperparts grayish brown. Red spot on wing. Tip of tail yellow. Underparts yellowish. Commonly in flocks, often seen catching insects on wing like Flycatcher.

SEXES: Alike.
VOICE: High thin lisp.
NESTS: Newfoundland to Alaska, south to southern Illinois, and east to Georgia.
WINTERS: Southern Ontario to southern British Columbia and south to Gulf.

LOGGERHEAD SHRIKE

(1) *Black mask on gray head.*
(2) *White below. Black wings; long black tail, white-edged.*

Solid-black hooked beak. Upperparts grayish. Usual perch is in the open on a wire or tip of tree. Shrikes, with their hooked beaks, eat large insects and grasshoppers, and sometimes other little birds. Easily distinguished by its black mask from Northern Mockingbird, which it resembles slightly.

SEXES: Alike.
VOICE: A subdued medley of many phrases.
NESTS: Central Canada to Gulf.
WINTERS: Mostly southern half of breeding range, occasionally farther north.

NORTHERN SHRIKE

(1) *Black mask on gray head.*
(2) *Grayish below, lightly barred; black tail, white-edged, and black wings.*

Upperparts pale grayish to white. White chin; base of bill usually pale. This is the rarer, larger, more northern cousin of the Loggerhead Shrike. (Immature is brown and barred below.)

FEMALE: Duller.
VOICE and HABITS: Similar to that of the Loggerhead Shrike.
NESTS: Labrador to Alaska south to central Canada.
WINTERS: As far south as Kentucky and Virginia.

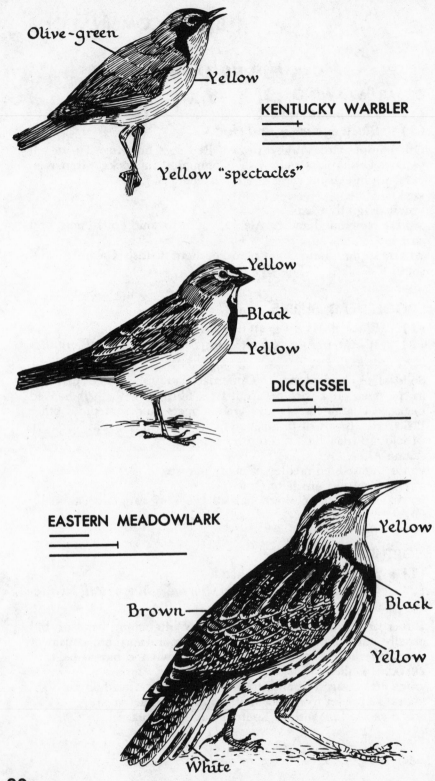

Olive-green

Yellow

KENTUCKY WARBLER

Yellow "spectacles"

Yellow

Black

Yellow

DICKCISSEL

EASTERN MEADOWLARK

Yellow

Brown

Black

Yellow

White

20

Patch Below Eye Black

KENTUCKY WARBLER*

(1)   *Underparts clear yellow, with black irregular patch below eye.*

(2)   *Yellow eye "spectacles."*

Upperparts olive-green. Top of head blackish. Distinguished from Common Yellowthroat, whose black mask entirely covers eye and forehead.

FEMALE: Black areas dusky; generally duller.

VOICE: A rapid loud *tury-tury-tury-tury*.

NESTS: Southeastern Nebraska to southwestern Connecticut and south to Gulf.

WINTERS: Mexico to northern South America.

Bib, Crescent, or V on Throat Black

DICKCISSEL

(1)   *Yellow breast.*

(2)   *Black bib.*

Brownish-striped upperparts; chestnut on shoulder. Yellow stripe above eye.

FEMALE: Much lighter throughout, no bib.

VOICE: A repetition of *dick-ciss-ciss-ciss*.

NESTS: Mostly western or plains. Canadian border states and provinces, south to Texas, and east to South Carolina. Often wanders to east coast.

WINTERS: Mexico to northern South America.

EASTERN MEADOWLARK*

(1)   *Broad black V on brilliant yellow underparts.*

(2)   *Outer feathers of short tail flash white in flight.*

Long slender bill. Upperparts brown-striped. Usually seen in open fields. Walks, does not hop.

FEMALE: Similar but smaller and duller.

VOICE: The loud beautiful-toned song of this large, conspicuous bird, with its one very common *spring is here*, makes it easily identifiable.

NESTS: Southeastern Canada to North Dakota, south to Arkansas, and east to North Carolina.

WINTERS: Mostly southern United States. Partly resident in Northeast.

NOTE: The Western Meadowlark, generally similar in appearance, has a very different song, of richer lower-pitched, whistled notes. It occurs in the Great Plains or western part of the area treated, but is spreading eastward.

21

Red

NORTHERN FLICKER

Black

Brown

Yellow in flight

White rump

Underside wings
and tail yellow

Brown

Brown-
striped

SONG SPARROW

Spot

Gray

Chestnut

LARK SPARROW Brownish

Spot

White

Bib, Crescent, or V on Throat Black

NORTHERN FLICKER*

(1)   *Black crescent and "mustache" on throat. Red cres-cent back of head.*

(2)   *White rump, prominent in flight. Underside of wings and tail yellow.*

Long Woodpecker bill. Upperparts brown, cross-striped. Under-parts with heavy black spots on whitish.

FEMALE: No "mustache."

VOICE: (1) A long succession of semi-musical, fast, far-reaching *kick's*. (2) A sort of squealing succession of *hickup's*. (3) An explosive, piercing *clear clear clear*. (4) A squeaky *eureka eureka eureka*.

NESTS: Alaska and Canada to southern Virginia and in moun-tains to North Carolina.

WINTERS: In limited numbers to northern limit of range and south to Gulf.

Spot on Breast Black

SONG SPARROW*

(1)   *Dark spot middle of breast where dark stripes con-verge.*

(2)   *Heavily brown-striped upperparts, breast, and sides. Gray belly.*

Brownish above, lighter below. Light line over eye. Brown crown. Commonly seen near ground in shrubbery and in moist places.

SEXES: Alike.

VOICE: Two to four drawn-out sweet notes ending in various lengthy trills in numberless variations.

NESTS: Northern Canada to Louisiana.

WINTERS: Southern fringe of Canada to Gulf.

LARK SPARROW

(1)   *Tail with white corners.*

(2)   *Black spot on clear whitish breast.*

Prominent chestnut patch on face. Black "whiskers" on side of chin.

Upperparts brownish-striped.

FEMALE: Similar.

VOICE: Sweet notes and trills with pauses between.

NESTS: Southwestern Canadian provinces as far east as western New York, south to southern Texas, and east to central Alabama.

WINTERS: Gulf coast and Mexico, occasionally farther north.

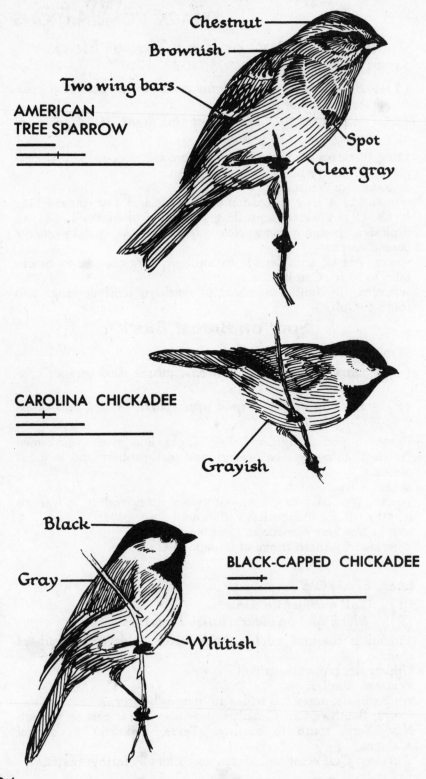

Chestnut

Brownish

Two wing bars

AMERICAN
TREE SPARROW

Spot

Clear gray

CAROLINA CHICKADEE

Grayish

Black

BLACK-CAPPED CHICKADEE

Gray

Whitish

Spot on Breast Black

AMERICAN TREE SPARROW

(1)   *Black spot on clear gray breast.*
(2)   *Chestnut crown.*

Dark line through eye. Two wing bars. Upperparts brownish-striped.

SEXES: Alike.
VOICE: Variable, starting with one or two high musical notes, then more rapid and lower in pitch.
NESTS: Northern Alaska and northern Canada.
WINTERS: Central Minnesota, southern fringe of Canada to Maine, south to Oklahoma, and east to North Carolina.

Throat and Top of Head Black

CAROLINA CHICKADEE

(1)   *Top of head and throat black.*
(2)   *White face.*

Underparts whitish to grayish, faintly buffy sides. Smaller than Black-capped Chickadee.

SEXES: Alike.
VOICE: (1) *chickadee* very fast and high. (2) Gentle, high, delightful

see me, see me, higher and faster than northern species.
RESIDENT: Central Illinois to central New Jersey and south to Gulf.

BLACK-CAPPED CHICKADEE*

(1)   *Black cap and throat.*
(2)   *White face.*

Upperparts gray. Breast white, rest of underparts tinged with buff. Often seen upside down. Resembles Carolina Chickadee but larger.

SEXES: Alike.
VOICE: (1) Often-repeated *chickadee-dee-dee.* (2) Delightful,

melodious languid *see me.*
RESIDENT: Alaska and Canada to central Illinois, east to northern New Jersey, and in mountains to Tennessee.

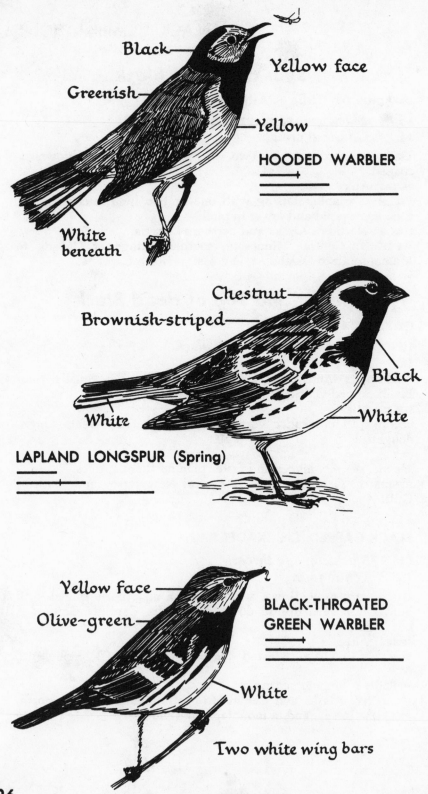

Black

Yellow face

Greenish

Yellow

HOODED WARBLER

White
beneath

Chestnut

Brownish-striped

Black

White

White

LAPLAND LONGSPUR (Spring)

Yellow face

BLACK-THROATED
GREEN WARBLER

Olive-green

White

Two white wing bars

Throat and Top of Head Black

HOODED WARBLER*

(1) *Bright yellow face within black hood.*
(2) *Belly yellow.*

Upperparts greenish. Tail feathers white below.
FEMALE: No black hood.
VOICE: Sprightly whistle: *hip, hip, horray.*
NESTS: Central Iowa to Rhode Island and south to Gulf.
WINTERS: West Indies and Central America.

LAPLAND LONGSPUR (Spring)

(1) *Black crown, throat, and sides.*
(2) *Chestnut collar back of neck.*

White or buffy band above and back of eye extends to chestnut and down to merge with white breast and belly. Back dark, heavily streaked with buff. Outer tail feathers white-edged. Light wing bars. Walks or creeps; does not hop. In winter practically all the black and chestnut markings are lacking.
FEMALE: Generally brownish above, heavily streaked. Breast and belly whitish, heavily streaked on sides.
VOICE: A rattly noise followed by a whistle.
NESTS: Greenland to northern Alaska.
WINTERS: To southern United States.

Throat Black

BLACK-THROATED GREEN WARBLER

(1) *Bright yellow face.*
(2) *Throat black, sides black-striped.*

Belly whitish. Upperparts olive-green. Two white wing bars. Usually found in heavy northern woods.
FEMALE: Similar to male but duller. Black areas on throat broken.
VOICE: A delicate, dreamy *zoo-zee-zoo-zoo-zee* or *zee-zee-zee-zoo-zee*, next-to-last note lower.
NESTS: Central Canada to Ohio, east to northern New Jersey, and in mountains to Georgia.
WINTERS: Mexico to Colombia.

Yellow

Gray

Whitish

GOLDEN-WINGED WARBLER

Yellow wing patch.
Black mask on
white face.

Dark blue

White

White
wing spot

BLACK-THROATED BLUE WARBLER

Blue-gray hood
Olive

Black

Yellow

MOURNING WARBLER

BLACK COMBINATIONS

Throat Black

GOLDEN-WINGED WARBLER

(1)   *Yellow wing patch and cap.*
(2)   *Black throat and black eye patch against white.*

Upperparts gray, underparts whitish.
FEMALE: Black replaced by gray.
VOICE: Four or five buzzy notes.
NESTS: Southern Ontario to southeastern Manitoba; south to southeastern Iowa, east to southern Connecticut, and in mountains to Georgia.
WINTERS: Central America and northern South America.

BLACK-THROATED BLUE WARBLER

(1)   *Black throat, extending along sides.*
(2)   *Upperparts dark blue.*

White wing spot. Belly white.
FEMALE: Olive or olive-brown above, no black markings. Yellowish below. Light eye stripe; small white wing spot.
VOICE: Three or four husky burred notes followed by high

clear note: *zur zur zur zree.*
NESTS: Southern Canada and Great Lakes States to northern New Jersey and in mountains to North Carolina.
WINTERS: Key West, mainly, and West Indies.

MOURNING WARBLER

(1)   *Blue-gray hood, blue-gray throat becoming black at edge of yellow.*
(2)   *Yellow underparts.*

Upperparts olive. Usually found in thickets near ground.
FEMALE: Hood light gray. No black on throat.
VOICE: Variable but usually loud, musical *cheery-cheery-chorry-chorry.*
NESTS: Central Canada to northeastern North Dakota, east to southern Maine, and in mountains to Virginia.
WINTERS: Central and South America.

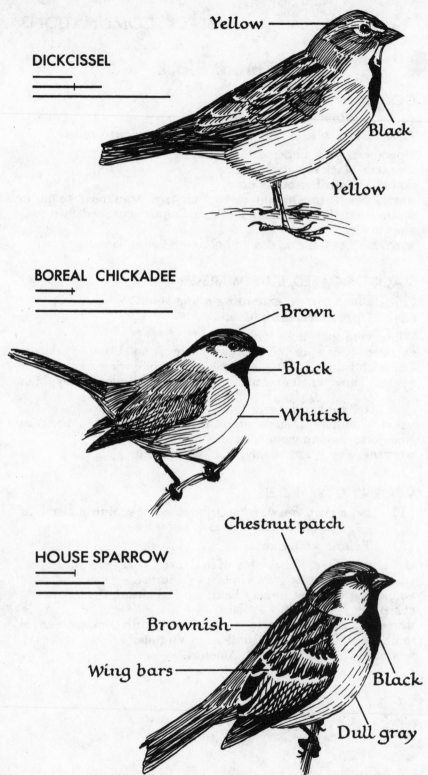

DICKCISSEL

Yellow

Black

Yellow

BOREAL CHICKADEE

Brown

Black

Whitish

HOUSE SPARROW

Chestnut patch

Brownish

Wing bars

Black

Dull gray

Throat Black

DICKCISSEL

(1) *Yellow breast.*
(2) *Black bib.*

Brownish-striped upperparts; chestnut on shoulder. Yellow stripe above eye.
FEMALE: Much lighter throughout, no bib.
VOICE: A repetition of *dick-ciss-ciss-ciss*.
NESTS: Mostly western or plains. Canadian border states and provinces, south to Texas, and east to South Carolina. Often wanders to east coast.
WINTERS: Mexico to northern South America.

BOREAL CHICKADEE

(1) *Brown cap above white face.*
(2) *Black throat.*

Upperparts brownish gray. Whitish below, washed with brown on sides.
SEXES: Alike.
VOICE: Harsh *dee-dee waah waah*.
RESIDENT: Northern Alaska, Canada, and northern fringe of border states, occasionally farther south in winter.

HOUSE SPARROW*

(1) *Brownish-striped above, black throat.*
(2) *Whitish patch between black throat and chestnut patch.*

Faint wing bars, short stubby bill characteristic of most sparrows. Underparts dingy gray. Mostly about houses and barns and in city streets.
FEMALE: No black on throat; no chestnut markings; dull whitish stripe over eye.
VOICE: A monotonous, everlasting *chirrup* or *chisick* or *cheep*.
RESIDENT: Northern Canada to Gulf.
NOTE: Formerly known as English Sparrow but called House Sparrow in latest A.O.U. Check List.

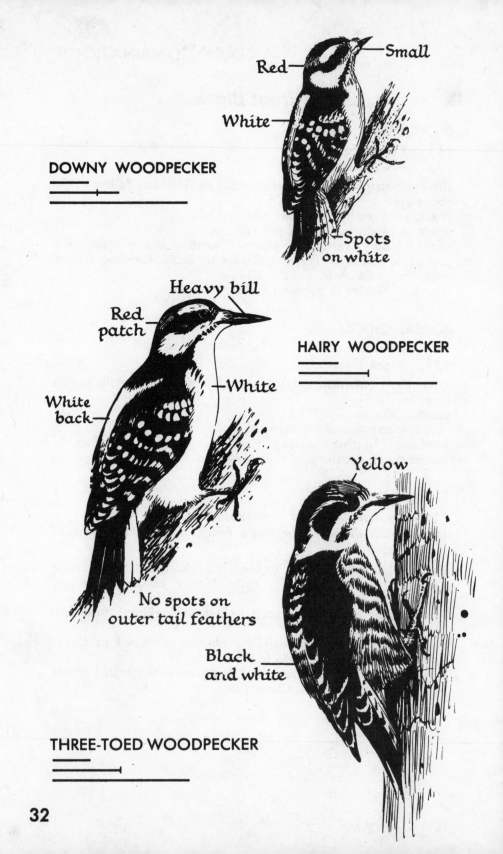

Red — Small

White

DOWNY WOODPECKER

Spots on white

Heavy bill

Red patch

White

White back

HAIRY WOODPECKER

Yellow

No spots on outer tail feathers

Black and white

THREE-TOED WOODPECKER

Upperparts Black-Barred or -Spotted

White Below

DOWNY WOODPECKER*

(1) *White back.*
(2) *Red spot back of head.*

Small bill. White spots on wings. Outer tail feathers white, spotted with black. Resembles Hairy Woodpecker but much smaller and with very small bill.

FEMALE: No red on head.

VOICE: (1) A light *keek keek*. (2) A musical succession of clear-cut high notes going down the scale.

RESIDENT: Alaska and Canada and south to Gulf.

HAIRY WOODPECKER*

(1) *Red spot on top of head, black crown. Black eye patch on white.*
(2) *White back, black wings and tail.*

Wings spotted white. Tail white-edged. White below. Distinguished from Downy Woodpecker by much larger size and large bill.

FEMALE: No red on head.

VOICE: (1) A rather loud, high *keek keek*. (2) A long, slurred high rattle, running together and descending at end.

RESIDENT: Alaska and Canada and south to Gulf.

THREE-TOED WOODPECKER

(1) *Upperparts black. Back barred black and white.*
(2) *Yellow cap.*

Throat and belly white. Sides black-barred on white. Narrow white stripe behind eye.

FEMALE: Crown not yellow; usually streaked black and white.

VOICE: A sharp *chirk;* a loud *queep;* a long squeal.

RESIDENT: From northern Canada to northern fringe of border states; occasionally in winter as far south as Massachusetts.

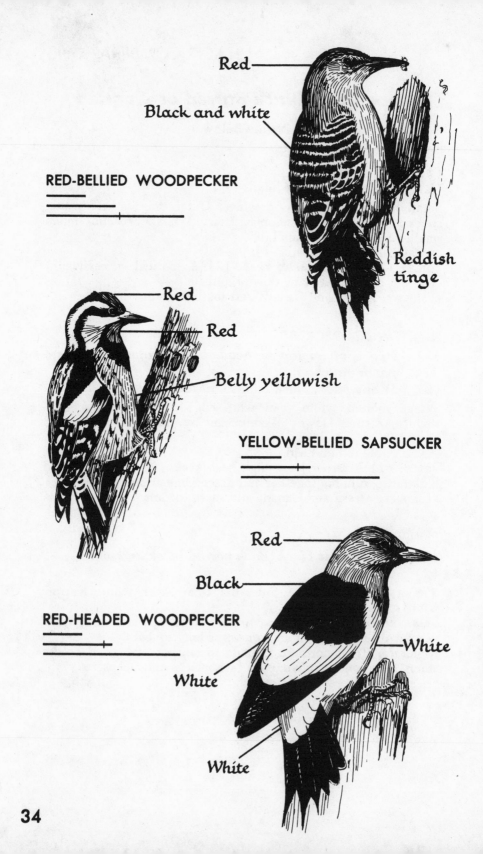

Red

Black and white

RED-BELLIED WOODPECKER

Reddish tinge

Red

Red

Belly yellowish

YELLOW-BELLIED SAPSUCKER

Red

Black

RED-HEADED WOODPECKER

White

White

White

BLACK COMBINATIONS

Upperparts Black-Barred or -Spotted

Gray to Reddish Below

RED-BELLIED WOODPECKER

(1) *Black upperparts heavily cross-barred with narrow white bars.*

(2) *Red crown.*

Tail black-barred in center. Throat and breast gray. Belly whitish with light reddish tinge.

FEMALE: Similar, except red patch on head smaller.

VOICE: (1) Harsh, loud *krrk krrk krrk*, rolling the *r*'s. (2) Loud, rattling *kack kack kack kack*, all on same pitch.

RESIDENT: Southeastern Minnesota through southwestern Ontario to western New York and south to Gulf. Occasionally New Jersey, Delaware, and Maryland.

Yellow or Yellowish Below

YELLOW-BELLIED SAPSUCKER*

(1) *Bright red crown and throat.*

(2) *Long white wing stripe.*

Yellowish below, light-spotted on sides. White stripe under and over black mask, which goes through eye. Back, wings, and tail black, white-spotted. Drills holes in trees for sap. Usually these Sapsucker holes are of little or no damage to trees unless heavily concentrated on one limb.

FEMALE: Has white throat.

VOICE: (1) A loud *ayow ayow* like mewing of a cat. (2) High-pitched slurred squeal.

NESTS: Labrador to British Columbia, south to eastern Missouri, east to northwestern Connecticut, and in mountains to Virginia.

WINTERS: Southern New England and Wisconsin south.

Black, White Wing Patch and Rump

White Below

RED-HEADED WOODPECKER*

(1) *Entire head red.*

(2) *Back and wings black.*

Large white patch on wing and rump. Underparts white.

SEXES: Alike.

VOICE: A loud *querr* or *queeah*.

NESTS: Southern Canada to Gulf. Rare east of Delaware and Hudson rivers.

WINTERS: Southern New England south.

Black

Orange-red wing patch and shoulder.

Orange-red

White

AMERICAN REDSTART

Whitish

Blackish brown

Dark

Dusky

Whitish

Buff

CLIFF SWALLOW

Steely blue

TREE SWALLOW

Pure white

Upperparts Solid Black
White or Whitish Below

AMERICAN REDSTART
(1) *Brilliant orange-red patches on sides, wings, and outer base of tail feathers.*
(2) *Belly white, throat black.*

FEMALE: Olive-gray replaces black; yellow replaces orange. Younger breeding males resemble females.

VOICE: High, weak *tēē tēē tēē tēē tuh uh,* sometimes ascending at end.
NESTS: Newfoundland to Alaska and south to northern half of Gulf States.
WINTERS: West Indies, Central and South America.

CLIFF SWALLOW*
(1) *Dark throat patch blending into buff and whitish belly.*
(2) *Forehead whitish.*

Blackish brown above. Buff rump. Tail almost square. Commonly seen in large flocks on telephone wires.
SEXES: Alike.
VOICE: (1) Alarm note: loud, down-sloping *eeyo.* (2) Call: a husky, squeaky *wee, wit,* or *wit-wit.*
NESTS: Southern Canada to Texas in West and Virginia in East. In gourdlike mud nests outside barns or on bridges or cliffs.
WINTERS: South America.

TREE SWALLOW*
(1) *Pure-white underparts.*
(2) *Steely blue back.*

Tail slightly forked. (Immatures are brown above.) Commonly seen in large flocks on telephone wires.
FEMALE: Usually duller.
VOICE: Clear musical whistle in two-note, sometimes three-note, phrases, often long-continued.
NESTS: Labrador to Alaska, south to northeastern Kansas in West and Maryland in East. Usually in tree cavities or birdhouses.
WINTERS: From Gulf north to Washington, occasionally to Massachusetts.

EASTERN KINGBIRD

Orange-red

Slate-black

White

White

Yellow

Black—

BLACK-BACKED
WOODPECKER

Chestnut

Blue-
black

Chestnut

Buff to
whitish

Long, forked

BARN SWALLOW

38

Upperparts Solid Black

White or Whitish Below

EASTERN KINGBIRD*

(1)   *Dark slate above appears black in field.*
(2)   *Tip of tail and belly white.*

Wing feathers slightly white-edged. Orange-red crown patch, rarely seen. Perches in open exposed places and chases insects on the wing.

SEXES: Similar.

VOICE: (1) Unmusical sputter. (2) A harsh *dzeeb*.

NESTS: Northern Ontario to northern British Columbia and south to Gulf.

WINTERS: Mostly Mexico and Central America.

BLACK-BACKED WOODPECKER

(1)   *Head and back solid black.*
(2)   *Yellow cap.*

Throat and outer sides of tail white. Sides barred black and white. Broad white stripe below ear and eye. Flight feathers white-spotted.

FEMALE: Lacks yellow crown.

VOICE: Sharp, shrill *chirk chirk;* also loud single call: *click-click*.

RESIDENT OR NESTS: Labrador to Alaska, south to northern fringe of border states to Maine and in mountains from northern New York to New Hampshire.

WINTERS: As far south as New Jersey.

NOTE: Northern Three-toed Woodpecker (rare) is similar to above but back is barred.

Buffy Below

BARN SWALLOW*

(1)   *Tail very deeply forked (swallow-tailed).*
(2)   *Forehead and throat chestnut. Underparts buffy.*

Upperparts blue-black. White spots on each tail feather. Commonly seen in large flocks on telephone wires.

FEMALE: Lighter underparts and forehead.

VOICE: Low musical chattering trill in medley of notes.

NESTS: Labrador to Alaska and south to Gulf. Usually inside barns.

WINTERS: Central America to central Chile and Argentina.

All black and white

BLACK-AND-WHITE WARBLER

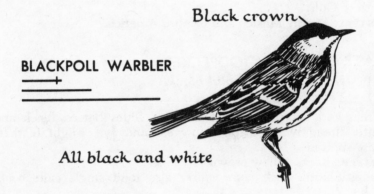

Black crown

BLACKPOLL WARBLER

All black and white

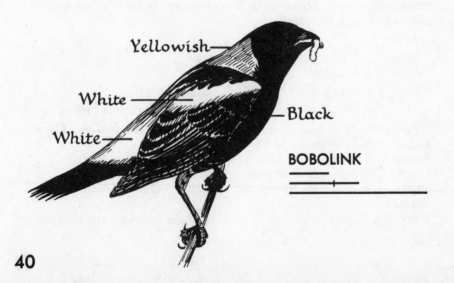

Yellowish

White

White

Black

BOBOLINK

Heavily Striped Black and White

BLACK-AND-WHITE WARBLER

(1) *Striped black and white above and on sides.*
(2) *Black eye patch bordered by white.*

Lower belly white. Two white wing bars. Usually seen creeping up limbs and trunks of trees.
FEMALE: Similar, except less black striping below.
VOICE: High-pitched *weesee-weesee-weesee* with variations.
NESTS: Northern Canada to Gulf States.
WINTERS: Mexico to South America.

BLACKPOLL WARBLER

(1) *Large black cap.*
(2) *Lower face white.*

Upperparts gray, yellowish-tinged, and black-striped. Underparts white, black-striped. Two wing bars. Black-and-white Warbler, which is similar, does not have solid-black crown.
FEMALE: Lower face gray, no black cap. Streaked with olive above. White below, lightly streaked.
VOICE: Thin, regular, high-pitched *zi-zi-zi-zi-zi-zi-zi*.
NESTS: Labrador to northern Alaska, south to Maine and high mountains of New York and New England.
WINTERS: South America.

Mostly Black Above and Below

BOBOLINK

(1) *Big white patches on wings and rump.*
(2) *Large yellowish patch back of head. Wing feathers white-edged.*

Solid black below. Found in meadows.
FEMALE: Yellowish line above eye and center of dark crown. Back heavily striped with brown.
VOICE: Delightful, rollicking, reedy, as if singing two or three songs at once in a sudden burst; often in flight.
NESTS: Nova Scotia to southern British Columbia, south to central Nebraska, and east to western Maryland.
WINTERS: South America.

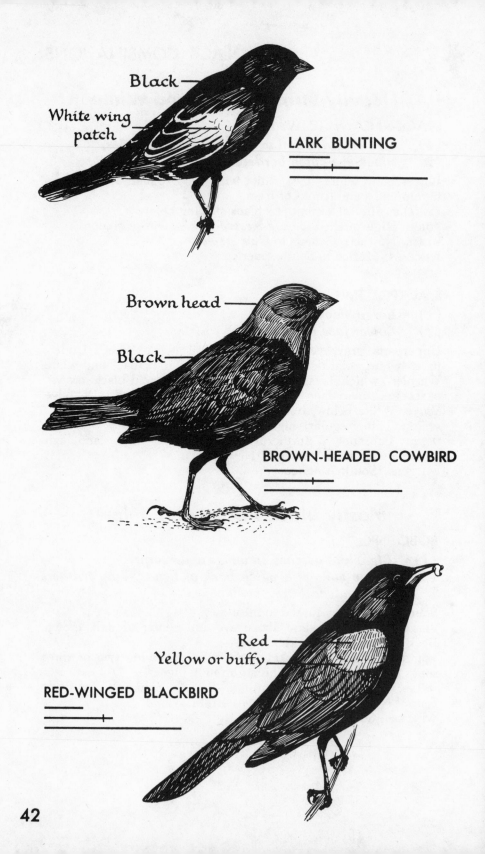

Black

White wing
patch

LARK BUNTING

Brown head

Black

BROWN-HEADED COWBIRD

Red
Yellow or buffy

RED-WINGED BLACKBIRD

Mostly Black Above and Below

LARK BUNTING

Solid black throughout except for conspicuous white wing patch and wing feathers white-edged.

In winter males lose most of black.
FEMALE: Brownish with striped breast.
VOICE: Soft sweet trills.
NESTS: Southwestern Canada to northern Texas and eastward to central Kansas.
WINTERS: Southwestern border states and Mexico.

BROWN-HEADED COWBIRD*

(1) *Solid black, except for brown head.*
(2) *Stubby bill.*

Commonly feeds on ground, often in flocks and associated with Blackbirds.
FEMALE: Uniform gray and lightly mottled.
VOICE: High, squeaky note followed by rattle and another squeak, such as *glub-glub-gleek*.
BREEDS: Southern Canada to Gulf. Lays eggs in other birds' nests.
WINTERS: Mostly in Southern States.

RED-WINGED BLACKBIRD*

(1) *Solid shiny black, except for red patch on wing with yellow or buffy border.*
(2) *Slender bill.*

FEMALE: Grayish brown, heavily striped.
VOICE: (1) Variety of notes. (2) Three-note phrase, first two

liquid, pure-toned, last note quavering and reedy: *conk ul reeee*.
NESTS: Central Canada to Gulf States, in damp and marshy places.
WINTERS: Mostly Southern States.

Yellow

White wing patch

YELLOW-HEADED BLACKBIRD

Red

Black

Red

White patch

PILEATED WOODPECKER

Mostly Black Above and Below

YELLOW-HEADED BLACKBIRD

(1) *Yellow head.*

(2) *Conspicuous white wing patch in flight. Body black.*

FEMALE: Brown, yellowish throat, streaked breast.

VOICE: An exceedingly raspy *caak,* and series of unmusical noises.

NESTS: Mostly western marshy places. Central Canada south to Nebraska. Occasionally wanders to east coast.

WINTERS: Western Gulf States and Mexico.

PILEATED WOODPECKER

(1) *Brilliant red crest.*

(2) *Mainly black, long white neck patch and wing patch.*

Very large sharp bill. Red streak behind bill.

FEMALE: No red streak behind bill. Front of crown grayish brown.

VOICE: Loud, deliberate, one-pitched *kuk-kuk-kukkuk-kuk-kuk,* similar to that of the Flicker but deeper-pitched. Often located by heavy chopping sound as it pecks huge oblong holes in decaying trees.

RESIDENT: Forested regions, southern Canada to Gulf.

Dusky
gray

CHIMNEY SWIFT

Body sooty black

Body
blue-black

PURPLE MARTIN

RUSTY BLACKBIRD

Solid black
Rusty only in fall
and winter.

All Black

CHIMNEY SWIFT*

(1)   "A cigar with wings."
(2)   Sooty black except for dusky grayish throat.

Stubby short tail. No markings. Narrow wings form crescent in flight and are held stiff. Rapid wingbeat in flying. Never perches out of doors.
FEMALE: Similar.
VOICE: Loud, rapid "chippering."
NESTS: Southern Canada to Gulf States. Usually in chimneys.
WINTERS: South America.

PURPLE MARTIN*

(1)   Blue-black above and below.
(2)   Very wide wings at base.

Notched tail. Catches insects on the wing.
FEMALE: Gray below, top of head and nape speckled gray and whitish. Immature males resembling females often breed.
VOICE: Sweet melodious whistle.
NESTS: Southern Canada to Gulf. In birdhouses or other cavities.
WINTERS: South America.

RUSTY BLACKBIRD*

(1)   Slaty black slightly glossed in spring.
(2)   Whitish eye.

Slender sharp bill. Tail not wedge-shaped. Rusty only in fall and winter. Can be distinguished from Grackles by much smaller size and smaller tail, which is neither wedge-shaped nor keel-shaped.
FEMALE: Uniform brownish gray with whitish eye.
VOICE: (1) A loud *chack*. (2) A creaky *coo-a-lee*.
NESTS: Alaska to Labrador, south to northern New York, and east to Maine.
WINTERS: Mostly Southern States.

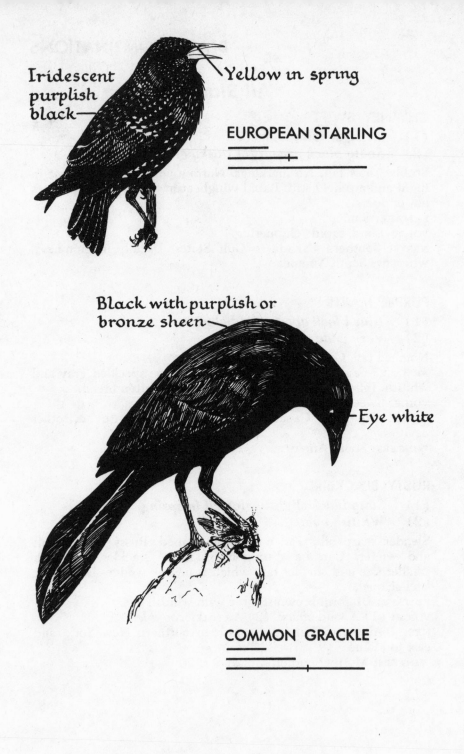

Iridescent purplish black—

Yellow in spring

EUROPEAN STARLING

Black with purplish or bronze sheen—

—Eye white

COMMON GRACKLE

All Black

EUROPEAN STARLING*

(1)   *Iridescent purplish black; back spotted.*
(2)   *Wings brownish-striped.*

Long sharp bill, yellow in spring. Usually in flocks and around towns and on lawns. Can be distinguished from other black-colored birds by heavy-set body, short tail, and long sharp bill.
FEMALE: Similar but duller.
VOICE: (1) *feee-u*, descending from high pitch. (2) A mixture of whistles and raspy notes, often imitating other birds.
NESTS OR RESIDENT: Southern Newfoundland to southern British Columbia and south to Gulf.

COMMON GRACKLE*

(1)   *Head and neck iridescent purplish.*
(2)   *Long wedge-shaped tail.*

Back and underparts black with either purplish or bronze sheen. White eye. Long down-curved bill. Commonly on ground in lawns or gardens.
FEMALE: Smaller, less iridescent.
VOICE: A squeaky *kuchakeweeke* going up the scale.
NESTS: Labrador to British Columbia and south to Gulf States.
WINTERS: Mostly Southern States.

Iridescent black——

BOAT-TAILED GRACKLE

All Black

BOAT-TAILED GRACKLE

(1) *Iridescent black throughout.*

(2) *Very long tail shaped like keel of boat.*

Large bill. Neck ruffled only in song. Often found near water.
FEMALE: Much smaller. Generally brown, dark above, buffy below. Dark line through eye.
VOICE: A harsh *check,* also a great variety of *cluck's* and loud whistles.
NESTS OR RESIDENT: Atlantic coast, New Jersey south, and Gulf States.

Solid black

FISH CROW

All Black

FISH CROW
(1)   *All black; smaller and glossier than American Crow.*
(2)   *Lives near tidewater.*
Distinguished from American Crow by its voice and habitat.
SEXES: Alike.
VOICE: Short and very different from that of the American Crow.
Sounds like the *ock* in "sock."
NESTS OR RESIDENT: Atlantic coast, Rhode Island to Florida.

Solid black

AMERICAN CROW

All Black

AMERICAN CROW*

(1)   *Solid black.*
(2)   *Large heavy bill.*

Usually in flocks.
SEXES: Alike.
VOICE: Loud *caw* or *cah*.
RESIDENT: Canada to Gulf.

Solid black

COMMON RAVEN

All Black

COMMON RAVEN

(1)   *Crow-like in appearance but larger, also with large heavy bill.*

(2)   *Tail wedge-shaped.*

Ruffled throat feathers often seen at close range. Often seen singly or in pairs rather than in flocks.

SEXES: Alike.

VOICE: Loud *cr-r-rawk* or *cruk,* with a rolling and repeated *r.*

RESIDENT: Rare in area covered by this guide. Northern Canada and south to Quebec, Maine, and northern edge of Great Lakes. Also south in mountains to Georgia.

Bald and black

BLACK VULTURE

Body black —

Tail
short and wide

All Black

BLACK VULTURE

(1) *Solid black except for prominent white areas under wings in flight.*

(2) *Short broad tail and very broad wings.*

Head bald and black, whereas Turkey Vulture's is red. Large hooked beak. Feeds largely on carrion. In flight from below can be distinguished from Turkey Vulture, which has longer narrow wings (lighter in the back) and a long tail. Black Vulture soars less and flaps wings more often than Turkey Vulture.

SEXES: Alike.

RESIDENT: Missouri to Maryland and south to Gulf. Casual north to Canadian border provinces.

TURKEY VULTURE

Bald and red

Body rusty black

All Black

TURKEY VULTURE*

(1) *Long narrow wings seen from below are two-toned, black in front, lighter behind.*

(2) *Wingspread six feet. Bare red head and neck.*

Usually seen soaring. Eats carrion.

SEXES: Alike.

VOICE: A weak hissing when angry, or a subdued croak, seldom heard.

NESTS: Southern Canada to Gulf.

WINTERS: As far north as southern New Jersey and Ohio Valley.

Bluish

Yellow

Chestnut

White

NORTHERN PARULA

Two wing bars

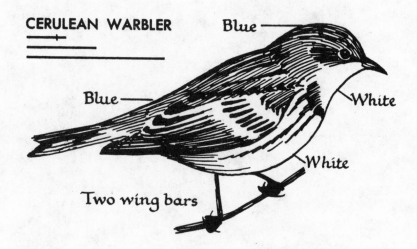

CERULEAN WARBLER

Blue

Blue

White

White

Two wing bars

BLUE-WINGED WARBLER

Yellow

Yellow

Wings bluish,
two wing bars

With Wing Bars

NORTHERN PARULA

(1) *Bluish above.*
(2) *Yellow throat and breast divided by dark chestnut chest band.*

White wing bars. Greenish patch middle of back. White belly. White patch near tips of outer tail feathers.
FEMALE: Similar but duller.
VOICE: Buzzing, rising trill ending in sharp lower *tup*, or buzzy notes ending in rising trill.
NESTS: Southern Canada to Gulf.
WINTERS: Mostly West Indies, also Central America and eastern Mexico.

CERULEAN WARBLER

(1) *Light-blue back, striped. Two wings bars. Underparts white.*
(2) *Dark line across breast.*

Striped on sides. White spots on tail feathers.
FEMALE: Lighter blue and faint stripes. Breast clear.
VOICE: Variable four to six buzzy notes on same pitch.
NESTS: Southeastern Nebraska to northern New Jersey and south to Louisiana.
WINTERS: South America.

BLUE-WINGED WARBLER

(1) *Face, fore crown, and underparts bright yellow. Black eye line.*
(2) *Bluish-gray wings; two wing bars.*

Rump yellowish. Other upperparts olive.
FEMALE: Similar to male but duller.
VOICE: Variable; commonest: two buzzy notes, second lower, with trilly *burr*.
NESTS: Central Nebraska to southeastern Massachusetts and south to northern Georgia, Missouri, and Kansas.
WINTERS: Central America and southeastern Mexico.

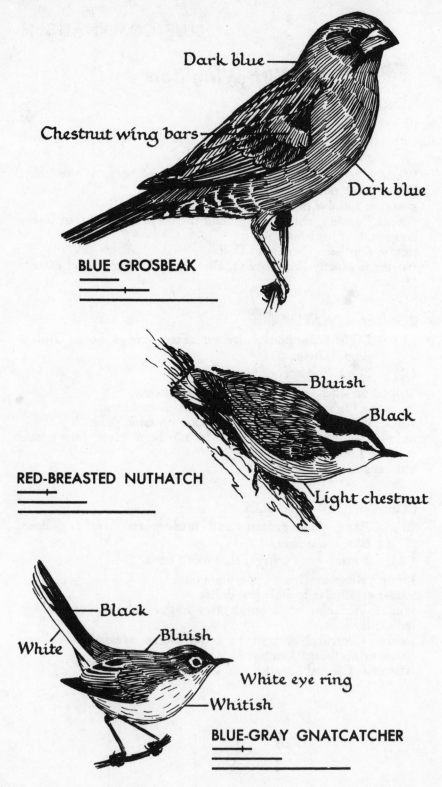

Dark blue

Chestnut wing bars

Dark blue

BLUE GROSBEAK

Bluish

Black

RED-BREASTED NUTHATCH

Light chestnut

Black

Bluish

White

White eye ring

Whitish

BLUE-GRAY GNATCATCHER

With Wing Bars

BLUE GROSBEAK
(1) *Deep blue above and below. Wings and tail black, feathers edged with buff and blue.*
(2) *Two chestnut wing bars.*
Heavy bill. Indigo Bunting is much smaller, has a much thinner bill, no chestnut wing bars.
FEMALE: Brown above and below. Two buff wing bars.
VOICE: Short sweet Finch-like warble.
NESTS: Oklahoma through Missouri, southern Illinois, southeastern Pennsylvania, and southwestern New Jersey, to Gulf. Casual north to Canadian border.
WINTERS: Central America.

No Wing Bars

RED-BREASTED NUTHATCH
(1) *Black cap, black eye line surmounted by white. White throat.*
(2) *Light chestnut underparts.*
Outer tail feathers white. Bluish above. "Upside-down" bird. Usually seen in evergreens.
FEMALE: Generally lighter.
VOICE: A sharp, high, nasal *ank-ank*.
NESTS OR RESIDENT: Alaska, Canada, northern edge of Great Lakes States, and in mountains to North Carolina.

BLUE-GRAY GNATCATCHER
(1) *Very slim with long black tail, white-edged.*
(2) *White eye ring.*
Bluish upperparts. Black line from base of bill over eye. Underparts whitish. Very nervous habits.
FEMALE: Similar, but less blue above.
VOICE: (1) Series of thin squeaky notes. (2) A wheezy *spee*.
NESTS: Eastern Nebraska to northern New Jersey and south to Gulf.
WINTERS: Central America and Mexico.

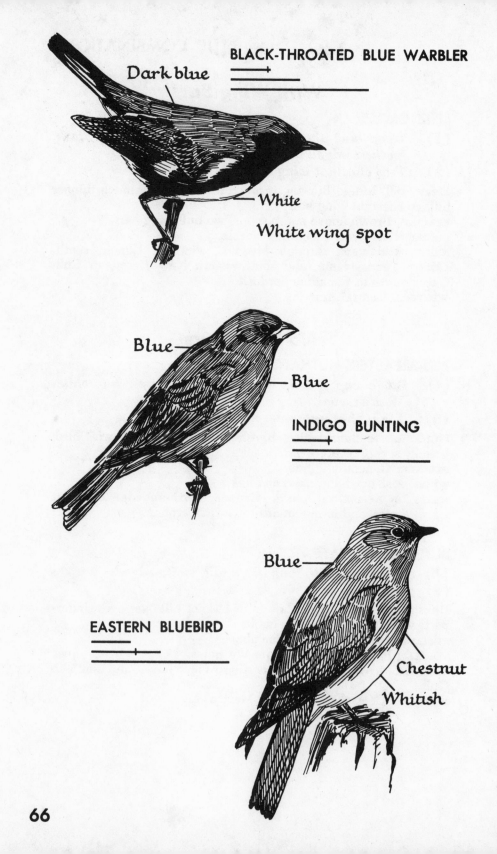

BLACK-THROATED BLUE WARBLER

Dark blue

White

White wing spot

Blue

Blue

INDIGO BUNTING

Blue

EASTERN BLUEBIRD

Chestnut

Whitish

No Wing Bars

BLACK-THROATED BLUE WARBLER
(1) *Black throat, extending along sides.*
(2) *Upperparts dark blue.*
White wing spot. Belly white.
FEMALE: Olive or olive-brown above, no black markings. Yellowish below. Light eye stripe; small white wing spot.
VOICE: Three or four husky burred notes followed by high clear note: *zur zur zur zree.*
NESTS: Southern Canada and Great Lakes States to northern New Jersey and in mountains to North Carolina.
WINTERS: Key West, mainly, and West Indies.

INDIGO BUNTING*
(1) *Solid blue above and below.*
(2) *Wings and tail darker. Bill small and stubby.*
Common in tree-grown fields. Blue Grosbeak is larger and duller blue with chestnut wing bars and much heavier bill.
FEMALE: Generally brownish and spotted below.
VOICE: (1) Sharp *tsick.* (2) Extremely high, gay, musical, in definite two-note (occasionally three-note) phrases usually from treetop:

tea tea tea tea tea tea teedleedlee.
NESTS: Southeastern Canada, south to South Dakota, east to Maine, and south to Gulf.
WINTERS: Central America.

EASTERN BLUEBIRD*
(1) *Solid blue above.*
(2) *Chestnut below.*
Belly whitish.
FEMALE: Paler and duller.
VOICE: (1) Note: often in flight; soft, sweet *cherwee.* (2) Song: rapid series of soft slurred notes.
NESTS: Southern Canada to Gulf.
WINTERS: From Central America north, occasionally as far north as southern New England and southern Great Lakes States.

BLUE JAY

Blue

Blue

Whitish

Whitish

BELTED KINGFISHER

Blue

White

Bluish

White

Crest Pronounced

BLUE JAY*

(1)   *High blue crest. Black necklace.*
(2)   *White bar and spots on bright blue wing.*

Outer tail feathers white-tipped. Gray-blue above, whitish below.
SEXES: Alike.
VOICE: (1) Harsh, screaming *jeay*. (2) A note like rusty hinge. (3) Variety of unmusical notes.
RESIDENT: Central Canada to Gulf.

BELTED KINGFISHER*

(1)   *High, ragged bluish-gray crest.*
(2)   *Underparts white, crossed by bluish-gray belt on breast. Upperparts blue. Very large, long bill.*

Found near water.
FEMALE: Chestnut band on sides and below blue-gray belt.
VOICE: Loud, harsh rattle; often in flight.
NESTS: Alaska and Canada and south to Gulf.
WINTERS: New Jersey, Ohio, and Illinois south.

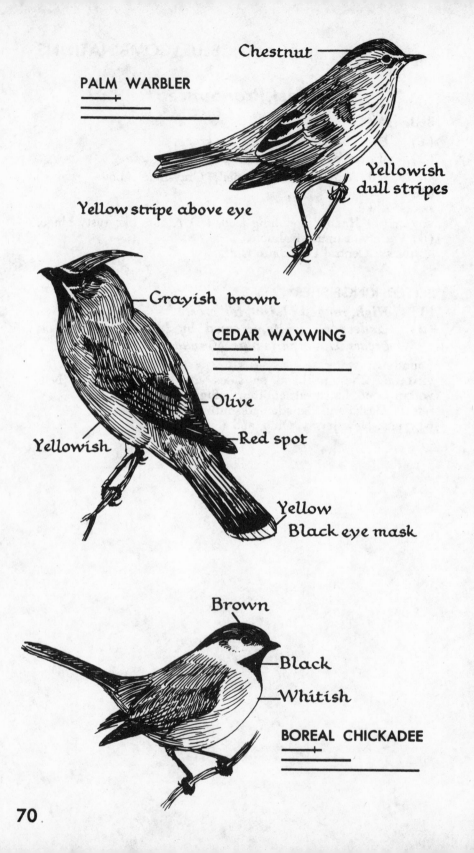

Chestnut

PALM WARBLER

Yellowish
dull stripes

Yellow stripe above eye

Grayish brown

CEDAR WAXWING

Olive

Red spot

Yellowish

Yellow
Black eye mask

Brown

Black

Whitish

BOREAL CHICKADEE

BROWN, RUFOUS, OR CHESTNUT COMBINATIONS

Crown Chestnut or Brown

Yellowish Underparts

PALM WARBLER
(1) *Chestnut cap. Yellow stripe over eye, dark stripe through eye.*
(2) *Constantly flicks tail up and down.*

Underparts yellowish, faintly striped. Undertail coverts bright yellow. Back dull olive-gray. Rump yellowish. Usually found on or near ground.
SEXES: Similar.
VOICE: Series of weak *thi-thi-thi-thi*'s.
NESTS: Southern Newfoundland to Mackenzie, south to northeastern Minnesota in West and Maine in East.
WINTERS: Southern States south into West Indies and Central America.

CEDAR WAXWING*
(1) *Prominent crest.*
(2) *Black eye mask and chin.*

Other upperparts grayish brown. Red spot on wing. Tip of tail yellow. Underparts yellowish. Commonly in flocks, often seen catching insects on wing like Flycatcher.
SEXES: Alike.
VOICE: High thin lisp.
NESTS: Newfoundland to Alaska, south to southern Illinois, and east to Georgia.
WINTERS: Southern Ontario to southern British Columbia and south to Gulf.

Black Throat

BOREAL CHICKADEE
(1) *Brown cap above white face.*
(2) *Black throat.*

Upperparts brownish gray. Whitish below, washed with brown on sides.
SEXES: Alike.
VOICE: Harsh *dee-dee waah waah*.
RESIDENT: Northern Alaska, Canada, and northern fringe of border states, occasionally farther south in winter.

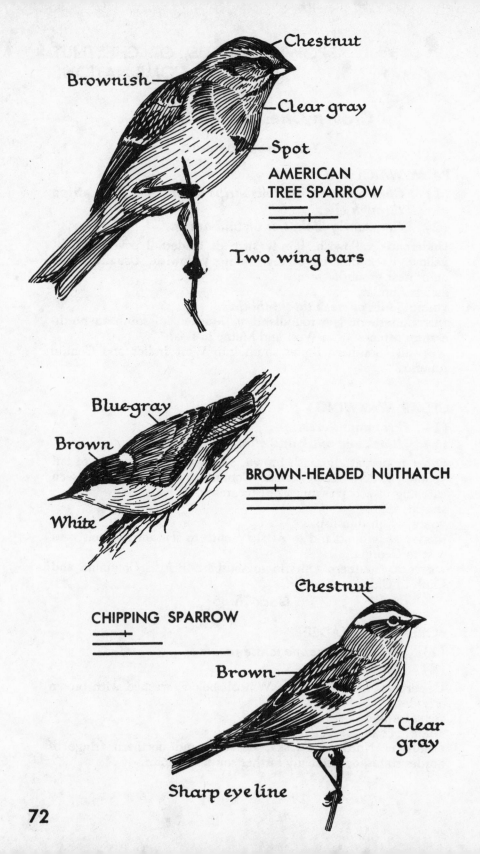

Chestnut

Brownish

Clear gray

Spot

AMERICAN
TREE SPARROW

Two wing bars

Bluegray

Brown

BROWN-HEADED NUTHATCH

White

CHIPPING SPARROW

Chestnut

Brown

Clear
gray

Sharp eye line

72

BROWN, RUFOUS, OR CHESTNUT COMBINATIONS

Crown Chestnut or Brown

Black Spot on Breast

AMERICAN TREE SPARROW

(1) *Black spot on clear gray breast.*
(2) *Chestnut crown.*

Dark line through eye. Two wing bars. Upperparts brownish-striped.

SEXES: Alike.

VOICE: Variable, starting with one or two high musical notes, then more rapid and lower in pitch.

NESTS: Northern Alaska and northern Canada.

WINTERS: Central Minnesota, southern fringe of Canada to Maine, south to Oklahoma, and east to North Carolina.

Clear Gray Underparts

BROWN-HEADED NUTHATCH

(1) *Top of head and back of neck brown.*
(2) *Works usually downhill.*

White spot near edge of brown. Chin white. Back blue-gray. Tail black, white spot on outer tail feather. Underparts whitish washed with buff or gray.

FEMALE: Similar.

VOICE: Musical whispering calls.

RESIDENT: Arkansas to southern Delaware and south to Gulf. Casual to New Jersey.

CHIPPING SPARROW*

(1) *Chestnut crown.*
(2) *White line above eye and black line through eye.*

Forked tail. Brown-streaked above. Clear gray below. Two inconspicuous wing bars. Commonly feeds on ground, often near houses.

SEXES: Similar.

VOICE: *Chip-chip-chip,* often long-continued on one pitch.

NESTS: Newfoundland to Alaska and south to Gulf.

WINTERS: Mainly Southern States.

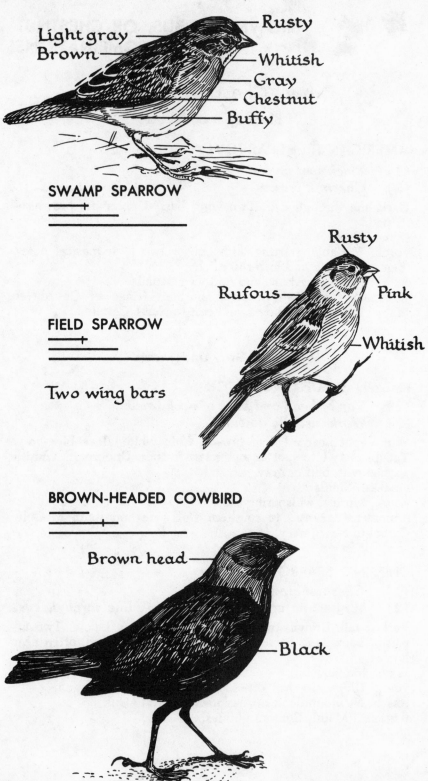

Rusty

Light gray
Brown

Whitish
Gray
Chestnut
Buffy

SWAMP SPARROW

FIELD SPARROW

Two wing bars

Rusty

Rufous

Pink

Whitish

BROWN-HEADED COWBIRD

Brown head

Black

BROWN, RUFOUS, OR CHESTNUT COMBINATIONS

Crown Chestnut or Brown

Clear Gray Underparts

SWAMP SPARROW
(1) *Rusty cap.*
(2) *Black line through eye, gray line above eye.*
Whitish throat. No wing bars. Brownish-streaked above. Clear grayish below. Chestnut on wings. Buffy flanks. Found chiefly in or near swamps or brushy meadows.
SEXES: Alike.
VOICE: (1) Sweet, fairly loud succession of trills, each changing in pitch. (2) A hard *chink*.
NESTS: Northern Canada south to eastern Nebraska and east to Delaware.
WINTERS: Southern New England to Mexico.

FIELD SPARROW*
(1) *Pink bill.*
(2) *Buffy eye ring and stripe behind eye.*
Rusty cap. Rufous-striped above. Whitish below, blending to brownish on upper breast and sides. Two wing bars. Generally light appearance.
SEXES: Alike.
VOICE: Three or four pure sweet whistles followed by shorter ones and ending in trill on one pitch:

—— —— —— —— — — — — - - ···

NESTS: Canadian border provinces to Gulf.
WINTERS: Mostly in Southern States.

Head Brown, Body Black

BROWN-HEADED COWBIRD*
(1) *Solid black, except for brown head.*
(2) *Stubby bill.*
Commonly feeds on ground, often in flocks and associated with Blackbirds.
FEMALE: Uniform gray and lightly mottled.
VOICE: High, squeaky note followed by rattle and another squeak, such as *glub-glub-gleek*.
BREEDS: Southern Canada to Gulf. Lays eggs in other birds' nests.
WINTERS: Mostly in Southern States.

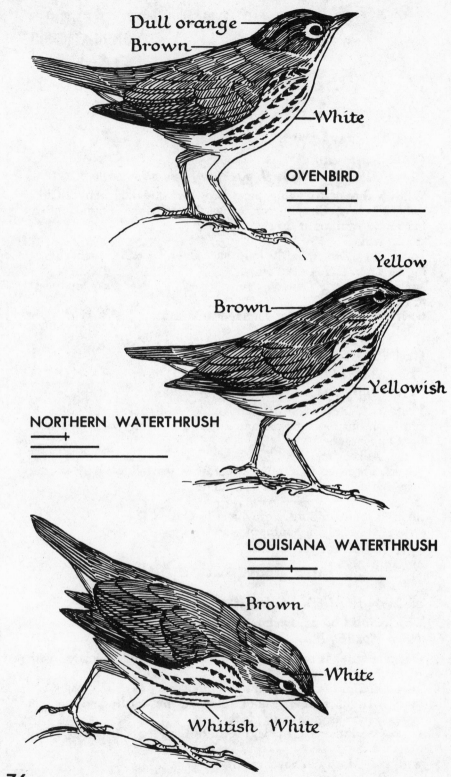

Dull orange
Brown

White

OVENBIRD

Yellow

Brown

Yellowish

NORTHERN WATERTHRUSH

LOUISIANA WATERTHRUSH

Brown

White

Whitish   White

BROWN, RUFOUS, OR CHESTNUT COMBINATIONS

Upperparts Solid Brown or Rufous Breast or Underparts Spotted

Orange Crown

OVENBIRD

(1) *Heavily spotted on whitish breast, chin and belly white.*

(2) *Eye ring and dull orange crown.*

Walks teetering in deep woods, often on logs.
FEMALE: Similar but duller.
VOICE: Metallic, penetrating, in two-note phrases starting softly and ending very loud:

— — — — — — — — — —

ka dee ka dee ka dee ka dee ka Dee KADEE!
NESTS: Newfoundland to British Columbia, south to North Dakota, and east to northern Georgia.
WINTERS: Central America and northern South America.

Pronounced Eye Line

NORTHERN WATERTHRUSH

(1) *Yellowish below, heavily streaked, including middle of throat.*

(2) *Conspicuous yellowish eye stripe. Brown above.*

Constantly teeters. Usually found near water.
SEXES: Alike.
VOICE: Ten or twelve liquid, ringing notes, accelerating at end and dropping in pitch.
NESTS: Northern Canada to northern Great Lakes region and east to Rhode Island.
WINTERS: West Indies, Central and South America.

LOUISIANA WATERTHRUSH

(1) *Conspicuous white eye stripe.*

(2) *White chin, rest below whitish, heavily streaked.*

Constantly teeters. Usually found in vicinity of wooded streams.
SEXES: Alike.
VOICE: Starts with three or four slow, up-slurred, ringing whistles followed by jumble of lowered whistles.
NESTS: Eastern Nebraska to Rhode Island and south to Gulf.
WINTERS: West Indies and Central America to northern South America.

WATER PIPIT

Grayish brown

Buffy

White

Walks, does not hop
Buffy wing bars

Brown

Bright rufous

Cream buff

Whitish

HERMIT THRUSH

Rufous

Olive-brown

Heavy spots
on white

WOOD THRUSH

Eye ring

BROWN, RUFOUS, OR CHESTNUT
COMBINATIONS
Upperparts Solid Brown or Rufous
Breast or Underparts Spotted

Dull Buffy Underparts

WATER PIPIT

(1)   *Upper breast and sides buffy, streaked or spotted with dark brown.*

(2)   *Tail, which constantly wags, is white-edged.*

Very light buffy wing bars. Grayish brown above. Slender bill. Light line through eye. Walks, does not hop.

SEXES: Alike.

VOICE: A thin *jee-ett.*

NESTS: Labrador, northern Canada, and northern Alaska.

WINTERS: Open country, New Jersey and Ohio south into Mexico and Central America.

Tail Rufous

HERMIT THRUSH

(1)   *Rufous tail brighter than brown upperparts.*

(2)   *Chest and lower cheeks pale cream buff, dusky-streaked and -spotted.*

Belly whitish. Slender bill. Dull whitish eye ring. At rest, cocks tail and lets it droop slowly. Usually found in wooded areas.

SEXES: Alike.

VOICE: A long ethereal opening note, followed by a series with tremolo effect. A pause between phrases.

NESTS: Wooded areas Alaska and Canada to Minnesota, east to Massachusetts, and in mountains to Maryland.

WINTERS: Southern States, Mexico, and Central America.

Head Rufous

WOOD THRUSH*

(1)   *Bright rufous head brighter than rest of body. Remaining upperparts olive-brown.*

(2)   *Breast and sides heavily spotted on white.*

Slender bill. Distinct eye ring. Larger and built heavier than other Thrushes.

SEXES: Alike.

VOICE: Lovely, unhurried, bell-like three-syllabled note with sputtering at end of each phrase if heard close: *ee o lee* (sputter) *o ee o* (sputter).

NESTS: Southern fringe of Canada to Gulf.

WINTERS: Florida and south into Central America.

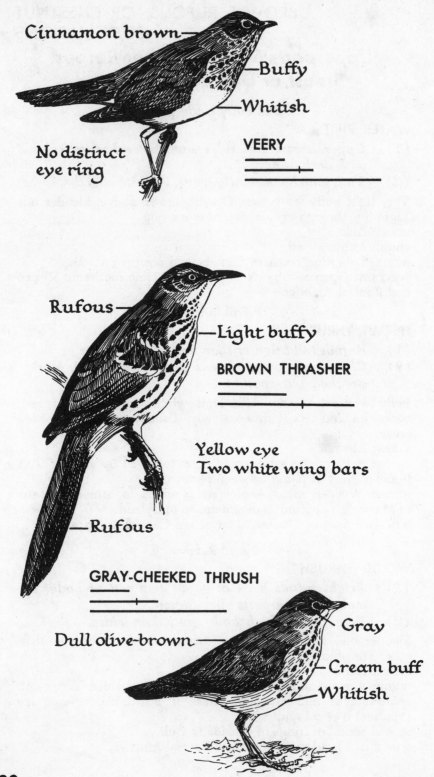

Cinnamon brown—

—Buffy

—Whitish

No distinct
eye ring

VEERY

Rufous—

—Light buffy

BROWN THRASHER

Yellow eye
Two white wing bars

—Rufous

GRAY-CHEEKED THRUSH

Dull olive-brown—

—Gray

—Cream buff

—Whitish

BROWN, RUFOUS, OR CHESTNUT COMBINATIONS

Upperparts Solid Brown or Rufous Breast or Underparts Spotted

Upperparts Bright Rufous

VEERY

(1) *Uniformly cinnamon or brown above.*
(2) *Indistinct, tawny spots on buffy throat.*

No distinct eye ring. Whitish below. Sides grayish-buffy.
SEXES: Alike.
VOICE: Exquisite, tremulous, echo-like notes sliding down the scale in two phrases: *veeur veeur veeur veeur*.
NESTS: Woods, southern Canada to Iowa, east to Maine, and in mountains to Georgia.
WINTERS: South America.

BROWN THRASHER*

(1) *Bright rufous above with long rufous tail. Buffy or whitish below, heavily streaked or spotted.*
(2) *Long down-curved bill, yellow eye.*

Two white wing bars.
SEXES: Alike.
VOICE: Loud burst of great variety of notes, long-continued, both musical and harsh and commonly in pairs.
NESTS: Southern fringe of Canada to Gulf.
WINTERS: Mostly in Southern States.

Upperparts Dull Olive-Brown

GRAY-CHEEKED THRUSH

(1) *Gray cheeks.*
(2) *Indistinct eye ring.*

Dull olive-brown above; not reddish. Spotted throat and breast, whitish belly, grayish olive on sides.
SEXES: Alike.
VOICE: Musical, thin, quavery, but tending downward, slightly resembling that of the Veery.
NESTS: Labrador to northern Alaska and south into mountains of New York and New England.
WINTERS: West Indies and northern South America.

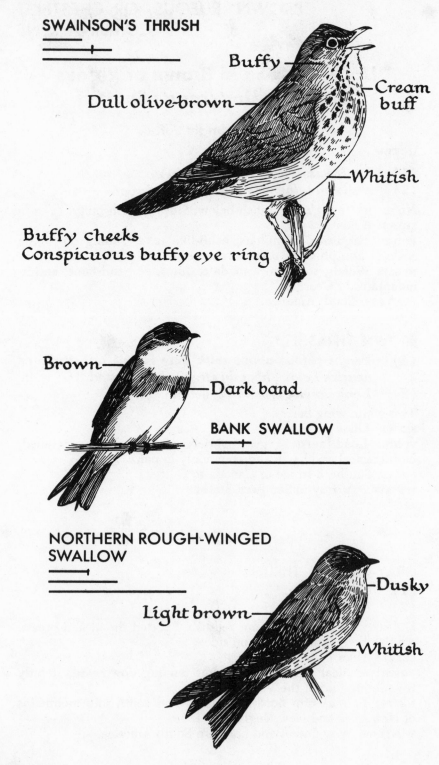

SWAINSON'S THRUSH

Buffy

Cream buff

Dull olive-brown

Whitish

Buffy cheeks
Conspicuous buffy eye ring

Brown

Dark band

BANK SWALLOW

NORTHERN ROUGH-WINGED
SWALLOW

Dusky

Light brown

Whitish

BROWN, RUFOUS, OR CHESTNUT COMBINATIONS

Upperparts Solid Brown or Rufous
Breast or Underparts Spotted

Upperparts Dull Olive-Brown

SWAINSON'S THRUSH

(1) *Buffy eye ring and cheeks.*
(2) *Dull olive-brown above, not reddish. Upper throat lightly spotted on cream buff.*

Belly whitish.
SEXES: Alike.
VOICE: Melodious, breezy, flutelike phrases tending to climb upward.
NESTS: Alaska, Canada, and northern half of Great Lakes States to Maine and in mountains to West Virginia.
WINTERS: Central and South America.
Note: This is the A.O.U. Check List name for the former Olive-backed Thrush.

Underparts Whitish

BANK SWALLOW*

(1) *Dark band across breast. Rest of underparts white.*
(2) *Back brown.*

Commonly seen in large flocks on telephone wires.
SEXES: Alike.
VOICE: A soft twitter.
NESTS: Labrador to Alaska, south to Arkansas in West and Virginia in East. In holes in sand banks.
WINTERS: South America.

NORTHERN ROUGH-WINGED SWALLOW*

(1) *Throat and breast dusky brown, belly whitish.*
(2) *Notched tail.*

Back light brown. No distinct band across breast as in Bank Swallow. Commonly seen in large flocks on telephone wires.
SEXES: Alike.
VOICE: Rough and burry *trit*, or *trit-trit*, often repetitious.
NESTS: Southern Canada to Gulf States. In holes in sand banks.
WINTERS: Southern States south into Central America.

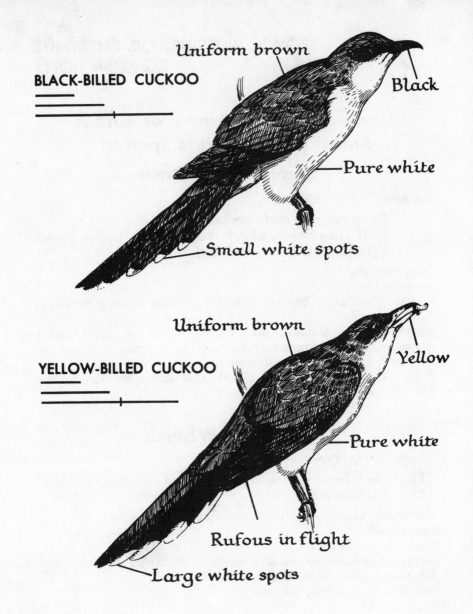

Uniform brown

BLACK-BILLED CUCKOO

Black

Pure white

Small white spots

Uniform brown

YELLOW-BILLED CUCKOO

Yellow

Pure white

Rufous in flight

Large white spots

BROWN, RUFOUS, OR CHESTNUT COMBINATIONS

Upperparts Solid Brown or Rufous Underparts Pure White

BLACK-BILLED CUCKOO*

(1) *Long, slim, with down-curved black bill and long tail.*

(2) *Gray under tail with small white spots.*

Tail feathers have dull white tips.

SEXES: Alike.

VOICE: Short, rapid, rather melodious groups of low throaty notes on one pitch. Like a Morse Code signal:

— — — —— —— ——

cook-cook-cook cook-cook-cook.

NESTS: Southern fringe of Canada to eastern Kansas and east to South Carolina.

WINTERS: Mostly South America.

YELLOW-BILLED CUCKOO*

(1) *Solid brown above, but outer wings rufous in flight. Slender with long tail. Lower half of bill yellow.*

(2) *Black under tail with large white spots. Outer edge of tail white.*

SEXES: Alike.

VOICE: A long sharp rattle (often not heard at a distance) followed by loud:

⅂ ⅂ ⅂ ⅂

kowk kowk kowk kowk.

NESTS: Southern fringe of Canada to Gulf.

WINTERS: South America.

Chestnut

Brown

Clear gray

CHIPPING SPARROW

Sharp eye line

Rusty

Light gray

Brown

Chestnut

Whitish

Gray

Buffy

SWAMP SPARROW

Rusty

Pink

Rufous

Whitish

FIELD SPARROW

Two wing bars

BROWN, RUFOUS, OR CHESTNUT COMBINATIONS

Upperparts Brown-Striped
Underparts Clear, Not Striped

Cap Chestnut

CHIPPING SPARROW*
(1)   *Chestnut crown.*
(2)   *White line above eye and black line through eye.*

Forked tail. Brown-streaked above. Clear gray below. Two inconspicuous wing bars. Commonly feeds on ground, often near houses.
SEXES: Similar.
VOICE: *Chip-chip-chip*, often long-continued on one pitch.
NESTS: Newfoundland to Alaska and south to Gulf.
WINTERS: Mainly Southern States.

SWAMP SPARROW
(1)   *Rusty cap.*
(2)   *Black line through eye, gray line above eye.*

Whitish throat. No wing bars. Brownish-streaked above. Clear grayish below. Chestnut on wings. Buffy flanks. Found chiefly in or near swamps or brushy meadows.
SEXES: Alike.
VOICE: (1) Sweet, fairly loud succession of trills, each changing in pitch. (2) A hard *chink*.
NESTS: Northern Canada south to eastern Nebraska and east to Delaware.
WINTERS: Southern New England to Mexico.

FIELD SPARROW*
(1)   *Pink bill.*
(2)   *Buffy eye ring and stripe behind eye.*

Rusty cap. Rufous-striped above. Whitish below, blending to brownish on upper breast and sides. Two wing bars. Generally light appearance.
SEXES: Alike.
VOICE: Three or four pure sweet whistles followed by shorter ones and ending in trill on one pitch:

— — — — — — — — — — — — — ···

NESTS: Canadian border provinces to Gulf.
WINTERS: Mostly in Southern States.

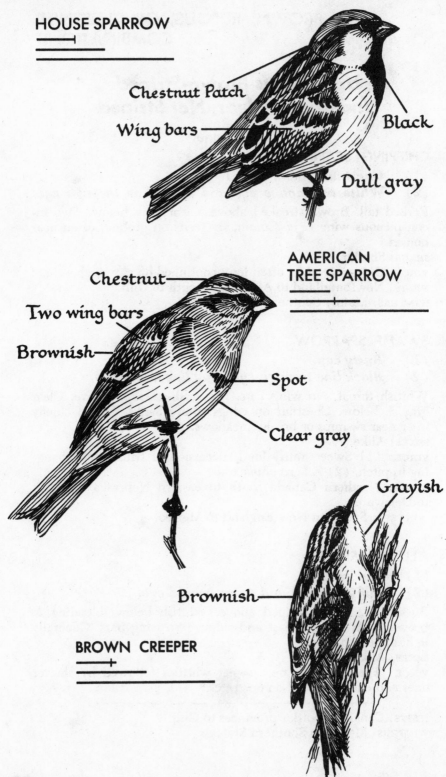

HOUSE SPARROW

Chestnut Patch

Wing bars

Black

Dull gray

AMERICAN
TREE SPARROW

Chestnut

Two wing bars

Brownish

Spot

Clear gray

Grayish

Brownish

BROWN CREEPER

BROWN, RUFOUS, OR CHESTNUT COMBINATIONS

Upperparts Brown-Striped
Underparts Clear, Not Striped

Cap Chestnut

HOUSE SPARROW*

(1) *Brownish-striped above, black throat.*
(2) *Whitish patch between black throat and chestnut patch.*

Faint wing bars, short stubby bill characteristic of most sparrows. Underparts dingy gray. Mostly about houses and barns and in city streets.

FEMALE: No black on throat; no chestnut markings; dull whitish stripe over eye.

VOICE: A monotonous, everlasting *chirrup* or *chisick* or *cheep*.

RESIDENT: Northern Canada to Gulf.

NOTE: Formerly known as English Sparrow but called House Sparrow in latest A.O.U. Check List.

AMERICAN TREE SPARROW

(1) *Black spot on clear gray breast.*
(2) *Chestnut crown.*

Dark line through eye. Two wing bars. Upperparts brownish-striped.

SEXES: Alike.

VOICE: Variable, starting with one or two high musical notes, then more rapid and lower in pitch.

NESTS: Northern Alaska and northern Canada.

WINTERS: Central Minnesota, southern fringe of Canada to Maine, south to Oklahoma, and east to North Carolina.

No Chestnut Cap

BROWN CREEPER

(1) *Creeps up tree trunks.*
(2) *Upperparts mottled brownish and buffy. Whitish to grayish below.*

Slender down-curved bill.

SEXES: Alike.

VOICE: (1) Call: very high *seeee*. (2) Song: five to six jumbled high, thin notes.

NESTS: Central Canada south to southeastern Nebraska, east to western Maryland, and in mountains to Tennessee.

WINTERS: Throughout most of its range.

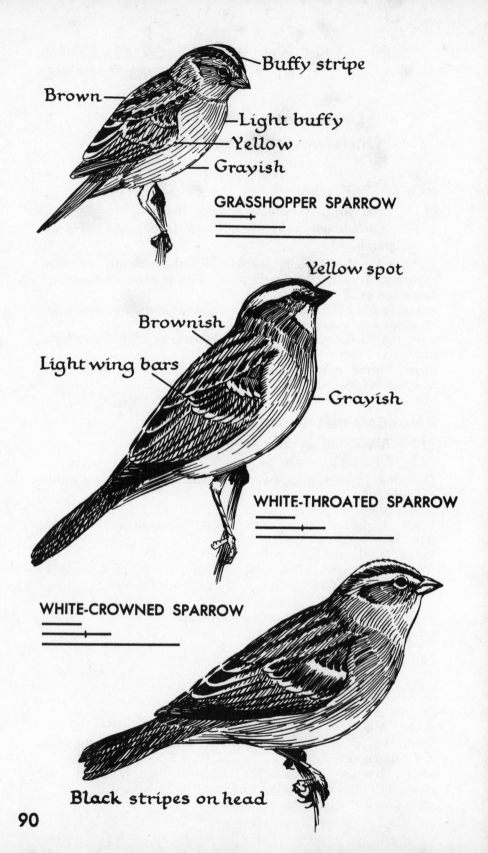

Buffy stripe

Brown

Light buffy

Yellow

Grayish

GRASSHOPPER SPARROW

Yellow spot

Brownish

Light wing bars

Grayish

WHITE-THROATED SPARROW

WHITE-CROWNED SPARROW

Black stripes on head

BROWN, RUFOUS, OR CHESTNUT COMBINATIONS

Upperparts Brown-Striped Underparts Clear, Not Striped

Prominent Head Stripes

GRASSHOPPER SPARROW

(1) *Light-buffy stripe through blackish crown and above eye.*

(2) *Short-tailed, flat-headed.*

Brownish above, heavily streaked. Throat light buff, unstreaked. Buffy eye spot and yellow streak on shoulder.

SEXES: Alike.

VOICE: Like an insect, a long *buzzz* with occasionally a few squeaks.

NESTS: Southern Canada south to Texas, Louisiana, and Georgia.

WINTERS: North Carolina and southern Illinois and south into South America.

WHITE-THROATED SPARROW*

(1) *Crown white, bordered by black stripes.*

(2) *White throat, yellow spot behind bill.*

Upperparts brownish-striped; two light wing bars; underparts grayish. (In immature, white lines are buffy and black lines are chestnut.)

FEMALE: Usually duller.

VOICE: Lovely plaintive whistle in minor key and long-drawn-out.

NESTS: Alaska and northern Canada to central Minnesota and east to Massachusetts.

WINTERS: Mostly Southern States to Mexico.

WHITE-CROWNED SPARROW*

(1) *White crown, bordered by heavy black stripes.*

(2) *White line over eye and thin black line behind eye.*

Upperparts brownish-striped. Light wing bars. Underparts clear grayish, no stripes. (Immature: White head stripes are buffy and black stripes reddish brown, giving chestnut-crown effect.)

FEMALE: Usually duller.

VOICE: Clear plaintive whistle followed by husky trilled whistle.

NESTS: Labrador to northern Alaska and south to southeastern Quebec.

WINTERS: Southern States to Mexico.

Light brown

SNOW BUNTING (Winter)

Pure white

Big white wing patch

Brown

Black

Whitish

BOREAL CHICKADEE

Chestnut patch

HOUSE SPARROW

Brownish

Black

Wing bars

Dull gray

92

BROWN, RUFOUS, OR CHESTNUT COMBINATIONS

Upperparts Brown-Striped
Underparts Clear, Not Striped

Underparts Pure White

SNOW BUNTING (Winter)

(1) *Underparts, including fore part of wings, almost pure white.*

(2) *Striped light brown above. Top of head and shoulders light-brownish.*

In early spring the brownish of males begins to turn to the black of breeding plumage. Usually travels on or close to the ground in flocks in open fields or on beaches.

FEMALE: Lighter in color.

VOICE: While flying, a melodious whistle followed by trill. Also a vibrant "purring" and *bzzt*.

NESTS: Greenland to Alaska; the farthest north of any land bird.

WINTERS: Southern Alaska and Canada south to Kansas and east to Virginia.

Throat Black

BOREAL CHICKADEE

(1) *Brown cap above white face.*

(2) *Black throat.*

Upperparts brownish gray. Whitish below, washed with brown on sides.

SEXES: Alike.

VOICE: Harsh *dee-dee waah waah*.

RESIDENT: Northern Alaska, Canada, and northern fringe of border states, occasionally farther south in winter.

HOUSE SPARROW*

(1) *Brownish-striped above, black throat.*

(2) *Whitish patch between black throat and chestnut patch.*

Faint wing bars, short stubby bill characteristic of most sparrows. Underparts dingy gray. Mostly about houses and barns and in city streets.

FEMALE: No black on throat; no chestnut markings; dull whitish stripe over eye.

VOICE: A monotonous, everlasting *chirrup* or *chisick* or *cheep*.

RESIDENT: Northern Canada to Gulf.

NOTE: Formerly known as English Sparrow but called House Sparrow in latest A.O.U. Check List.

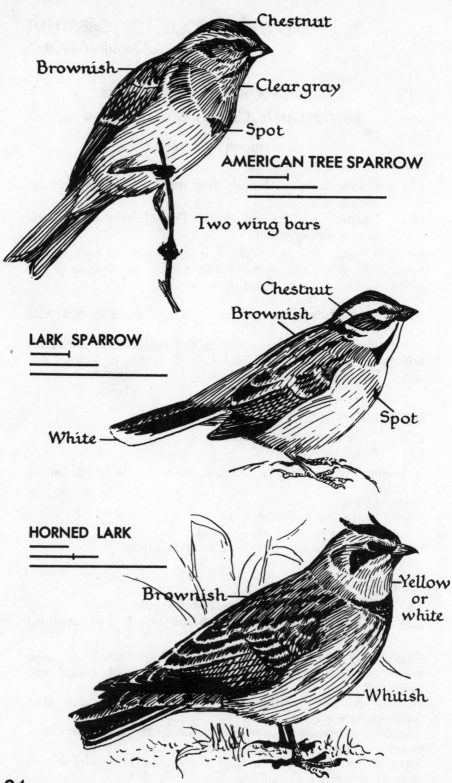

Chestnut

Brownish

Clear gray

Spot

AMERICAN TREE SPARROW

Two wing bars

Chestnut
Brownish

LARK SPARROW

White

Spot

HORNED LARK

Brownish

Yellow
or
white

Whitish

94

BROWN, RUFOUS, OR CHESTNUT COMBINATIONS

Upperparts Brown-Striped
Underparts Clear, Not Striped

Black Spot on Breast
AMERICAN TREE SPARROW
(1) *Black spot on clear gray breast.*
(2) *Chestnut crown.*

Dark line through eye. Two wing bars. Upperparts brownish-striped.
SEXES: Alike.
VOICE: Variable, starting with one or two high musical notes, then more rapid and lower in pitch.
NESTS: Northern Alaska and northern Canada.
WINTERS: Central Minnesota, southern fringe of Canada to Maine, south to Oklahoma, and east to North Carolina.

LARK SPARROW
(1) *Tail with white corners.*
(2) *Black spot on clear whitish breast.*

Prominent chestnut patch on face. Black "whiskers" on side of chin.
Upperparts brownish-striped.
FEMALE: Similar.
VOICE: Sweet notes and trills with pauses between.
NESTS: Southwestern Canadian provinces as far east as western New York, south to southern Texas, and east to central Alabama.
WINTERS: Gulf coast and Mexico, occasionally farther north.

Throat, Mask, and Crown Black
HORNED LARK
(1) *Black mask and throat patch on yellow or white.*
(2) *Black patch top of head ending in "horns," often hard to see.*

Brownish-striped above. Usually seen on ground in open country.
FEMALE: Similar but smaller and duller. No black on top of head.
VOICE: Often long, high-pitched, tinkling; frequently in flight.
NESTS: Arctic coast of North America, south to eastern Kansas in West and North Carolina in East.
WINTERS: South to Gulf States.

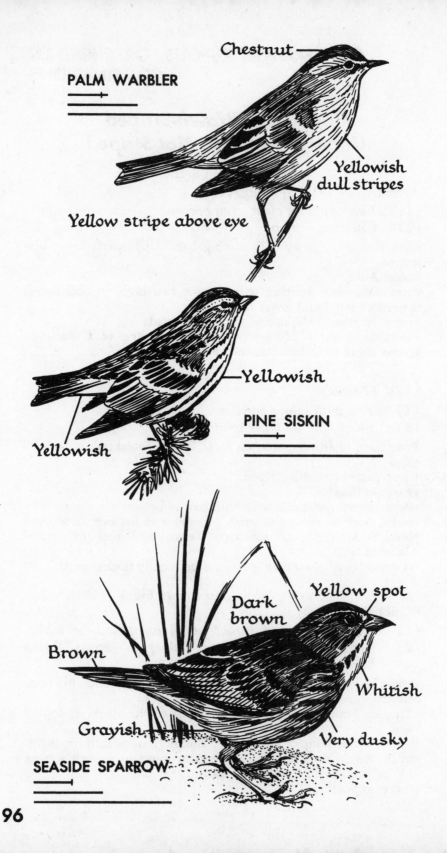

Chestnut

PALM WARBLER

Yellowish dull stripes

Yellow stripe above eye

Yellowish

PINE SISKIN

Yellowish

Dark brown

Yellow spot

Brown

Whitish

Grayish

Very dusky

SEASIDE SPARROW

96

BROWN, RUFOUS, OR CHESTNUT COMBINATIONS

Upperparts Brown-Striped
Underparts Striped

Yellow Markings

PALM WARBLER

(1) *Chestnut cap. Yellow stripe over eye, dark stripe through eye.*
(2) *Constantly flicks tail up and down.*

Underparts yellowish, faintly striped. Undertail coverts bright yellow. Back dull olive-gray. Rump yellowish. Usually found on or near ground.
SEXES: Similar.
VOICE: Series of weak *thi-thi-thi-thi*'s.
NESTS:Southern Newfoundland to Mackenzie, south to northeastern Minnesota in West and Maine in East.
WINTERS: Southern States south into West Indies and Central America.

PINE SISKIN

(1) *Heavily striped above and below.*
(2) *Small yellow patch on wing and upper tail, often hard to see.*

Wing feathers yellow-edged. Small short bill. Tail forked. Usually in flocks whether in trees or flying.
SEXES: Similar.
VOICE: High, resembling that of the Goldfinch.
NESTS: Labrador to Alaska, south to Kansas and east to Connecticut.
WINTERS: At lower altitudes throughout its range.

SEASIDE SPARROW

(1) *Very dark appearance.*
(2) *Yellow patch in front of eye and yellow at bend of wing.*

Upperparts olive-brown with indistinct striping. White line at bend of jaw. Upper breast dusky-streaked; remaining underparts grayish, lightly streaked. Found in coastal salt marshes. Very shy.
SEXES: Alike.
VOICE: Short *zhe-eeee*.
RESIDENT: Massachusetts south, near Atlantic coast.

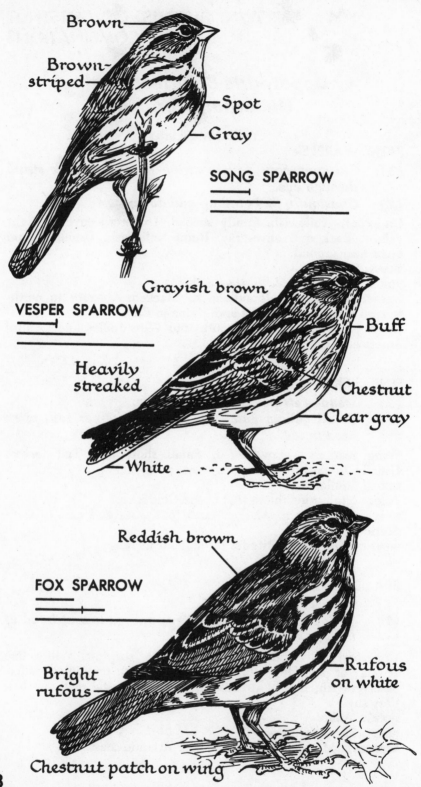

Brown

Brown-
striped

Spot

Gray

SONG SPARROW

Grayish brown

Buff

VESPER SPARROW

Heavily
streaked

Chestnut

Clear gray

White

Reddish brown

FOX SPARROW

Bright
rufous

Rufous
on white

Chestnut patch on wing

BROWN, RUFOUS, OR CHESTNUT COMBINATIONS

Upperparts Brown-Striped
Underparts Striped

Black Spot on Breast

SONG SPARROW*

(1) *Dark spot middle of breast where dark stripes converge.*

(2) *Heavily brown-striped upperparts, breast, and sides. Gray belly.*

Brownish above, lighter below. Light line over eye. Brown crown. Commonly seen near ground in shrubbery and in moist places.

SEXES: Alike.

VOICE: Two to four drawn-out sweet notes ending in various lengthy trills in numberless variations.

NESTS: Northern Canada to Louisiana.

WINTERS: Southern fringe of Canada to Gulf.

White Outer Tail Feathers

VESPER SPARROW*

(1) *White outer tail feathers most conspicuous in flight. Chestnut on shoulder.*

(2) *Striped on back, upper breast, and sides. Grayish belly.*

Found mostly on ground in fields. Has "wide-eyed" appearance.

SEXES: Alike.

VOICE: Two long, clear melodious whistles followed by two higher ones and ending in descending trill.

NESTS: Central Canada south to central Missouri and east to North Carolina.

WINTERS: Southern Illinois to Connecticut and south to Gulf.

Bright Rufous

FOX SPARROW

(1) *Bright rufous tail, but body heavily striped reddish brown above and below.*

(2) *Heavy, Sparrow-like bill. Wing with chestnut patch.*

Usually found in hedges or thickets.

SEXES: Alike.

VOICE: Loud, melodious short clear notes and sliding whistles.

NESTS: Labrador to Alaska south to southern Canada.

WINTERS: Massachusetts, Ohio, and Indiana south to Gulf.

HENSLOW'S SPARROW

Olive

Yellowish

Brown

Buffy

Rufous

Blackish

Dark buff

Dark buff

Gray-brown

Buffy

Yellow

Whitish

SHARP-TAILED SPARROW

Brown

LINCOLN'S SPARROW

Fine
streaks

BROWN, RUFOUS, OR CHESTNUT COMBINATIONS

Upperparts Brown-Striped Underparts Striped

Olive or Buff on Head

HENSLOW'S SPARROW

(1) *Short-tailed, flat-headed, with black-striped rufous wings and olive head.*
(2) *Throat buffy and lightly streaked. Belly whitish.*
Dark line behind eye. Back heavily striped.
SEXES: Alike.
VOICE: Short double-noted *flee-sic,* often heard at night.
NESTS: Northeastern Massachusetts to central Minnesota, south to central Kansas, and east to South Carolina.
WINTERS: Southeastern States.

SHARP-TAILED SPARROW

(1) *Buff stripe over eye and surrounding gray cheek patch.*
(2) *Short tail.*
Whitish underparts with distinct streakings on breast and sides. Edge of wing pale yellow. Lives in marshes. Shy. In Atlantic States restricted to salt marshes.
SEXES: Alike.
VOICE: Buzzing *tup-tup-sheeee.*
NESTS: Salt marshes southern Quebec to North Carolina, and fresh-water marshes central Canada to South Dakota.
WINTERS: Long Island south.

Finely Striped Throat

LINCOLN'S SPARROW

(1) *Light creamy, finely streaked band across breast.*
(2) *Striped above and below with fine, narrow, dark stripes.*
Upper throat and belly gray, unstreaked. On migration usually on ground at edge of deep thickets. Very shy.
SEXES: Alike.
VOICE: Sweet warble starting low, rising, and dropping at end.
NESTS: Labrador to Alaska and south to Canadian border states.
WINTERS: Oklahoma to Central America, occasionally farther north along Atlantic coast.

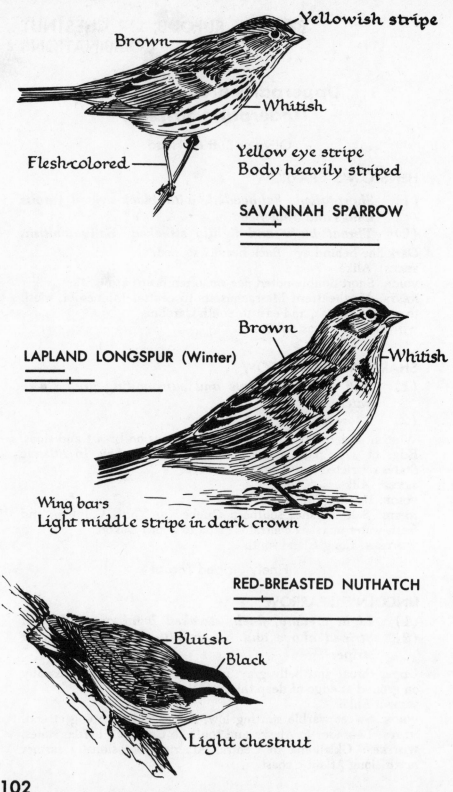

Brown

Yellowish stripe

Whitish

Flesh-colored

Yellow eye stripe
Body heavily striped

SAVANNAH SPARROW

Brown

Whitish

LAPLAND LONGSPUR (Winter)

Wing bars
Light middle stripe in dark crown

RED-BREASTED NUTHATCH

Bluish

Black

Light chestnut

BROWN, RUFOUS, OR CHESTNUT COMBINATIONS

Upperparts Brown-Striped Underparts Striped

Yellow Stripe over Eye

SAVANNAH SPARROW

(1) *Heavily striped above and below, but no black breast spot as in Song Sparrow.*

(2) *Yellow stripe above eye.*

Short notched tail. Belly whitish. Pinkish legs. On ground in open places, beaches, near thickets.

SEXES: Alike.

VOICE: Two to five short notes followed by two buzzy trills.

NESTS: Northern Canada south to southern Minnesota and east to southeastern New York.

WINTERS: Southern New York and southern Indiana south.

Whitish Throat and Cheek

LAPLAND LONGSPUR (Winter)

(1) *Whitish throat with dark patch.*

(2) *Brown above with two wing bars on dark wing.*

Whitish cheek marked with black angle. Dark crown, with lighter middle stripe. Narrow black streakings on sides. Walks or creeps, does not hop.

FEMALE: Similar.

VOICE: A rattly noise followed by a whistle.

NESTS: Greenland to northern Alaska.

WINTERS: To southern United States.

Underparts Solid Chestnut or Brown

RED-BREASTED NUTHATCH

(1) *Black cap, black eye line surmounted by white. White throat.*

(2) *Light chestnut underparts.*

Outer tail feathers white. Bluish above. "Upside-down" bird. Usually seen in evergreens.

FEMALE: Generally lighter.

VOICE: A sharp, high, nasal *ank-ank*.

NESTS OR RESIDENT: Alaska, Canada, northern edge of Great Lakes States, and in mountains to North Carolina.

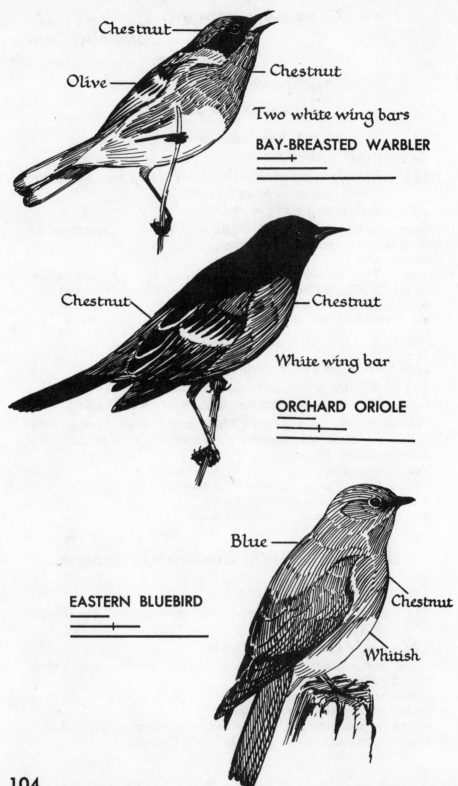

Chestnut

Olive

Chestnut

Two white wing bars

BAY-BREASTED WARBLER

Chestnut

Chestnut

White wing bar

ORCHARD ORIOLE

Blue

Chestnut

Whitish

EASTERN BLUEBIRD

BROWN, RUFOUS, OR CHESTNUT COMBINATIONS

Underparts Solid Chestnut or Brown

BAY-BREASTED WARBLER
(1) *Chestnut crown, upper breast, and sides.*
(2) *Prominent white area behind black mask.*

Back olive-streaked. Two white wing bars. Belly whitish.
FEMALE: Similar but markings much paler and less distinct.
VOICE: Commonly short, wiry, high, on one pitch.
NESTS: Central Canada to northeastern Minnesota and east to southern Maine.
WINTERS: Panama and northern South America.

ORCHARD ORIOLE
(1) *Chestnut underparts and rump.*
(2) *Black head, extending down back, black tail and wings.*

White wing bar and feather edgings.
FEMALE: Olive above, yellow below, no black markings. Immature males resemble females, but have black throats.
VOICE: Long, high, sweet warble, Robin-like but of much finer quality, almost like Purple Finch.
NESTS: South-central Canada to North Dakota, east to central New York, and south to Gulf.
WINTERS: Central and South America.

EASTERN BLUEBIRD*
(1) *Solid blue above.*
(2) *Chestnut below.*

Belly whitish.
FEMALE: Paler and duller.
VOICE: (1) Note: often in flight; soft, sweet *cherwee.* (2) Song: rapid series of soft slurred notes.
NESTS: Southern Canada to Gulf.
WINTERS: From Central America north, occasionally as far north as southern New England and southern Great Lakes States.

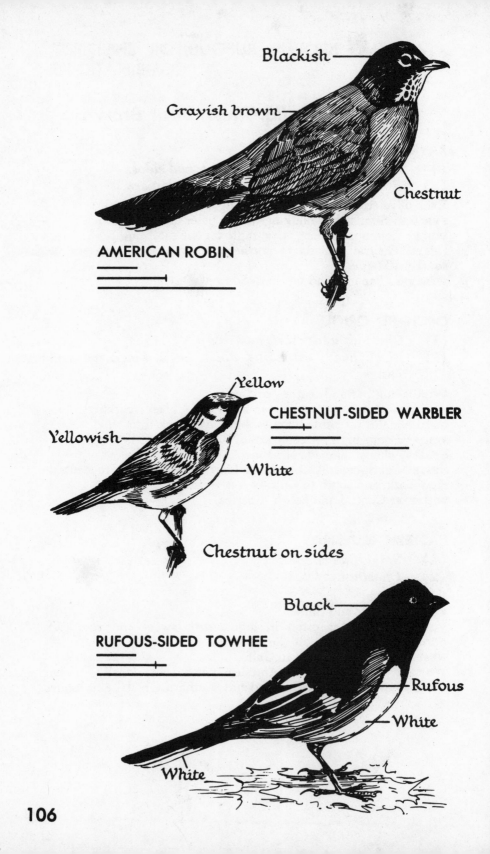

Blackish

Grayish brown

Chestnut

AMERICAN ROBIN

Yellow

Yellowish

CHESTNUT-SIDED WARBLER

White

Chestnut on sides

Black

RUFOUS-SIDED TOWHEE

Rufous

White

White

BROWN, RUFOUS, OR CHESTNUT COMBINATIONS

Underparts Solid Chestnut or Brown

AMERICAN ROBIN*

(1)   *Chestnut underparts.*
(2)   *Blackish head.*

Chin with fine black and white stripes, lower belly white. Tail corners white. Breast actually chestnut, not red. Commonly feeds on lawns around houses.
FEMALE: Paler above and below.
VOICE: Varies greatly in individual birds. A loud rich, prolonged warble consisting of two or more notes each, with notes running into each other:

NESTS: Northern Alaska and Canada to Gulf.
WINTERS: Southern States to Mexico and Central America; occasionally in Northeast.

Sides Chestnut or Rufous

CHESTNUT-SIDED WARBLER*

(1)   *White below with broad chestnut stripe on side.*
(2)   *Yellow crown.*

Black patch through and under eye in front of white patch. Striped black and yellow above. Two yellowish wing bars.
FEMALE: Similar to male but with less chestnut and black.
VOICE: (1) High, musical

pleased pleased pleased ta meecha.
(2)*you may see me maybe?* and variations.
NESTS: Nova Scotia to Saskatchewan, south to eastern Nebraska in West, to Maryland in East, and in mountains to South Carolina.
WINTERS: Central America.

RUFOUS-SIDED TOWHEE*

(1)   *Chestnut sides.*
(2)   *Black head, back, wings, and tail.*

Wings and outer tips of tail white-edged. White belly. Commonly seen, and heard, scratching around on ground in low shrubbery.
FEMALE: Brown replaces black markings.

VOICE: (1) *tow hee.* (2) *drink your teeee.* Last note high and wavering.
NESTS: Southeastern Canada to Gulf States.
WINTERS: Mostly in Southern States.

107

White "window"

COMMON NIGHTHAWK

White bar

White

Black and gray barred

White

White

Mottled gray and brown

WHIP-POOR-WILL*

108

Body Dusky Brown, Heavily Mottled
(Birds Mostly Seen Flying)

COMMON NIGHTHAWK*

(1)   *White throat and wing patches and white tail band.*
(2)   *Mottled gray above, barred below.*

Wings long, slim. Flies at dusk or daybreak, catching insects while in flight over open places.

FEMALE: Throat patch less conspicuous and no white band on tail.

VOICE: Loud sharp *peent* while flying. Often while dive-bombing a loud booming noise caused by air rushing through wings.

NESTS: Northern Canada and Alaska to Gulf States. In open country on bare rock or ground. Sometimes on rooftops.

WINTERS: South America.

WHIP-POOR-WILL*

(1)   *Dark throat with white chest band.*
(2)   *Breast mottled buffy.*

Tail barred with large patches of white on ends of outer tail feathers. Short stubby bill. Mottled brownish back roughly barred resembles bark of tree. Nocturnal. During day sits on ground, rocks, or branch of tree.

FEMALE: Similar, but tail spots buffy and smaller.

VOICE: Strong, repeated *whip-poor-will;* heard at night.

NESTS: Central Canada to Gulf States.

WINTERS: Mostly Gulf States and eastern Mexico.

Tawny

White

Tawny

Light buff

CHUCK-WILL'S-WIDOW

Tawny black-mottled

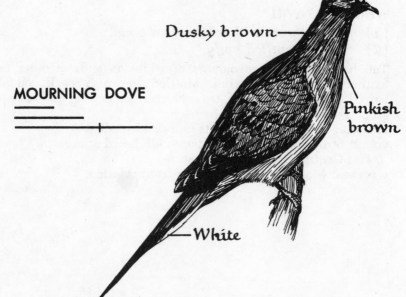

Dusky brown

MOURNING DOVE

Pinkish brown

White

BROWN, RUFOUS, OR CHESTNUT COMBINATIONS

Body Dusky Brown, Heavily Mottled (Birds Mostly Seen Flying)

CHUCK-WILL'S-WIDOW
(1) *Tawny-streaked and spotted with black.*
(2) *Outer tail feathers tawny.*

Band on throat buffy. Much larger than Whip-poor-will, whose throat band and outer tail feathers are white. Usually found in woodlands.

FEMALE: Similar.

VOICE: Repetitious, resembling name: *chuck will's widow.*

NESTS: Eastern Kansas to southern New Jersey and south to Gulf.

WINTERS: Louisiana and Florida south.

Body Light Brownish Gray

MOURNING DOVE*
(1) *Long pointed tail white on outside in flight.*
(2) *Small round head.*

Dusky brown above, lighter pinkish brown below. Dark spot on neck.

FEMALE: Similar but smaller and duller.

VOICE: Soft, melodious, in minor key:

oo oh ooo oo oo.

NESTS: Southern fringe of Canada to Gulf.

WINTERS: Northern tier of states south.

Brownish-mottled

Russet

AMERICAN WOODCOCK

BROWN, RUFOUS, OR CHESTNUT COMBINATIONS

Body Russet, Heavily Mottled (Very Long Bill)

AMERICAN WOODCOCK

(1) *Extremely long bill.*
(2) *Chunky, almost neckless, russet-colored.*

Brownish, mottled, resembling dry leaves on forest floor. Short tail. The long bill is used to dig up worms in moist woods or thickets.

FEMALE: Similar.

VOICE: A low nasal *peent*. Sometimes a musical chippering in flight.

NESTS: Newfoundland and southern Canada to Gulf.

WINTERS: Southern States, occasionally farther north.

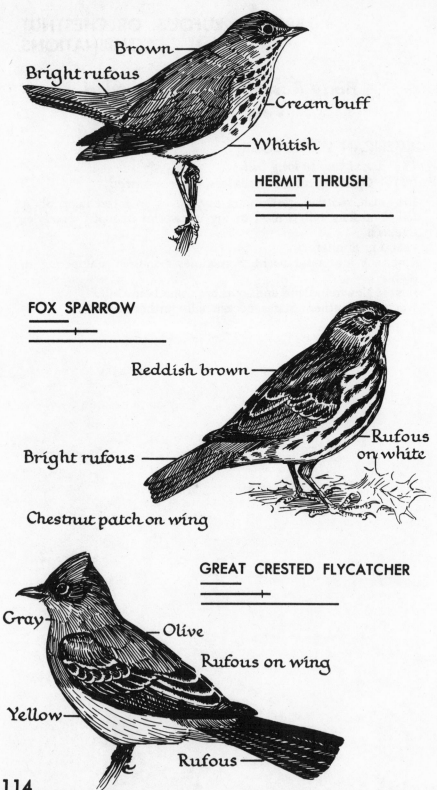

Brown

Bright rufous

Cream buff

Whitish

HERMIT THRUSH

FOX SPARROW

Reddish brown

Bright rufous

Rufous on white

Chestnut patch on wing

GREAT CRESTED FLYCATCHER

Gray

Olive

Rufous on wing

Yellow

Rufous

BROWN, RUFOUS, OR CHESTNUT COMBINATIONS

Tail Chestnut or Rufous

HERMIT THRUSH
(1) *Rufous tail brighter than brown upperparts.*
(2) *Chest and lower cheeks pale cream buff, dusky-streaked and -spotted.*

Belly whitish. Slender bill. Dull whitish eye ring. At rest, cocks tail and lets it droop slowly. Usually found in wooded areas.
SEXES: Alike.
VOICE: A long ethereal opening note, followed by a series with tremolo effect. A pause between phrases.
NESTS: Wooded areas Alaska and Canada to Minnesota, east to Massachusetts, and in mountains to Maryland.
WINTERS: Southern States, Mexico, and Central America.

FOX SPARROW
(1) *Bright rufous tail, but body heavily striped reddish brown above and below.*
(2) *Heavy, Sparrow-like bill. Wing with chestnut patch.*
Usually found in hedges or thickets.
SEXES: Alike.
VOICE: Loud, melodious short clear notes and sliding whistles.
NESTS: Labrador to Alaska south to southern Canada.
WINTERS: Massachusetts, Ohio, and Indiana south to Gulf.

GREAT CRESTED FLYCATCHER*
(1) *Conspicuous rufous tail and side of wing.*
(2) *Belly yellow.*

Throat gray. Back and head olive. Head with crest. Two wing bars, and wing feathers white-edged.
FEMALE: Underparts grayish. Crown and back gray, washed with yellow on shoulder.
VOICE: Loud, clear *wheeep*, rising at end with seemingly scolding notes. Also loud, harsh, burred *kur, kur, kur, kur, kur.*
NESTS: Central Canada to Gulf.
WINTERS: Florida, Mexico, and Central America.

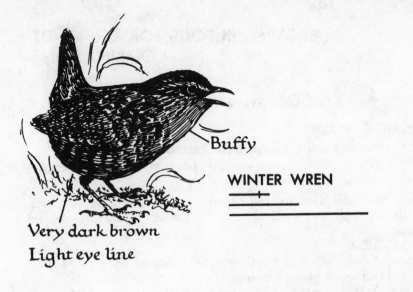

Buffy

WINTER WREN

Very dark brown

Light eye line

Finely white
streaked

Whitish
bordered
by buff

SEDGE WREN

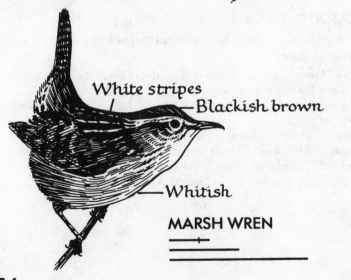

White stripes

Blackish brown

Whitish

MARSH WREN

116

Tiny Brown Birds

Finely Barred Wings and Tail (Usually Cocked Up)

WINTER WREN

(1) *Dark-brownish mottled underparts, lighter on breast. Barred wings and tail.*

(2) *Light line over eye.*

Stubby, "over-back" tail. Bobs head often. Usually skulks around brush heaps, etc. Often near streams.

SEXES: Alike.

VOICE: Long succession of beautiful high notes and trills.

NESTS: Central Canada south to central Minnesota, east to Maine, and in mountains to western Maryland.

WINTERS: Massachusetts to Nebraska and south to Gulf.

SEDGE WREN

(1) *Brownish above, streaked and barred with black and fine white lines.*

(2) *Whitish below, bordered by light buff. Crown streaked. Short "over-back" tail, finely barred.*

Short bill. Narrow buffy eye stripe. Usually found in grassy and sedgy marshes.

SEXES: Similar.

VOICE: Dry, unmusical chattering, ending in buzzy trill. Resembles sound of pebbles being struck together.

NESTS: Southern Canada south to eastern Kansas and east to southeastern Virginia.

WINTERS: Maryland to Tennessee and south to Gulf and Mexico.

MARSH WREN

(1) *Crown dark blackish brown: rump light brown; white stripes on dark-brown back.*

(2) *Pronounced white stripe above eye.*

Whitish below, blending to brown on sides. Cross-barred wings and tail, which tilts up sharply. Mainly in cattail and reedy marshes.

SEXES: Alike.

VOICE: Series of short rapid notes, rattly and guttural.

NESTS OR RESIDENT: Southern fringe of Canada south to Gulf.

WINTERS: Mostly Southern States and into Mexico.

Clear gray

HOUSE WREN

Dark

White

No stripes

White eye line

BEWICK'S WREN

Whitish

Long, heavy eye line

Rufous red

Buffy

CAROLINA WREN

BROWN, RUFOUS, OR CHESTNUT COMBINATIONS
Tiny Brown Birds
Finely Barred Wings and Tail (Usually Cocked Up)

HOUSE WREN*
(1) *No distinct eye stripe. Brown above, lightly cross-barred, including tail.*
(2) *Clear gray breast merging into dark belly.*
Very small, energetic, cocks tail over back. Commonly seen around yards and houses.
SEXES: Alike.
VOICE: Short burst of rapid, musical notes, falling at end.
NESTS: Southern Canada south to Arkansas and east to Georgia.
WINTERS: Southern Atlantic States, Gulf States, and Mexico.

BEWICK'S WREN*
(1) *Long tail white-spotted in corners, whitish below.*
(2) *Sharp white line above eye.*
Brown back, no stripes. Cross-barred wings and tail, which is carried erect above back. Commonly seen around houses and lawns.
SEXES: Alike.
VOICE: Loud, melodious clear high notes (usually two or three), then lower burry note ending in trill.
NESTS OR RESIDENT: Central Pennsylvania to southeastern Nebraska and south to Gulf.

CAROLINA WREN*
(1) *Rufous-red above.*
(2) *Conspicuous white stripe above and back of eye.*
Buffy below. Wings and tail lightly cross-barred. Much larger than other Wrens.
SEXES: Alike.
VOICE: Loud, ringing, musical. Three distinct songs. (1) Rather deliberate:

tu wee lee, tu wee lee, tu wee lee.
(2) Somewhat faster:

o will ye will ye will ye we.
(3) Very fast:

cheer-i-ly cheer-i-ly cheer-i-ly.
RESIDENT: As far north as southern New York, Ohio, and southeastern Nebraska, and south to Mexico.

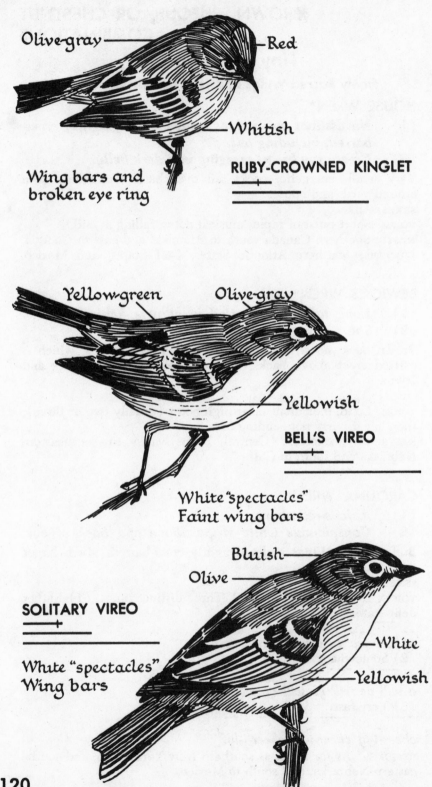

Olive-gray — Red

Whitish

Wing bars and
broken eye ring

RUBY-CROWNED KINGLET

Yellow-green — Olive-gray

Yellowish

BELL'S VIREO

White "spectacles"
Faint wing bars

Bluish
Olive

SOLITARY VIREO

White
Yellowish

White "spectacles"
Wing bars

GRAY, OLIVE-GRAY, OR OLIVE-GREEN COMBINATIONS

Both Wing Bars and Eye Ring

RUBY-CROWNED KINGLET*

(1) *Tiny, with broken white eye ring and two pale wing bars.*
(2) *Ruby crown, often hard to see. Olive-gray above, whitish below.*

FEMALE: No ruby crown.
VOICE: (1) Husky *ji-dit*. (2) Variable; loud, high *zee-zee-zee's*, lower *kew, kew, kew's*, then tinkling three-note phrases going up the scale.
NESTS: Labrador to Alaska south to northern Michigan in West and Maine in East.
WINTERS: Mostly southern United States.

BELL'S VIREO

(1) *White eye ring forms "spectacles."*
(2) *Faint wing bars.*

Top of head olive-gray. Yellow-green back. Throat white. Belly and sides yellowish. Distinguished from White-eyed Vireo, which has yellow "spectacles," and from Solitary Vireo, which has bluish head and pure-white throat and belly.
SEXES: Alike.
VOICE: Low three-syllabled phrases at short intervals, first phrase rising and second falling at end.
NESTS: Southeastern South Dakota to northeastern Illinois, south to central Texas, and east to Gulf and Tennessee.
WINTERS: Mainly in Mexico.

SOLITARY VIREO

(1) *Blue-gray head, white eye ring in "spectacle" form.*
(2) *Wings darker, white-edged, and two wing bars. Back and rump olive.*

Pure-white throat and belly. Yellowish sides. Tail white-edged.
SEXES: Similar.
VOICE: Variable, sweet, high, clear, slow, often in four-note phrases with a pause in between: *teeay-taweeta*, etc.
NESTS: Newfoundland to British Columbia, south through Great Lakes States to northern New Jersey, and in mountains to northern Georgia.
WINTERS: South Carolina to Gulf States and Central America.

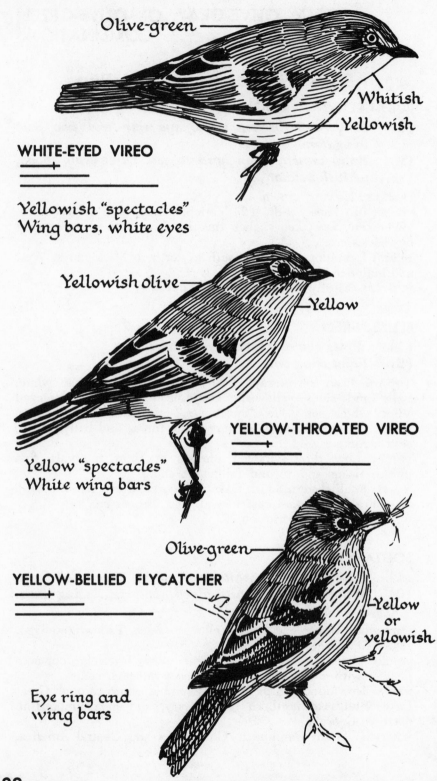

Olive-green

Whitish

Yellowish

WHITE-EYED VIREO

Yellowish "spectacles"
Wing bars, white eyes

Yellowish olive

Yellow

YELLOW-THROATED VIREO

Yellow "spectacles"
White wing bars

YELLOW-BELLIED FLYCATCHER

Olive-green

Yellow
or
yellowish

Eye ring and
wing bars

Both Wing Bars and Eye Ring

WHITE-EYED VIREO*
(1) *Yellowish eye ring forms "spectacles."*
(2) *Two wing bars and white eyes.*

Whitish throat. Yellowish sides. Olive-green above. Immature has dark eye.
SEXES: Alike.
VOICE: Variable, commonly *chip-per-weo-chick*, ending like crack of whip.
NESTS: Southern Nebraska east to southern Connecticut and south to Gulf.
WINTERS: North to South Carolina.

YELLOW-THROATED VIREO
(1) *Yellow eye ring forms "spectacles."*
(2) *Bright yellow throat, whitish belly.*

Gray rump. Rest of upperparts yellowish olive. White wing bars. Wings darker. Wing feathers and outer tail feathers white-edged. Usually found in deep woods or swamps.
FEMALE: Similar.
VOICE: (1) Call: harsh, scolding. (2) Song: deliberate, reedy, burred notes, often interpreted as saying *three-eight.*
NESTS: Southern fringe of Canada to Gulf.
WINTERS: Mexico into South America.

YELLOW-BELLIED FLYCATCHER
(1) *Uniform yellowish below, throat to belly. Olive-green above.*
(2) *Eye ring and two wing bars. Lower mandible yellow.*

Flycatchers perch on exposed twigs and catch insects on the wing.
SEXES: Alike.
VOICE: Plaintive, soft *pur weee;* also *killick.*
NESTS: Newfoundland to northern British Columbia, south to North Dakota, and east on border to mountains and Pennsylvania and New York.
WINTERS: Mexico and Central America.

Olive-gray — — Whitish

— Gray

WILLOW FLYCATCHER

— Yellowish

Eye ring and
two wing bars — Whitish

Olive-green —

ACADIAN FLYCATCHER

Eye ring
and two wing bars

Gray

Olive-gray —

LEAST FLYCATCHER

Whitish

Eye ring and
two wing bars

GRAY, OLIVE-GRAY, OR OLIVE-GREEN COMBINATIONS

Both Wing Bars and Eye Ring

WILLOW FLYCATCHER

(1)   *Eye ring rather indistinct and two wing bars, some wing feathers white-edged. Olive-gray back, whitish chin, olive-gray throat, yellowish belly.*

(2)   *Voice.*

In field distinguishable from Least Flycatcher only by voice. Usually in low thickets or damp places.

SEXES: Alike.

VOICE: A hoarse, burry *we-be-o* or *fitz-bew*.

NESTS: Newfoundland to Alaska, south to northeastern Oklahoma, and east to eastern New York and New Jersey and south to Maryland.

WINTERS: Central and South America.

ACADIAN FLYCATCHER

(1)   *Eye ring and wing bars.*

(2)   *Throat whitish.*

Remaining underparts whitish to yellowish. Olive-green above. Wing feathers white-edged. Similar to Least Flycatcher and Willow Flycatcher, distinguishable by its habitat in southern part of area and by its voice. Usually in rich woodland.

SEXES: Alike.

VOICE: A sharp, explosive *we-see!* or *spit-chee!* Also a thin *peet*.

NESTS: South Dakota to Connecticut and south to Gulf. Mostly southern, rare in Northeast.

WINTERS: Central America and northern South America.

LEAST FLYCATCHER*

(1)   *Eye ring, two wing bars. Some wing feathers white-edged.*

(2)   *Voice.*

Olive-gray above, light below, slightly yellowish. In field distinguishable from Willow Flycatcher only by voice.

SEXES: Alike.

VOICE: Constantly repeated *kerik kerik kerik*.

NESTS: Northern Ontario to Alaska, south to northeastern Kansas in West and northwestern Georgia in East.

WINTERS: Mexico and Central America.

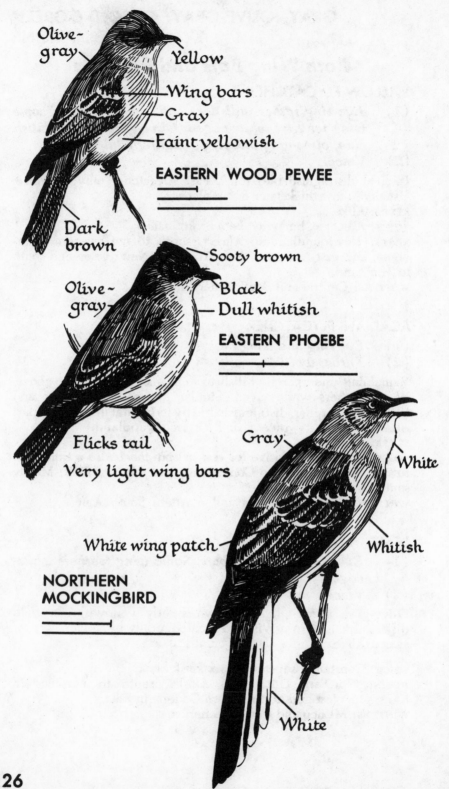

Olive-gray

Yellow

Wing bars

Gray

Faint yellowish

EASTERN WOOD PEWEE

Dark brown

Sooty brown

Olive-gray

Black

Dull whitish

EASTERN PHOEBE

Flicks tail

Very light wing bars

Gray

White

White wing patch

Whitish

NORTHERN MOCKINGBIRD

White

GRAY, OLIVE-GRAY, OR OLIVE-GREEN COMBINATIONS

Wing Bars and No Eye Ring

EASTERN WOOD PEWEE*

(1)   *Two whitish wing bars, and feathers white-edged.*
(2)   *Lower mandible yellow.*

Olive-gray above, wings and tail dark brown. Chin and throat whitish; belly slightly yellowish. No eye ring. Perches on open branches.

SEXES: Alike.

VOICE: (1) Wistful, sweet *pee uh weee.* (2) A delicate, musical *pee ur.*

NESTS: Southern Canada to Gulf in woodland.

WINTERS: Central and South America.

EASTERN PHOEBE*

(1)   *Constantly flicks tail.*
(2)   *Olive-gray above, head sooty brown.*

Dull whitish below, often with yellowish tinge. Black bill. Light wing bars, often not visible. Sits upright like Flycatcher. Nests under bridges and in corners of buildings.

SEXES: Alike.

VOICE: (1) Often-repeated high *fee bee fee bee* or *fee bee fee be it.*

NESTS: Northern Canada to Gulf States.

WINTERS: Throughout the South and Mexico.

NOTE: Phoebes' wing bars are variable, actually invisible in some birds and noticeable in others.

NORTHERN MOCKINGBIRD*

(1)   *Two white wing patches and white outer tail feathers prominent in flight.*
(2)   *Solid gray above. Whitish below. Slender body and bill and long tail.*

FEMALE: Similar, but white areas smaller.

VOICE: Succession—often day and night—of loud notes and phrases, often accurately imitating other birds in the vicinity.

RESIDENT: Nebraska to southeastern Massachusetts and south to Gulf. Rare in winter in northern part of its range.

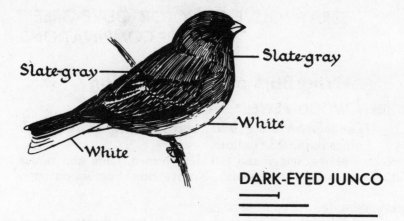

Slate-gray

Slate-gray

White

White

DARK-EYED JUNCO

Bluish gray

Whitish

Rusty

TUFTED TITMOUSE

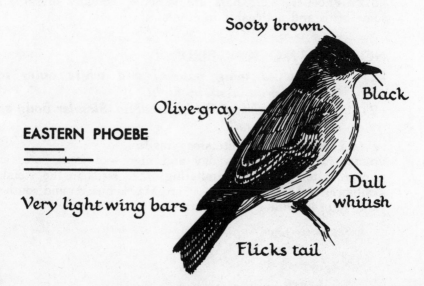

Sooty brown

Olive-gray

Black

EASTERN PHOEBE

Dull whitish

Very light wing bars

Flicks tail

GRAY, OLIVE-GRAY, OR OLIVE-GREEN COMBINATIONS

Neither Wing Bars Nor Eye Ring

DARK-EYED JUNCO*
(1) *Slate-gray throughout, except for white belly and white outer tail feathers.*
(2) *Short, Sparrow-like bill.*

FEMALE: Slate color lighter and more brownish.
VOICE: Loose, quavering trill.
NESTS: Labrador to Alaska, south to Minnesota, east to Massachusetts, and in mountains to South Carolina.
WINTERS: Canada to Gulf.

TUFTED TITMOUSE*
(1) *Pronounced crest.*
(2) *Solid bluish gray above, whitish below, reddish buff on sides.*

SEXES: Alike.
VOICE: (1) Fast, loud, unmusical *Peter Peter Peter Peter*
(2) Extremely rapid, with upward inflection,

Dear? Dear? Dear?
RESIDENT: Southeastern Nebraska to southwestern Connecticut and south to Gulf States; irregularly farther north.

EASTERN PHOEBE*
(1) *Constantly flicks tail.*
(2) *Olive-gray above, head sooty brown.*

Dull whitish below, often with yellowish tinge. Black bill. Light wing bars, often not visible. Sits upright like Flycatcher. Nests under bridges and in corners of buildings.
SEXES: Alike.
VOICE: (1) Often-repeated high *fee bee fee bee* or *fee bee*

fee be it.
NESTS: Northern Canada to Gulf States.
WINTERS: Throughout the South and Mexico.
NOTE: Phoebes' wing bars are variable, actually invisible in some birds and noticeable in others.

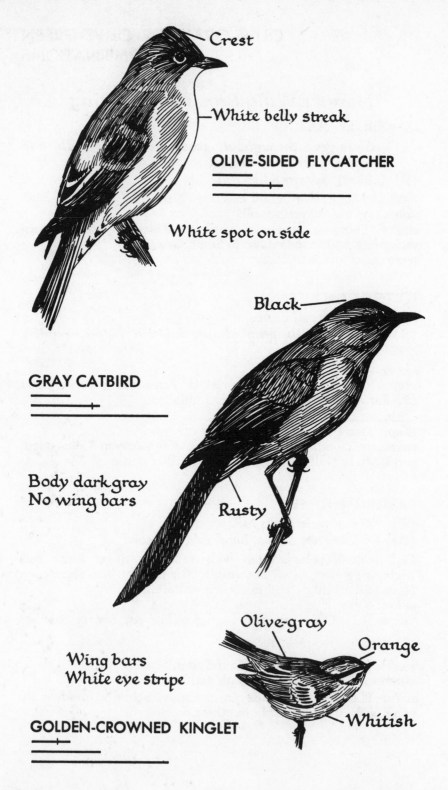

Crest

White belly streak

OLIVE-SIDED FLYCATCHER

White spot on side

Black

GRAY CATBIRD

Body dark gray
No wing bars

Rusty

Olive-gray

Orange

Wing bars
White eye stripe

Whitish

GOLDEN-CROWNED KINGLET

GRAY, OLIVE-GRAY, OR OLIVE-GREEN COMBINATIONS

Neither Wing Bars Nor Eye Ring

OLIVE-SIDED FLYCATCHER*

(1) *White throat and white center stripe on dark belly. White patches, not always visible, behind wings. Body olive-gray.*

(2) *Large head and bill.*

Perches on dead branches and catches insects on the wing.

SEXES: Alike.

VOICE: Often-repeated *quick three beers.*

NESTS: Newfoundland to northern Alaska, south through North Dakota, and east along Canadian border and mountains to western North Carolina.

WINTERS: South America.

GRAY CATBIRD*

(1) *Solid dark gray throughout.*

(2) *Black cap.*

No white marking. Rusty under long tail. Commonly seen in low bushes or shrubbery.

SEXES: Alike.

VOICE: (1) A catlike *mayow,* slurred downward. (2) Great variety of whistles, frequently harsh. Often resembles that of the Northern Mockingbird.

NESTS: Nova Scotia to southern British Columbia and south to Gulf States.

WINTERS: Usually in southern United States to Central America; few in Northeast.

White Eye Stripe

GOLDEN-CROWNED KINGLET

(1) *Bright orange crown bordered by yellow-and-black stripe.*

(2) *Whitish wing bars and white eye stripe. Wing feathers yellow-edged.*

Olive-gray above. Whitish to gray below. Is very confiding.

FEMALE: Crown yellow.

VOICE: (1) Call: a high, wiry *see-see-see.* (2) Song: high thin notes, going up and ending in low chatter.

NESTS: Northern Canada south to northern fringe of border states and in mountains to South Carolina.

WINTERS: Southern Minnesota to southern Newfoundland and south to Gulf.

131

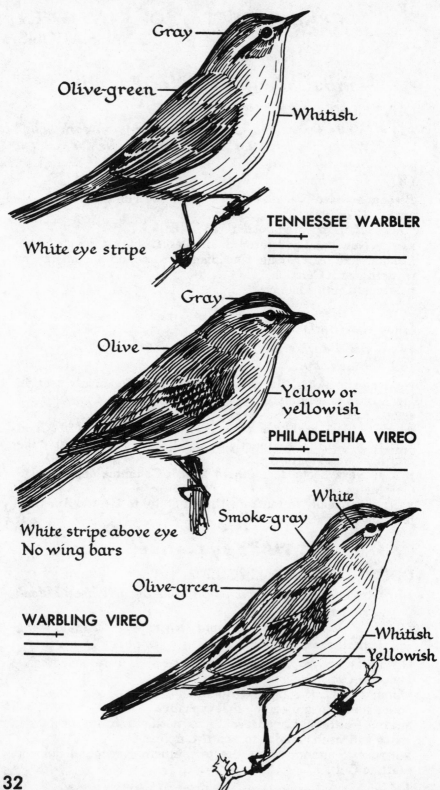

Gray

Olive-green

Whitish

White eye stripe

TENNESSEE WARBLER

Gray

Olive

Yellow or
yellowish

PHILADELPHIA VIREO

White stripe above eye
No wing bars

WARBLING VIREO

White

Smoke-gray

Olive-green

Whitish

Yellowish

GRAY, OLIVE-GRAY, OR OLIVE-GREEN COMBINATIONS

White Eye Stripe

TENNESSEE WARBLER

(1)   *White stripe above and black stripe through eye. Whitish underparts. Gray head, back olive-green.*
(2)   *No wing bars.*

Resembles Vireos but more slender and active, and with slender pointed bill.
FEMALE: Similar markings. Crown olive-green, underparts yellowish-tinged .
VOICE: Variable, very loud short *zit-zit-zit*, etc., lower at end.
NESTS: Labrador to Yukon, south to northern Minnesota in West and southern Maine in East.
WINTERS: South and Central America.

PHILADELPHIA VIREO

(1)   *White stripe above eye.*
(2)   *Underparts light yellowish to white. No wing bars.*

Gray head, olive back. Dark spot in front of eye. Yellowish underparts distinguish it from Red-eyed Vireo and Warbling Vireo.
SEXES: Similar.
VOICE: Similar to that of the Red-eyed Vireo, but higher-pitched, weaker, and more deliberate.
NESTS: Central Canada south to North Dakota in West and central Maine in East.
WINTERS: Central and South America.

WARBLING VIREO*

(1)   *White eye stripe but no wing bars.*
(2)   *Whitish breast, slightly yellowish on sides.*

Top of head and back of neck smoke-gray. Back olive-green.
SEXES: Alike.
VOICE: (1) Wheezy, questioning *whee*. (2) Rather brilliant short warble; resembles somewhat the song of the Purple Finch.
NESTS: Central Canada to Gulf. Rare in coastal plain from New Jersey to Virginia.
WINTERS: Central America.

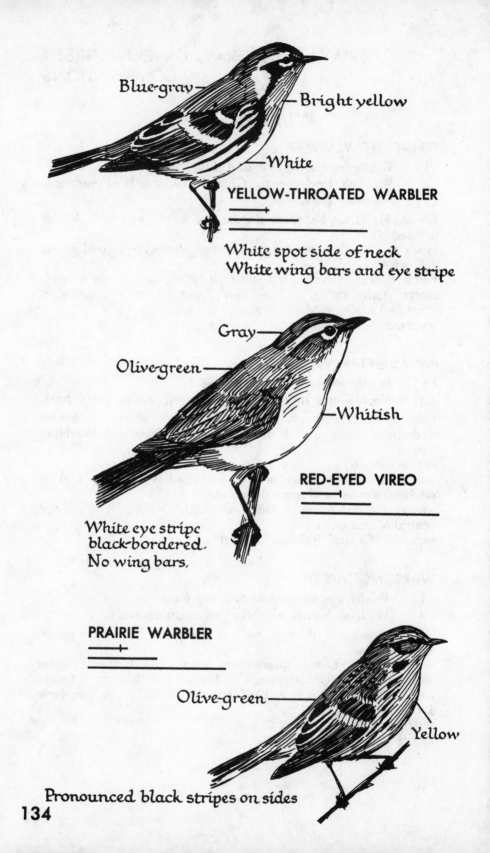

Blue-gray

Bright yellow

White

YELLOW-THROATED WARBLER

White spot side of neck
White wing bars and eye stripe

Gray

Olive-green

Whitish

RED-EYED VIREO

White eye stripe
black-bordered.
No wing bars.

PRAIRIE WARBLER

Olive-green

Yellow

Pronounced black stripes on sides

GRAY, OLIVE-GRAY, OR OLIVE-GREEN COMBINATIONS

White Eye Stripe

YELLOW-THROATED WARBLER

(1) *Bright yellow throat, white belly.*

(2) *Black on forehead, below and behind eye, and in stripes on sides. White stripe above eye and white patch on side of neck.*

Two wing bars. Upperparts blue-gray. Underparts whitish.

SEXES: Similar.

VOICE: Series of clear notes, slurred and dropping in pitch. Last note higher.

NESTS: Southern Ohio to central New Jersey (rare) and south to Gulf.

WINTERS: Southern States southward into Central America.

RED-EYED VIREO*

(1) *White stripe above eye bordered on top by black and below by black stripe through eye.*

(2) *Gray cap.*

Reddish eye at close range. No wing bars. Olive-green above; whitish below, slightly yellow on sides. Found in woods, parks, and suburbs, usually in treetops.

SEXES: Alike.

VOICE: Monotonous, endless, unmusical repetition of generally two- or three-note phrases with definite pause between phrases. Often nicknamed "Preacher Bird."

NESTS: Central Canada to Gulf.

WINTERS: South America.

Yellow Eye Stripe

PRAIRIE WARBLER

(1) *Bright yellow below, with heavy black stripes on sides. Black line through eye and black line under eye.*

(2) *Yellow stripe above eye.*

Olive-green above. Reddish-mottled in middle of back. Two inconspicuous wing bars. Wags tail (an important field mark).

FEMALE: Similar but duller.

VOICE: Thin, distinct *zee-zee-zee-zee-zee-zee-zee-zee*, going up the scale.

NESTS: Southeastern South Dakota east through northern Great Lakes region to southern New Hampshire and south to Gulf.

WINTERS: West Indies.

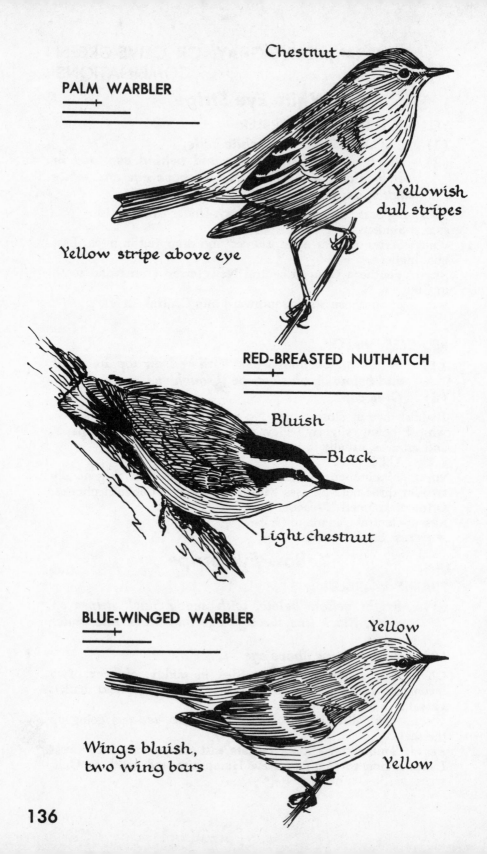

PALM WARBLER

Chestnut

Yellowish dull stripes

Yellow stripe above eye

RED-BREASTED NUTHATCH

Bluish

Black

Light chestnut

BLUE-WINGED WARBLER

Yellow

Wings bluish, two wing bars

Yellow

136

GRAY, OLIVE-GRAY, OR OLIVE-GREEN COMBINATIONS
Yellow Eye Stripe

PALM WARBLER

(1)   *Chestnut cap. Yellow stripe over eye, dark stripe through eye.*

(2)   *Constantly flicks tail up and down.*

Underparts yellowish, faintly striped. Undertail coverts bright yellow. Back dull olive-gray. Rump yellowish. Usually found on or near ground.

SEXES: Similar.

VOICE: Series of weak *thi-thi-thi-thi*'s.

NESTS: Southern Newfoundland to Mackenzie, south to northeastern Minnesota in West and Maine in East.

WINTERS: Southern States south into West Indies and Central America.

Black Eye Stripe or Mask

RED-BREASTED NUTHATCH

(1)   *Black cap, black eye line surmounted by white. White throat.*

(2)   *Light chestnut underparts.*

Outer tail feathers white. Bluish above. "Upside-down" bird. Usually seen in evergreens.

FEMALE: Generally lighter.

VOICE: A sharp, high, nasal *ank-ank*.

NESTS OR RESIDENT: Alaska, Canada, northern edge of Great Lakes States, and in mountains to North Carolina.

BLUE-WINGED WARBLER

(1)   *Face, fore crown, and underparts bright yellow. Black eye line.*

(2)   *Bluish-gray wings; two wing bars.*

Rump yellowish. Other upperparts olive.

FEMALE: Similar to male but duller.

VOICE: Variable; commonest: two buzzy notes, second lower, with trilly *burr*.

NESTS: Central Nebraska to southeastern Massachusetts and south to northern Georgia, Missouri, and Kansas.

WINTERS: Central America and southeastern Mexico.

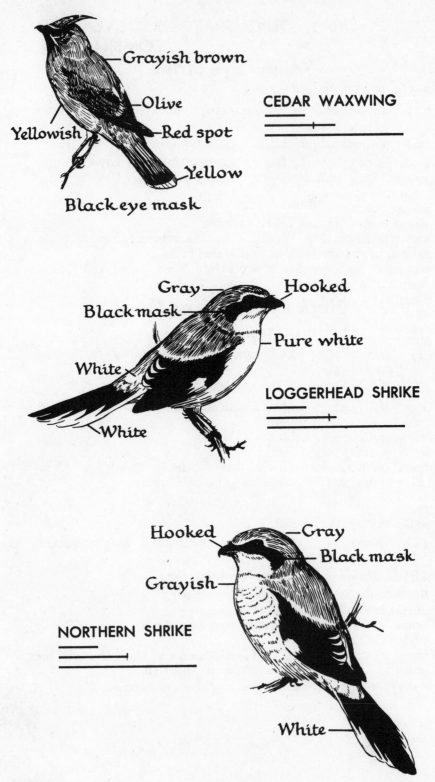

Grayish brown

Olive

CEDAR WAXWING

Yellowish

Red spot

Yellow

Black eye mask

Gray

Hooked

Black mask

Pure white

White

LOGGERHEAD SHRIKE

White

Hooked

Gray

Black mask

Grayish

NORTHERN SHRIKE

White

GRAY, OLIVE-GRAY, OR OLIVE-GREEN COMBINATIONS

Black Eye Stripe or Mask

CEDAR WAXWING*

(1) *Prominent crest.*
(2) *Black eye mask and chin.*

Other upperparts grayish brown. Red spot on wing. Tip of tail yellow. Underparts yellowish. Commonly in flocks, often seen catching insects on wing like Flycatcher.

SEXES: Alike.
VOICE: High thin lisp.
NESTS: Newfoundland to Alaska, south to southern Illinois, and east to Georgia.
WINTERS: Southern Ontario to southern British Columbia and south to Gulf.

LOGGERHEAD SHRIKE

(1) *Black mask on gray head.*
(2) *White below. Black wings; long black tail, white-edged.*

Solid-black hooked beak. Upperparts grayish. Usual perch is in the open on a wire or tip of tree. Shrikes, with their hooked beaks, eat large insects and grasshoppers, and sometimes other little birds. Easily distinguished by its black mask from Northern Mockingbird, which it resembles slightly.

SEXES: Alike.
VOICE: A subdued medley of many phrases.
NESTS: Central Canada to Gulf.
WINTERS: Mostly southern half of breeding range, occasionally farther north.

NORTHERN SHRIKE

(1) *Black mask on gray head.*
(2) *Grayish below, lightly barred; black tail, white-edged, and black wings.*

Upperparts pale grayish to white. White chin; base of bill usually pale. This is the rarer, larger, more northern cousin of the Loggerhead Shrike. (Immature is brown and barred below.)

FEMALE: Duller.
VOICE and HABITS: Similar to that of the Loggerhead Shrike.
NESTS: Labrador to Alaska south to central Canada.
WINTERS: As far south as Kentucky and Virginia.

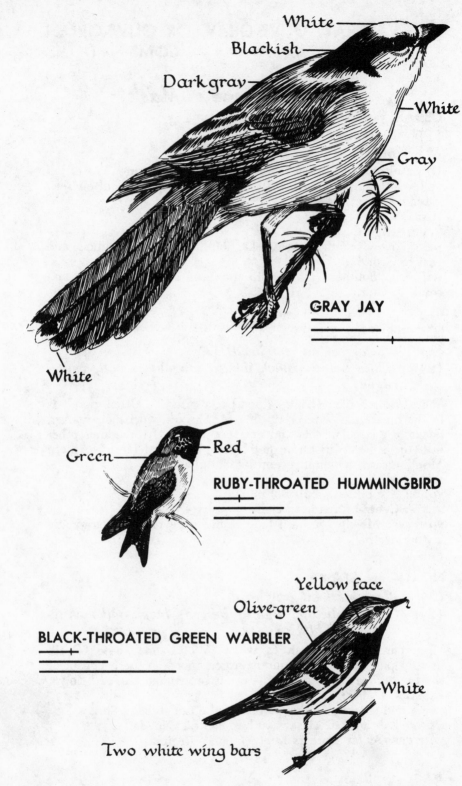

White

Blackish

Dark gray

White

Gray

GRAY JAY

White

Green — Red

RUBY-THROATED HUMMINGBIRD

Yellow face

Olive-green

BLACK-THROATED GREEN WARBLER

White

Two white wing bars

GRAY, OLIVE-GRAY, OR OLIVE-GREEN COMBINATIONS

Black Eye Stripe or Mask

GRAY JAY

(1) *Black eye line enlarges to blackish patch back of head, bordered by white collar.*

(2) *White forehead, side of neck, and throat.*

Dark gray above, tail feathers white-tipped. Gray belly.

FEMALE: Slightly lighter than male.

VOICE: Variable; a loud *whee-ah* and other sounds, harsh or pleasant.

RESIDENT: New Brunswick to northern British Columbia, south to northern Minnesota, and east through northern fringe of border states to northern Maine.

GREEN COMBINATIONS

RUBY-THROATED HUMMINGBIRD*

(1) *Metallic green above.*

(2) *Glowing red throat. Smallest of birds.*

Feeds on nectar of flowers, and some insects.

FEMALE: White throat.

VOICE: A shrill *chick-we-we-a* when fighting. Staccato chips.

NESTS: Central Canada to Gulf.

WINTERS: Florida south.

BLACK-THROATED GREEN WARBLER

(1) *Bright yellow face.*

(2) *Throat black, sides black-striped.*

Belly whitish. Upperparts olive-green. Two white wing bars. Usually found in heavy northern woods.

FEMALE: Similar to male but duller. Black areas on throat broken.

VOICE: A delicate, dreamy *zoo-zee-zoo-zoo-zee* or *zee-zee-zee-zoo-zee*, next-to-last note lower.

NESTS: Central Canada to Ohio, east to northern New Jersey, and in mountains to Georgia.

WINTERS: Mexico to Colombia.

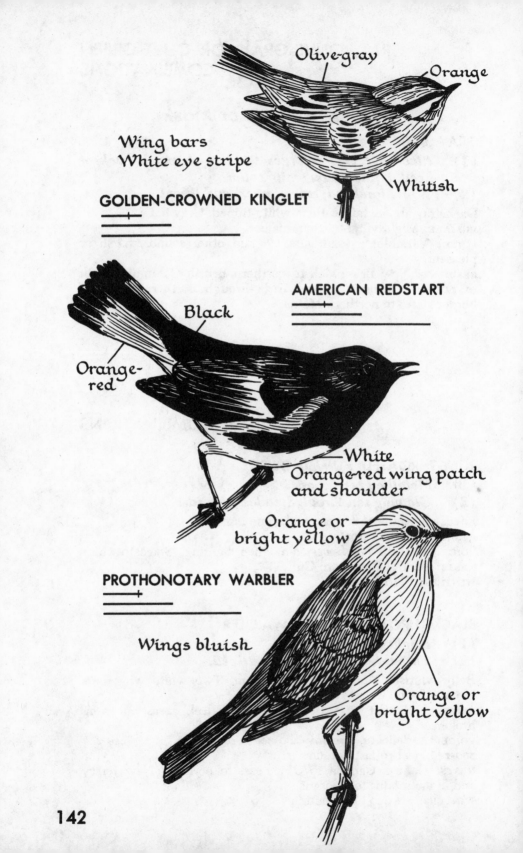

Olive-gray

Orange

Wing bars
White eye stripe

GOLDEN-CROWNED KINGLET

Whitish

Black

AMERICAN REDSTART

Orange-
red

White
Orange-red wing patch
and shoulder

Orange or
bright yellow

PROTHONOTARY WARBLER

Wings bluish

Orange or
bright yellow

GOLDEN-CROWNED KINGLET

(1) *Bright orange crown bordered by yellow-and-black stripe.*

(2) *Whitish wing bars and white eye stripe. Wing feathers yellow-edged.*

Olive-gray above. Whitish to gray below. Is very confiding.
FEMALE: Crown yellow.
VOICE: (1) Call: a high, wiry *see-see-see*. (2) Song: high thin notes, going up and ending in low chatter.
NESTS: Northern Canada south to northern fringe of border states and in mountains to South Carolina.
WINTERS: Southern Minnesota to southern Newfoundland and south to Gulf.

AMERICAN REDSTART

(1) *Brilliant orange-red patches on sides, wings, and outer base of tail feathers.*

(2) *Belly white, throat black.*

FEMALE: Olive-gray replaces black; yellow replaces orange. Younger breeding males resemble females.

VOICE: High, weak *tee tee tee tee tuh uh*, sometimes ascending at end.
NESTS: Newfoundland to Alaska and south to northern half of Gulf States.
WINTERS: West Indies, Central and South America.

PROTHONOTARY WARBLER

(1) *Entire head and breast varying from deep yellow to light orange.*

(2) *Wings blue-gray.*

FEMALE: Duller.
VOICE: Sharp *weet, weet, weet, weet,* on one pitch.
NESTS: Central Minnesota east through central New York to New Jersey and south to Gulf. Rare in northern part of range.
WINTERS: Central and South America.

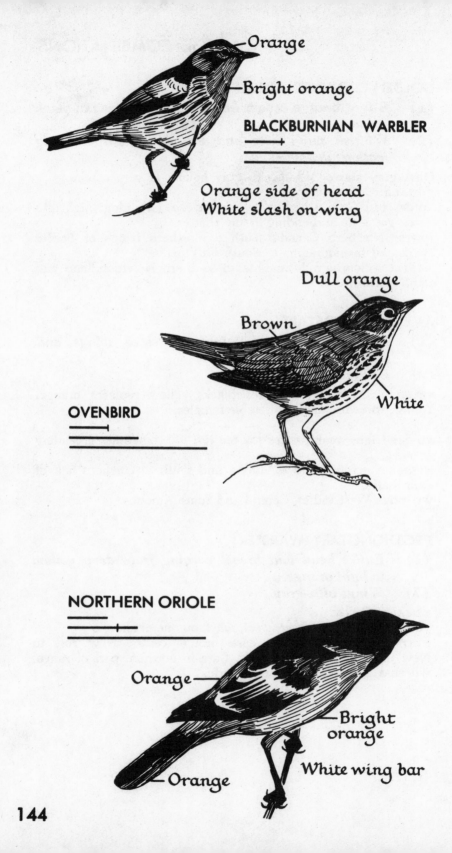

Orange

Bright orange

BLACKBURNIAN WARBLER

Orange side of head
White slash on wing

Dull orange

Brown

White

OVENBIRD

NORTHERN ORIOLE

Orange

Bright
orange

Orange

White wing bar

BLACKBURNIAN WARBLER
(1) *Brilliant orange throat.*
(2) *Upperparts black with white streaks.*
Yellow crown patch and yellow line over eye. Yellowish to whitish below, with black streaks on sides. Slash of white on wing.
FEMALE: Similar but duller. Gray replaces black on head.
VOICE: Thin, wiry warble climbing the scale. Also two to four notes climbing the scale, followed by trill lower on the scale.
NESTS: Northern Ontario to Saskatchewan, south to Minnesota in West, Maine in East, and mountains to South Carolina.
WINTERS: Mexico, Central and South America.

OVENBIRD
(1) *Heavily spotted on whitish breast, chin and belly white.*
(2) *Eye ring and dull orange crown.*
Walks teetering in deep woods, often on logs.
FEMALE: Similar but duller.
VOICE: Metallic, penetrating, in two-note phrases starting softly and ending very loud:

ka dee ka dee ka dee ka dee ka Dee KADEE!
NESTS: Newfoundland to British Columbia, south to North Dakota, and east to northern Georgia.
WINTERS: Central America and northern South America.

NORTHERN ORIOLE*
(1) *Brilliant orange underparts, rump, and outer tail tips.*
(2) *Black head, back, wings, and tail center.*
White wing bar, wing feathers white-edged.
FEMALE: Olive-brown above, yellow below, spotted throat. Top of head and back often blackish.
VOICE: (1) Several rich rolling whistles very distinctive in quality. (2) A rounded chatter.
NESTS: Central Canada to Gulf States.
WINTERS: Mostly Mexico to Colombia.

NORTHERN ORIOLE

White

Yellow

Bright orange

Small

Red

White

DOWNY WOODPECKER

Heavy bill

Red patch

Spots on white

White

White back

HAIRY WOODPECKER

No spots on outer tail feathers

ORANGE COMBINATIONS

NORTHERN ORIOLE
(1) *Brilliant orange cheeks and underparts.*
(2) *Prominent white wing patches.*
Top of head, throat, and back black. Yellow rump and tail edges.
FEMALE: Yellowish underparts, and edges on tail; whitish belly; olive-gray upperparts. Two white wing bars.
VOICE: Loud melodious whistles.
NESTS: Southwestern Canadian provinces south to central Texas and east to western Kansas.
WINTERS: Mexico to Costa Rica.

RED COMBINATIONS

Head with Red Markings

Woodpeckers

DOWNY WOODPECKER*
(1) *White back.*
(2) *Red spot back of head.*
Small bill. White spots on wings. Outer tail feathers white, spotted with black. Resembles Hairy Woodpecker but much smaller and with very small bill.
FEMALE: No red on head.
VOICE: (1) A light *keek keek*. (2) A musical succession of clear-cut high notes going down the scale.
RESIDENT: Alaska and Canada and south to Gulf.

HAIRY WOODPECKER*
(1) *Red spot on top of head, black crown. Black eye patch on white.*
(2) *White back, black wings and tail.*
Wings spotted white. Tail white-edged. White below. Distinguished from Downy Woodpecker by much larger size and large bill.
FEMALE: No red on head.
VOICE: (1) A rather loud, high *keek keek*. (2) A long, slurred high rattle, running together and descending at end.
RESIDENT: Alaska and Canada and south to Gulf.

Red
Red

YELLOW-BELLIED SAPSUCKER

Belly yellowish
White stripe on wing

Red —
Black —
White —
— White

RED-HEADED WOODPECKER

White

Red —
Gray —
Black
and
white —
— Reddish tinge

RED-BELLIED WOODPECKER

Head with Red Markings

Woodpeckers

YELLOW-BELLIED SAPSUCKER*

(1) *Bright red crown and throat.*
(2) *Long white wing stripe.*

Yellowish below, light-spotted on sides. White stripe under and over black mask, which goes through eye. Back, wings, and tail black, white-spotted. Drills holes in trees for sap. Usually these Sapsucker holes are of little or no damage to trees unless heavily concentrated on one limb.
FEMALE: Has white throat.

VOICE: (1) A loud *ayow ayow* like mewing of a cat. (2) High-pitched slurred squeal.
NESTS: Labrador to British Columbia, south to eastern Missouri, east to northwestern Connecticut, and in mountains to Virginia.
WINTERS: Southern New England and Wisconsin south.

RED-HEADED WOODPECKER*

(1) *Entire head red.*
(2) *Back and wings black.*

Large white patch on wing and rump. Underparts white.
SEXES: Alike.
VOICE: A loud *querr* or *queeah.*
NESTS: Southern Canada to Gulf. Rare east of Delaware and Hudson rivers.
WINTERS: Southern New England south.

RED-BELLIED WOODPECKER

(1) *Black upperparts heavily cross-barred with narrow white bars.*
(2) *Red crown.*

Tail black-barred in center. Throat and breast gray. Belly whitish with light reddish tinge.
FEMALE: Similar, except red patch on head smaller.
VOICE: (1) Harsh, loud *krrk krrk krrk,* rolling the *r*'s.
(2) Loud, rattling *kack kack kack kack,* all on same pitch.
RESIDENT: Southeastern Minnesota through southwestern Ontario to western New York and south to Gulf. Occasionally New Jersey, Delaware, and Maryland.

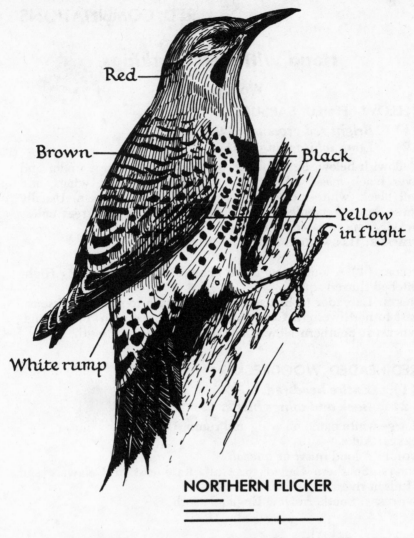

Red

Brown

Black

Yellow
in flight

White rump

NORTHERN FLICKER

Underside wings and tail yellow

Head with Red Markings

Woodpeckers

NORTHERN FLICKER*

(1) *Black crescent and "mustache" on throat. Red crescent back of head.*

(2) *White rump, prominent in flight. Underside of wings and tail yellow.*

Long Woodpecker bill. Upperparts brown, cross-striped. Underparts with heavy black spots on whitish.

FEMALE: No "mustache."

VOICE: (1) A long succession of semi-musical, fast, far-reaching *kick*'s. (2) A sort of squealing succession of *hickup*'s. (3) An explosive, piercing *clear clear clear*. (4) A squeaky *eureka eureka eureka*.

NESTS: Alaska and Canada to southern Virginia and in mountains to North Carolina.

WINTERS: In limited numbers to northern limit of range and south to Gulf.

Red

Red

Black

White patch

PILEATED WOODPECKER

Head with Red Markings

Woodpeckers

PILEATED WOODPECKER

(1) *Brilliant red crest.*
(2) *Mainly black, long white neck patch and wing patch.*

Very large sharp bill. Red streak behind bill.

FEMALE: No red streak behind bill. Front of crown grayish brown.

VOICE: Loud, deliberate, one-pitched *kuk-kuk-kukkuk-kuk-kuk*, similar to that of the Flicker but deeper-pitched. Often located by heavy chopping sound as it pecks huge oblong holes in decaying trees.

RESIDENT: Forested regions, southern Canada to Gulf.

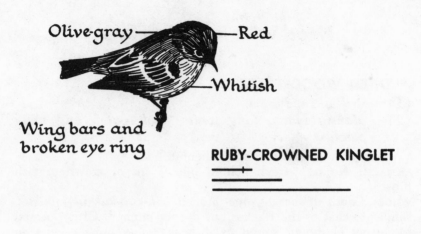

Olive-gray — Red

— Whitish

Wing bars and
broken eye ring

RUBY-CROWNED KINGLET

COMMON REDPOLL

— Red

— Black

Brown-striped —

— Pinkish

PURPLE FINCH

Dull red —

— Dull
red

Purplish red —

Unstreaked
below

Head with Red Markings

Other Than Woodpeckers

RUBY-CROWNED KINGLET*
(1) *Tiny, with broken white eye ring and two pale wing bars.*
(2) *Ruby crown, often hard to see. Olive-gray above, whitish below.*

FEMALE: No ruby crown.
VOICE: (1) Husky *ji-dit*. (2) Variable; loud, high *zee-zee-zee's*, lower *kew, kew, kew's*, then tinkling three-note phrases going up the scale.
NESTS: Labrador to Alaska south to northern Michigan in West and Maine in East.
WINTERS: Mostly southern United States.

COMMON REDPOLL
(1) *Forward part of body pinkish, bright red forehead.*
(2) *Brown-striped upperparts, lighter below, striped on sides.*

Black chin. Forked tail. Found usually in open country in weedy areas.
FEMALE: Lighter and less reddish.
VOICE: In flight a rattling *chut-chut-chut*.
NESTS: Greenland and Newfoundland to Alaska.
WINTERS: Irregularly in northern tier of states. Winter plumage of lighter color.
NOTE: The Hoary Redpoll, which is very rare, is a subarctic bird with a white rump, wintering, though only rarely, as far south as the northern United States.

PURPLE FINCH*
(1) *Head, breast, and rump purplish red.*
(2) *Wings and tail brownish.*

Brown back with reddish stripes. Whitish belly, not streaked as in House Finch.
FEMALE: No red, heavy brown stripes. Has whitish stripe above and behind eye.
VOICE: (1) Call: A dull, metallic *click*. (2) Song: beautiful, extremely rapid, Canary-like long-sustained warble.
NESTS: Nova Scotia to British Columbia south to North Dakota in West and northern New Jersey in East.
WINTERS: Canadian border to Gulf.

Bright red —

Bright red

Bright
red —

HOUSE FINCH

Streaked below

RED-WINGED BLACKBIRD

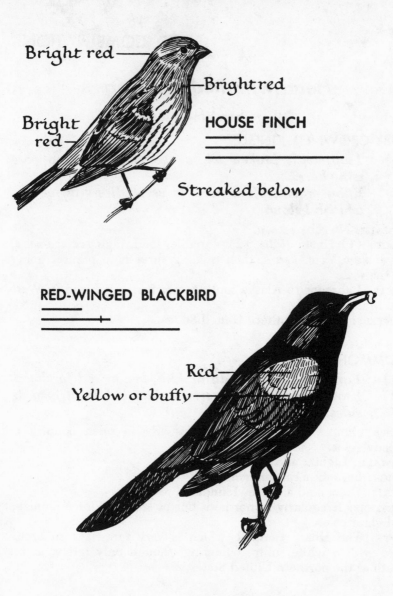

Red —

Yellow or buffy —

RUBY-THROATED HUMMINGBIRD

Green — — Red

Head with Red Markings

Other Than Woodpeckers

HOUSE FINCH

(1) *Bright red head, breast, and rump.*

(2) *Heavy short bill.*

Back darker. Wings brown-streaked. Belly whitish, heavily brown-streaked. Most easily distinguished from Purple Finch by brighter red, streaked underparts, and very different song.
FEMALE: Heavily brown-streaked on dull-gray background.
VOICE: High musical warble resembling Purple Finch but has distinctive energetic "schweer" at end.
RESIDENT: A western bird introduced in the East but, being pugnacious and resourceful, is already common around New York and Connecticut.

Shoulder Red

RED-WINGED BLACKBIRD*

(1) *Solid shiny black, except for red patch on wing with yellow or buffy border.*

(2) *Slender bill.*

FEMALE: Grayish brown, heavily striped.
VOICE: (1) Variety of notes. (2) Three-note phrase, first two liquid, pure-toned, last note quavering and reedy: *conk ul reeee.*
NESTS: Central Canada to Gulf States, in damp and marshy places.
WINTERS: Mostly Southern States.

Breast or Throat Red

RUBY-THROATED HUMMINGBIRD*

(1) *Metallic green above.*

(2) *Glowing red throat. Smallest of birds.*

Feeds on nectar of flowers, and some insects.
FEMALE: White throat.
VOICE: A shrill *chick-we-we-a* when fighting. Staccato chips.
NESTS: Central Canada to Gulf.
WINTERS: Florida south.

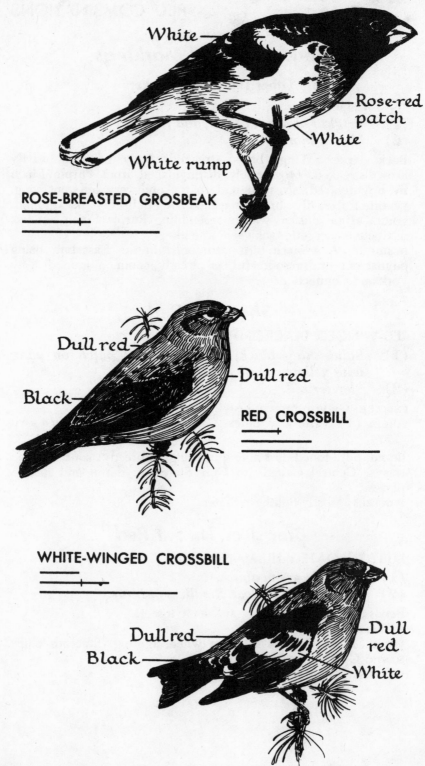

White

Rose-red
patch

White

White rump

ROSE-BREASTED GROSBEAK

Dull red

Black

Dull red

RED CROSSBILL

WHITE-WINGED CROSSBILL

Dull red

Black

Dull
red

White

Breast or Throat Red

ROSE-BREASTED GROSBEAK*
(1) *Brilliant red throat patch.*
(2) *Black head, back, wings, and tail.*

Large stubby bill. White wing bars, rump, and belly.
FEMALE: Brownish-striped, white line above eye and on top of head.
VOICE: A beautiful full-toned warble, notes running into each other similar to that of the American Robin.

NESTS: Northern and central Canada, south to Missouri, and east to northern Georgia.
WINTERS: Southern Mexico to South America.

Mostly Red

RED CROSSBILL
(1) *Dull red above and below.*
(2) *Wings and tail black.*

No wing bars. Bill crossed when seen close. Some males are dull orange. Usually in flocks in pine or spruce.
FEMALE: Resembles male, but dull yellowish replaces red.
VOICE: (1) Call: a hard *kip-kip-kip*. (2) Song: Finch-like warbles, *too-tee, too-tee-tee-tee;* also elaborate flight song.
NESTS: Newfoundland to Alaska, south to border states, and in mountains to North Carolina.
WINTERS: Erratically to Southern States.

WHITE-WINGED CROSSBILL
(1) *Dull red above and below.*
(2) *Black wings and tail with conspicuous white wing bars.*

Cross-billed.
FEMALE: Pink replaced by dull yellow.
VOICE: (1) Call: a single *cheep* or loud whistled *wheat-wheat-wheat*. (2) Song: series of beautiful loud whistles, trills, and twitters.
NESTS OR RESIDENT: Labrador to northern Alaska south to northern Minnesota in West and Maine in East.
WINTERS: Erratically as far south as North Carolina.

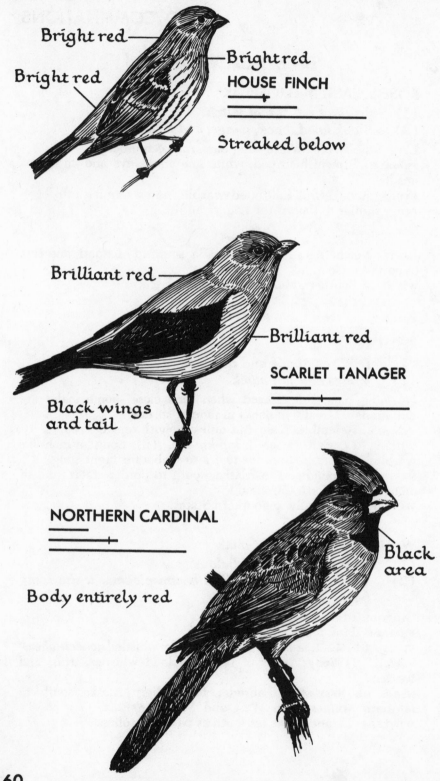

Bright red

Bright red

Bright red
HOUSE FINCH

Streaked below

Brilliant red

Brilliant red

SCARLET TANAGER

Black wings
and tail

NORTHERN CARDINAL

Black
area

Body entirely red

Mostly Red

HOUSE FINCH

(1)   *Bright red head, breast, and rump.*
(2)   *Heavy short bill.*

Back darker. Wings brown-streaked. Belly whitish, heavily brown-streaked. Most easily distinguished from Purple Finch by brighter red, streaked underparts, and very different song.
FEMALE: Heavily brown-streaked on dull-gray background.
VOICE: High musical warble resembling Purple Finch but has distinctive energetic "schweer" at end.
RESIDENT: A western bird introduced in the East but, being pugnacious and resourceful, is already common around New York and Connecticut.

SCARLET TANAGER*

(1)   *Brilliant, glowing red.*
(2)   *Jet-black wings and tail.*

No wing bars.
FEMALE: Plain olive above, yellow below.
VOICE: Robin-like, but strongly burred.
NESTS: Southern Canada to southeastern Oklahoma in West and South Carolina in East.
WINTERS: South America.

NORTHERN CARDINAL*

(1)   *Bright red with high crest.*
(2)   *Black area at base of bill.*

Heavy stout bill.
FEMALE: Yellowish brown with red tinge on crown, wings, and tail. No black area at base of bill.
VOICE: (1) Call: sharp, loud *tsip*. (2) Songs: brilliant, loud, musical whistles interspersed with short notes.
(*a*) Whistle, like whistling for a dog.

(*b*) A down-slurred whistle.

(*c*) *hip hooray hip hooray*.

(*d*) A fast *wurdy wurdy wurdy wurdy wurdy*.
RESIDENT: Southeastern South Dakota in West to southwestern Connecticut in East and south to Gulf.

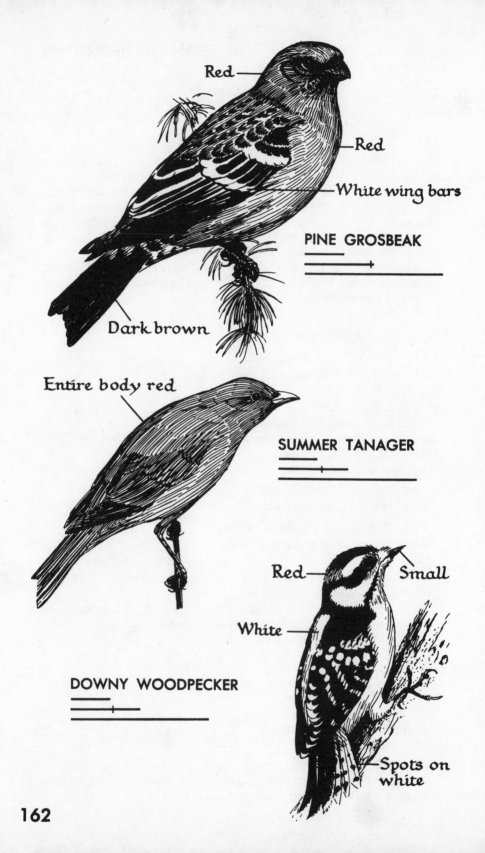

Red

Red

White wing bars

PINE GROSBEAK

Dark brown

Entire body red

SUMMER TANAGER

Red — Small

White

DOWNY WOODPECKER

Spots on white

Mostly Red

PINE GROSBEAK

(1) *Red with dusky wings and tail.*

(2) *Two white wing bars.*

Wing feathers white-edged. Heavy stubby bill.

FEMALE: Gray. Head and rump dull yellow.

VOICE: (1) Flight call: several loud whistles. (2) Song: variable; most commonly a loud whistle, *tee-tee-tew*. Others, ventriloquial in sweet warble.

NESTS: Northern Labrador to Alaska and south to northern New Hampshire and central Maine.

WINTERS: Erratically in southern part of area.

All Red

SUMMER TANAGER*

(1) *All red, slightly darker on wings and tail.*

(2) *No crest.*

Distinguished from Northern Cardinal by: (1) being more slender; (2) having slender instead of short stout bill and having no black area at base of bill.

FEMALE: Olive above, yellow below, with more orange tone than female Scarlet Tanager.

VOICE: Loud long series, Robin-like.

NESTS: Southeastern Nebraska in West to southern Delaware in East and south to Gulf.

WINTERS: Central and South America.

WHITE MARKINGS IMPORTANT IN IDENTIFICATION

Rump or Back White

DOWNY WOODPECKER*

(1) *White back.*

(2) *Red spot back of head.*

Small bill. White spots on wings. Outer tail feathers white, spotted with black. Resembles Hairy Woodpecker but much smaller and with very small bill.

FEMALE: No red on head.

VOICE: (1) A light *keek keek*. (2) A musical succession of clear-cut high notes going down the scale.

RESIDENT: Alaska and Canada and south to Gulf.

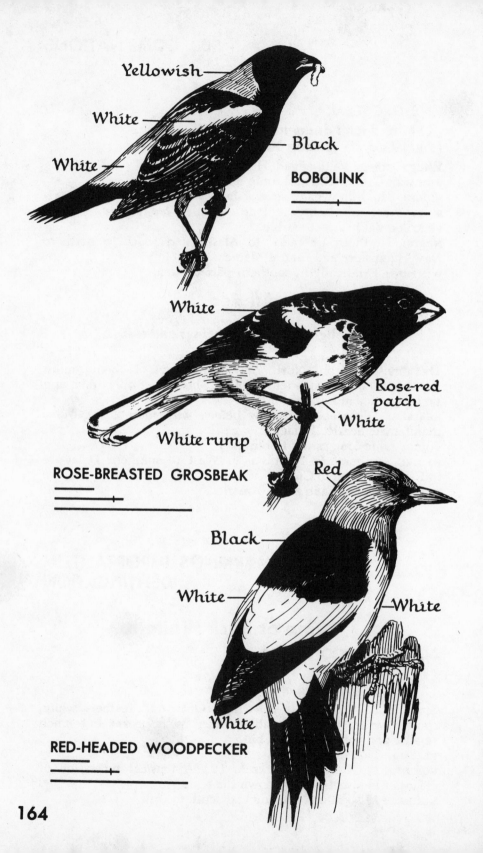

Yellowish—

White—

White—

—Black

BOBOLINK

White—

Rose-red
patch

—White

White rump

ROSE-BREASTED GROSBEAK

Red—

Black—

White—

—White

White—

RED-HEADED WOODPECKER

WHITE MARKINGS IMPORTANT IN IDENTIFICATION

Rump or Back White

BOBOLINK
(1) *Big white patches on wings and rump.*
(2) *Large yellowish patch back of head. Wing feathers white-edged.*

Solid black below. Found in meadows.
FEMALE: Yellowish line above eye and center of dark crown. Back heavily striped with brown.
VOICE: Delightful, rollicking, reedy, as if singing two or three songs at once in a sudden burst; often in flight.
NESTS: Nova Scotia to southern British Columbia, south to central Nebraska, and east to western Maryland.
WINTERS: South America.

ROSE-BREASTED GROSBEAK*
(1) *Brilliant red throat patch.*
(2) *Black head, back, wings, and tail.*

Large stubby bill. White wing bars, rump, and belly.
FEMALE: Brownish-striped, white line above eye and on top of head.
VOICE: A beautiful full-toned warble, notes running into each other similar to that of the American Robin.

NESTS: Northern and central Canada, south to Missouri, and east to northern Georgia.
WINTERS: Southern Mexico to South America.

RED-HEADED WOODPECKER*
(1) *Entire head red.*
(2) *Back and wings black.*

Large white patch on wing and rump. Underparts white.
SEXES: Alike.
VOICE: A loud *querr* or *queeah*.
NESTS: Southern Canada to Gulf. Rare east of Delaware and Hudson rivers.
WINTERS: Southern New England south.

Red patch

Heavy bill

White back

White

HAIRY WOODPECKER

No spots on outer tail feathers

Hooked

Gray

Black mask

Grayish

NORTHERN SHRIKE

White

Gray

Hooked

Black mask

Pure white

White

LOGGERHEAD SHRIKE

White

WHITE MARKINGS IMPORTANT IN IDENTIFICATION

Rump or Back White

HAIRY WOODPECKER*

(1)   *Red spot on top of head, black crown. Black eye patch on white.*

(2)   *White back, black wings and tail.*

Wings spotted white. Tail white-edged. White below. Distinguished from Downy Woodpecker by much larger size and large bill.

FEMALE: No red on head.

VOICE: (1) A rather loud, high *keek keek*. (2) A long, slurred high rattle, running together and descending at end.

RESIDENT: Alaska and Canada and south to Gulf.

NORTHERN SHRIKE

(1)   *Black mask on gray head.*

(2)   *Grayish below, lightly barred; black tail, white-edged, and black wings.*

Upperparts pale grayish to white. White chin; base of bill usually pale. This is the rarer, larger, more northern cousin of the Loggerhead Shrike. (Immature is brown and barred below.)

FEMALE: Duller.

VOICE and HABITS: Similar to that of the Loggerhead Shrike.

NESTS: Labrador to Alaska south to central Canada.

WINTERS: As far south as Kentucky and Virginia.

LOGGERHEAD SHRIKE

(1)   *Black mask on gray head.*

(2)   *White below. Black wings; long black tail, white-edged.*

Solid-black hooked beak. Upperparts grayish. Usual perch is in the open on a wire or tip of tree. Shrikes, with their hooked beaks, eat large insects and grasshoppers, and sometimes other little birds. Easily distinguished by its black mask from Northern Mockingbird, which it resembles slightly.

SEXES: Alike.

VOICE: A subdued medley of many phrases.

NESTS: Central Canada to Gulf.

WINTERS: Mostly southern half of breeding range, occasionally farther north.

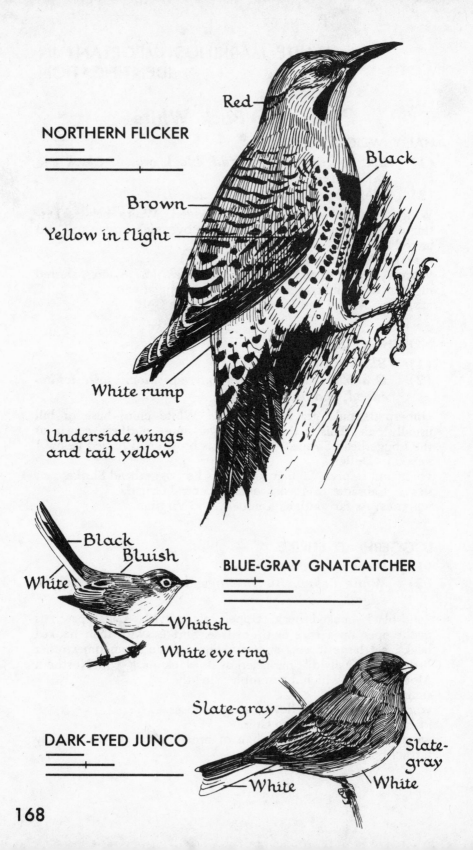

NORTHERN FLICKER

Red

Black

Brown

Yellow in flight

White rump

Underside wings
and tail yellow

Black

Bluish

White

BLUE-GRAY GNATCATCHER

Whitish

White eye ring

Slate-gray

Slate-
gray

DARK-EYED JUNCO

White

White

WHITE MARKINGS IMPORTANT IN IDENTIFICATION

Rump or Back White

NORTHERN FLICKER*
(1) *Black crescent and "mustache" on throat. Red crescent back of head.*
(2) *White rump, prominent in flight. Underside of wings and tail yellow.*

Long Woodpecker bill. Upperparts brown, cross-striped. Underparts with heavy black spots on whitish.
FEMALE: No "mustache."
VOICE: (1) A long succession of semi-musical, fast, far-reaching *kick*'s. (2) A sort of squealing succession of *hickup*'s. (3) An explosive, piercing *clear clear clear*. (4) A squeaky *eureka eureka eureka*.
NESTS: Alaska and Canada to southern Virginia and in mountains to North Carolina.
WINTERS: In limited numbers to northern limit of range and south to Gulf.

Outer Tail Feathers White

BLUE-GRAY GNATCATCHER
(1) *Very slim with long black tail, white-edged.*
(2) *White eye ring.*

Bluish upperparts. Black line from base of bill over eye. Underparts whitish. Very nervous habits.
FEMALE: Similar, but less blue above.
VOICE: (1) Series of thin squeaky notes. (2) A wheezy *spee*.
NESTS: Eastern Nebraska to northern New Jersey and south to Gulf.
WINTERS: Central America and Mexico.

DARK-EYED JUNCO*
(1) *Slate-gray throughout, except for white belly and white outer tail feathers.*
(2) *Short, Sparrow-like bill.*

FEMALE: Slate color lighter and more brownish.
VOICE: Loose, quavering trill.
NESTS: Labrador to Alaska, south to Minnesota, east to Massachusetts, and in mountains to South Carolina.
WINTERS: Canada to Gulf.

169

VESPER SPARROW

Grayish brown
Heavily streaked

Buff

Chestnut

Clear gray

White

WATER PIPIT

Grayish brown

Buffy

White

Walks, does not hop
Buffy wing bars

Chestnut

Brownish

LARK SPARROW

Spot

White

WHITE MARKINGS IMPORTANT IN
IDENTIFICATION

Outer Tail Feathers White

VESPER SPARROW*

(1) *White outer tail feathers most conspicuous in flight. Chestnut on shoulder.*

(2) *Striped on back, upper breast, and sides. Grayish belly.*

Found mostly on ground in fields. Has "wide-eyed" appearance.

SEXES: Alike.

VOICE: Two long, clear melodious whistles followed by two higher ones and ending in descending trill.

NESTS: Central Canada south to central Missouri and east to North Carolina.

WINTERS: Southern Illinois to Connecticut and south to Gulf.

WATER PIPIT

(1) *Upper breast and sides buffy, streaked or spotted with dark brown.*

(2) *Tail, which constantly wags, is white-edged.*

Very light buffy wing bars. Grayish brown above. Slender bill. Light line through eye. Walks, does not hop.

SEXES: Alike.

VOICE: A thin *jee-ett*.

NESTS: Labrador, northern Canada, and northern Alaska.

WINTERS: Open country, New Jersey and Ohio south into Mexico and Central America.

LARK SPARROW

(1) *Tail with white corners.*

(2) *Black spot on clear whitish breast.*

Prominent chestnut patch on face. Black "whiskers" on side of chin.

Upperparts brownish-striped.

FEMALE: Similar.

VOICE: Sweet notes and trills with pauses between.

NESTS: Southwestern Canadian provinces as far east as western New York, south to southern Texas, and east to central Alabama.

WINTERS: Gulf coast and Mexico, occasionally farther north.

Chestnut

Brownish-striped

Black

LAPLAND LONGSPUR
(Spring)

White

White

Yellow

Brown

Black

Yellow

EASTERN MEADOWLARK

White

Gray

White

White wing patch

Whitish

NORTHERN MOCKINGBIRD

White

WHITE MARKINGS IMPORTANT IN IDENTIFICATION
Outer Tail Feathers White

LAPLAND LONGSPUR (Spring)

(1) *Black crown, throat, and sides.*

(2) *Chestnut collar back of neck.*

White or buffy band above and back of eye extends to chestnut and down to merge with white breast and belly. Back dark, heavily streaked with buff. Outer tail feathers white-edged. Light wing bars. Walks or creeps; does not hop. In winter practically all the black and chestnut markings are lacking.

FEMALE: Generally brownish above, heavily streaked. Breast and belly whitish, heavily streaked on sides.

VOICE: A rattly noise followed by a whistle.

NESTS: Greenland to northern Alaska.

WINTERS: To southern United States.

EASTERN MEADOWLARK*

(1) *Broad black V on brilliant yellow underparts.*

(2) *Outer feathers of short tail flash white in flight.*

Long slender bill. Upperparts brown-striped. Usually seen in open fields. Walks, does not hop.

FEMALE: Similar but smaller and duller.

VOICE: The loud beautiful-toned song of this large, conspicuous bird, with its one very common *spring is here,* makes it easily identifiable.

NESTS: Southeastern Canada to North Dakota, south to Arkansas, and east to North Carolina.

WINTERS: Mostly southern United States. Partly resident in Northeast.

NOTE: The Western Meadowlark, generally similar in appearance, has a very different song, of richer lower-pitched, whistled notes. It occurs in the Great Plains or western part of the area treated, but is spreading eastward.

NORTHERN MOCKINGBIRD*

(1) *Two white wing patches and white outer tail feathers prominent in flight.*

(2) *Solid gray above. Whitish below. Slender body and bill and long tail.*

FEMALE: Similar, but white areas smaller.

VOICE: Succession—often day and night—of loud notes and phrases, often accurately imitating other birds in the vicinity.

RESIDENT: Nebraska to southeastern Massachusetts and south to Gulf. Rare in winter in northern part of its range.

LOGGERHEAD SHRIKE

Hooked

Gray

Black mask

White

White

Pure white

Hooked

Gray

Black mask

NORTHERN SHRIKE

Grayish

White

Dusky brown

Pinkish brown

MOURNING DOVE

White

WHITE MARKINGS IMPORTANT IN IDENTIFICATION

Outer Tail Feathers White

LOGGERHEAD SHRIKE

(1)   *Black mask on gray head.*
(2)   *White below. Black wings; long black tail, white-edged.*

Solid-black hooked beak. Upperparts grayish. Usual perch is in the open on a wire or tip of tree. Shrikes, with their hooked beaks, eat large insects and grasshoppers, and sometimes other little birds. Easily distinguished by its black mask from Northern Mockingbird, which it resembles slightly.
SEXES: Alike.
VOICE: A subdued medley of many phrases.
NESTS: Central Canada to Gulf.
WINTERS: Mostly southern half of breeding range, occasionally farther north.

NORTHERN SHRIKE

(1)   *Black mask on gray head.*
(2)   *Grayish below, lightly barred; black tail, white-edged, and black wings.*

Upperparts pale grayish to white. White chin; base of bill usually pale. This is the rarer, larger, more northern cousin of the Loggerhead Shrike. (Immature is brown and barred below.)
FEMALE: Duller.
VOICE and HABITS: Similar to that of the Loggerhead Shrike.
NESTS: Labrador to Alaska south to central Canada.
WINTERS: As far south as Kentucky and Virginia.

MOURNING DOVE*

(1)   *Long pointed tail white on outside in flight.*
(2)   *Small round head.*

Dusky brown above, lighter pinkish brown below. Dark spot on neck.
FEMALE: Similar but smaller and duller.
VOICE: Soft, melodious, in minor key:

oo oh ooo oo oo.
NESTS: Southern fringe of Canada to Gulf.
WINTERS: Northern tier of states south.

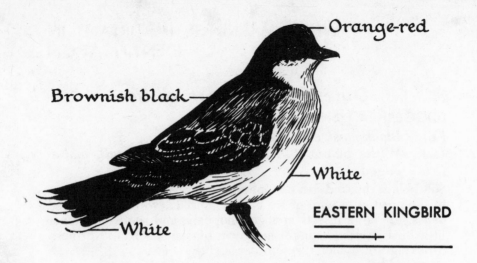

Orange-red

Brownish black—

White

—White

EASTERN KINGBIRD

Light brown

SNOW BUNTING (Winter)

Pure white

Big white wing patch

Tip of Tail White

EASTERN KINGBIRD*

(1)   *Dark slate above appears black in field.*
(2)   *Tip of tail and belly white.*

Wing feathers slightly white-edged. Orange-red crown patch, rarely seen. Perches in open exposed places and chases insects on the wing.

SEXES: Similar.

VOICE: (1) Unmusical sputter. (2) A harsh *dzeeb*.

NESTS: Northern Ontario to northern British Columbia and south to Gulf.

WINTERS: Mostly Mexico and Central America.

Mostly White

SNOW BUNTING (Winter)

(1)   *Underparts, including fore part of wings, almost pure white.*
(2)   *Striped light brown above. Top of head and shoulders light-brownish.*

In early spring the brownish of males begins to turn to the black of breeding plumage. Usually travels on or close to the ground in flocks in open fields or on beaches.

FEMALE: Lighter in color.

VOICE: While flying, a melodious whistle followed by trill. Also a vibrant "purring" and *bzzt*.

NESTS: Greenland to Alaska; the farthest north of any land bird.

WINTERS: Southern Alaska and Canada south to Kansas and east to Virginia.

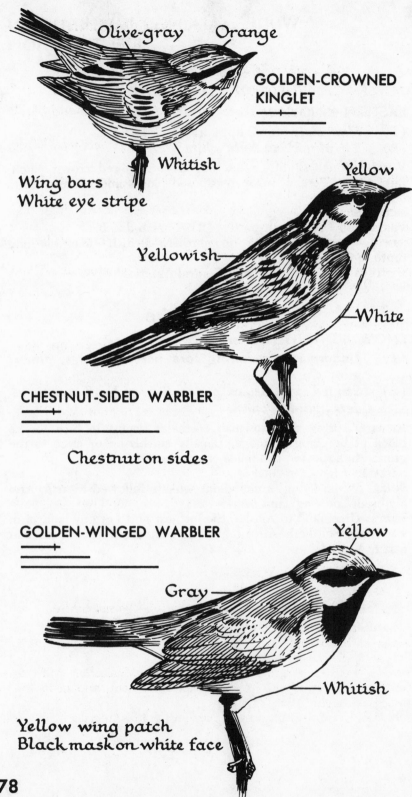

Olive-gray   Orange

**GOLDEN-CROWNED
KINGLET**

Whitish

Wing bars
White eye stripe

Yellow

Yellowish

White

CHESTNUT-SIDED WARBLER

Chestnut on sides

GOLDEN-WINGED WARBLER

Yellow

Gray

Whitish

Yellow wing patch
Black mask on white face

Crown Yellow or Orange

GOLDEN-CROWNED KINGLET

(1) *Bright orange crown bordered by yellow-and-black stripe.*

(2) *Whitish wing bars and white eye stripe. Wing feathers yellow-edged.*

Olive-gray above. Whitish to gray below. Is very confiding.
FEMALE: Crown yellow.
VOICE: (1) Call: a high, wiry *see-see-see*. (2) Song: high thin notes, going up and ending in low chatter.
NESTS: Northern Canada south to northern fringe of border states and in mountains to South Carolina.
WINTERS: Southern Minnesota to southern Newfoundland and south to Gulf.

CHESTNUT-SIDED WARBLER*

(1) *White below with broad chestnut stripe on side.*
(2) *Yellow crown.*

Black patch through and under eye in front of white patch. Striped black and yellow above. Two yellowish wing bars.
FEMALE: Similar to male but with less chestnut and black.
VOICE: (1) High, musical ___ _

pleased pleased pleased ta meecha.

(2)*you may see me maybe?* and variations.
NESTS: Nova Scotia to Saskatchewan, south to eastern Nebraska in West, to Maryland in East, and in mountains to South Carolina.
WINTERS: Central America.

GOLDEN-WINGED WARBLER

(1) *Yellow wing patch and cap.*
(2) *Black throat and black eye patch against white.*

Upperparts gray, underparts whitish.
FEMALE: Black replaced by gray.
VOICE: Four or five buzzy notes.
NESTS: Southern Ontario to southeastern Manitoba; south to southeastern Iowa, east to southern Connecticut, and in mountains to Georgia.
WINTERS: Central America and northern South America.

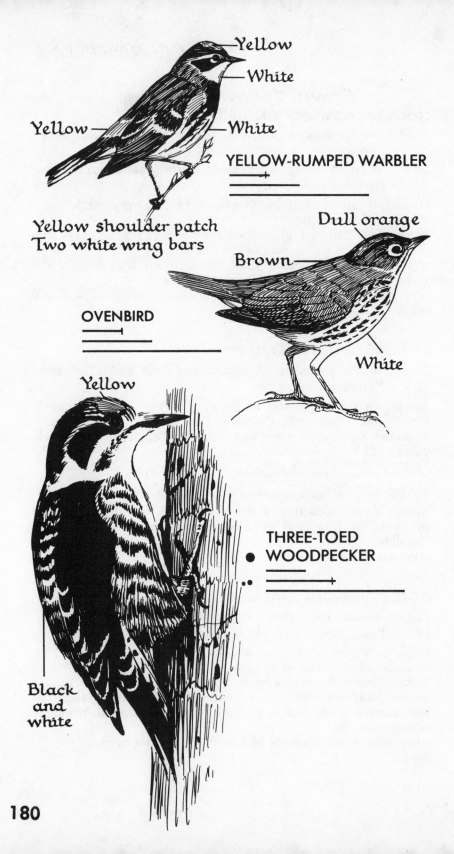

Yellow

White

Yellow

White

YELLOW-RUMPED WARBLER

Yellow shoulder patch
Two white wing bars

Dull orange

Brown

White

OVENBIRD

Yellow

**THREE-TOED
WOODPECKER**

Black
and
white

Crown Yellow or Orange

YELLOW-RUMPED WARBLER*
(1) *Yellow crown spot, rump, and sides of breast.*
(2) *Black mask, surmounted by short white line.*

White chin. Underparts white with heavy black stripes. Two white wing bars. Above bluish slate-gray, streaked black. White outer tail tips. Magnolia Warbler easily distinguished from Yellow-rumped Warbler by yellow instead of white underparts.
FEMALE: Duller and more brownish above.
VOICE: Clear warble of about eight notes.
NESTS: Labrador to Alaska, south to northern part of Great Lakes States, and east to Maine.
WINTERS: Frequently in Northeast, mostly southern United States to Central America.

OVENBIRD
(1) *Heavily spotted on whitish breast, chin and belly white.*
(2) *Eye ring and dull orange crown.*

Walks teetering in deep woods, often on logs.
FEMALE: Similar but duller.
VOICE: Metallic, penetrating, in two-note phrases starting softly and ending very loud:

ka dee ka dee ka dee ka dee ka Dee KADEE!

NESTS: Newfoundland to British Columbia, south to North Dakota, and east to northern Georgia.
WINTERS: Central America and northern South America.

THREE-TOED WOODPECKER
(1) *Upperparts black. Back barred black and white.*
(2) *Yellow cap.*

Throat and belly white. Sides black-barred on white. Narrow white stripe behind eye.
FEMALE: Crown not yellow; usually streaked black and white.
VOICE: A sharp *chirk*; a loud *queep*; a long squeal.
RESIDENT: From northern Canada to northern fringe of border states; occasionally in winter as far south as Massachusetts.

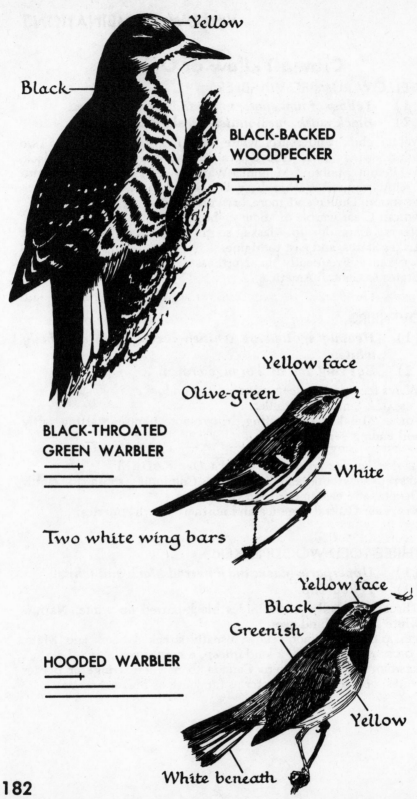

Yellow

Black

**BLACK-BACKED
WOODPECKER**

Yellow face

Olive-green

**BLACK-THROATED
GREEN WARBLER**

White

Two white wing bars

Yellow face

Black

Greenish

HOODED WARBLER

Yellow

White beneath

182

Crown Yellow or Orange

BLACK-BACKED WOODPECKER

(1)   *Head and back solid black.*
(2)   *Yellow cap.*

Throat and outer sides of tail white. Sides barred black and white. Broad white stripe below ear and eye. Flight feathers white-spotted.

FEMALE: Lacks yellow crown.

VOICE: Sharp, shrill *chirk chirk;* also loud single call: *click-click.*

RESIDENT OR NESTS: Labrador to Alaska, south to northern fringe of border states to Maine and in mountains from northern New York to New Hampshire.

WINTERS: As far south as New Jersey.

NOTE: Three-toed Woodpecker (rare) is similar to above but back is barred.

Face Yellow

BLACK-THROATED GREEN WARBLER

(1)   *Bright yellow face.*
(2)   *Throat black, sides black-striped.*

Belly whitish. Upperparts olive-green. Two white wing bars. Usually found in heavy northern woods.

FEMALE: Similar to male but duller. Black areas on throat broken.

VOICE: A delicate, dreamy *zoo-zee-zoo-zoo-zee* or *zee-zee-zee-zoo-zee*, next-to-last note lower.

NESTS: Central Canada to Ohio, east to northern New Jersey, and in mountains to Georgia.

WINTERS: Mexico to Colombia.

HOODED WARBLER*

(1)   *Bright yellow face within black hood.*
(2)   *Belly yellow.*

Upperparts greenish. Tail feathers white below.

FEMALE: No black hood.

VOICE: Sprightly whistle: *hip, hip, horray.*

NESTS: Central Iowa to Rhode Island and south to Gulf.

WINTERS: West Indies and Central America.

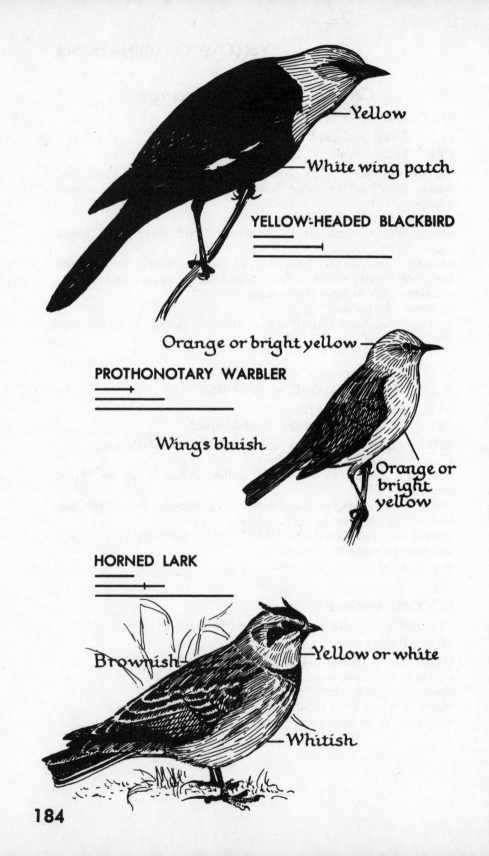

Yellow

White wing patch

YELLOW-HEADED BLACKBIRD

Orange or bright yellow

PROTHONOTARY WARBLER

Wings bluish

Orange or
bright
yellow

HORNED LARK

Brownish

Yellow or white

Whitish

Head Yellow or Orange-Yellow

Body Black

YELLOW-HEADED BLACKBIRD

(1) *Yellow head.*

(2) *Conspicuous white wing patch in flight. Body black.*

FEMALE: Brown, yellowish throat, streaked breast.

VOICE: An exceedingly raspy *caak*, and series of unmusical noises.

NESTS: Mostly western marshy places. Central Canada south to Nebraska. Occasionally wanders to east coast.

WINTERS: Western Gulf States and Mexico.

Underparts Bright Yellow

PROTHONOTARY WARBLER

(1) *Entire head and breast varying from deep yellow to light orange.*

(2) *Wings blue-gray.*

FEMALE: Duller.

VOICE: Sharp *weet, weet, weet, weet,* on one pitch.

NESTS: Central Minnesota east through central New York to New Jersey and south to Gulf. Rare in northern part of range.

WINTERS: Central and South America.

Face and Throat Yellow *(Black Mask and Bib)*

HORNED LARK

(1) *Black mask and throat patch on yellow or white.*

(2) *Black patch top of head ending in "horns," often hard to see.*

Brownish-striped above. Usually seen on ground in open country.

FEMALE: Similar but smaller and duller. No black on top of head.

VOICE: Often long, high-pitched, tinkling; frequently in flight.

NESTS: Arctic coast of North America, south to eastern Kansas in West and North Carolina in East.

WINTERS: South to Gulf States.

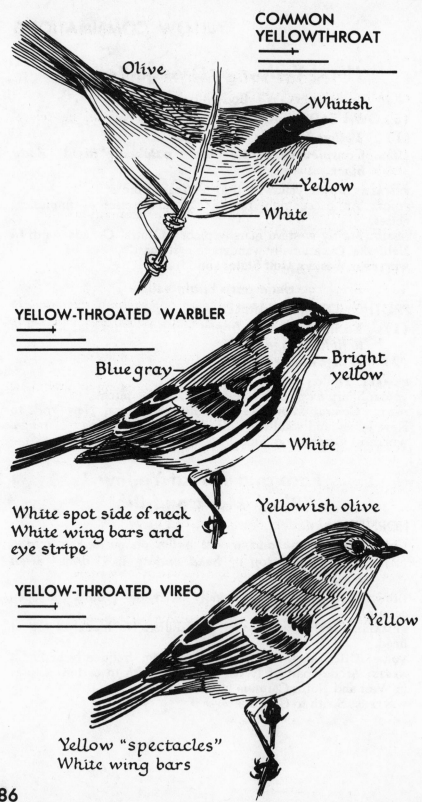

COMMON YELLOWTHROAT

Olive

Whitish

Yellow

White

YELLOW-THROATED WARBLER

Blue gray

Bright yellow

White

White spot side of neck
White wing bars and
eye stripe

Yellowish olive

Yellow

YELLOW-THROATED VIREO

Yellow "spectacles"
White wing bars

186

Throat Solid Bright Yellow

COMMON YELLOWTHROAT*

(1) *Black mask bounded above and behind by white.*

(2) *Yellow throat. White belly.*

Uniform olive above. No wing bars. Usually found in low shrubs in moist places.

FEMALE: Grayish mask. Brownish above, duller below.

VOICE: *witchity-witchity-witchity-witch.*

NESTS: Newfoundland to southern Alaska and south to Gulf.

WINTERS: Southern States.

YELLOW-THROATED WARBLER

(1) *Bright yellow throat, white belly.*

(2) *Black on forehead, below and behind eye, and in stripes on sides. White stripe above eye and white patch on side of neck.*

Two wing bars. Upperparts blue-gray. Underparts whitish.

SEXES: Similar.

VOICE: Series of clear notes, slurred and dropping in pitch. Last note higher.

NESTS: Southern Ohio to central New Jersey (rare) and south to Gulf.

WINTERS: Southern States southward into Central America.

YELLOW-THROATED VIREO

(1) *Yellow eye ring forms "spectacles."*

(2) *Bright yellow throat, whitish belly.*

Gray rump. Rest of upperparts yellowish olive. White wing bars. Wings darker. Wing feathers and outer tail feathers white-edged. Usually found in deep woods or swamps.

FEMALE: Similar.

VOICE: (1) Call: harsh, scolding. (2) Song: deliberate, reedy, burred notes, often interpreted as saying *three-eight.*

NESTS: Southern fringe of Canada to Gulf.

WINTERS: Mexico into South America.

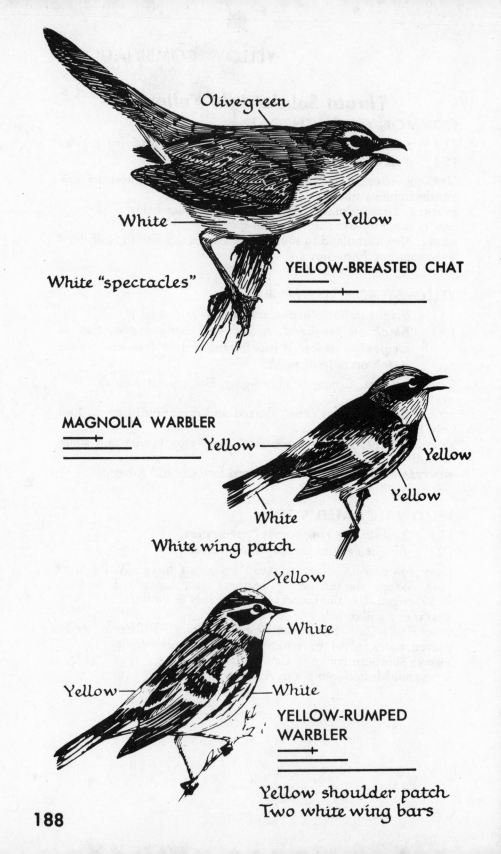

Olive-green

White   Yellow

White "spectacles"   YELLOW-BREASTED CHAT

MAGNOLIA WARBLER

Yellow   Yellow

Yellow

White

White wing patch

Yellow

White

Yellow   White

YELLOW-RUMPED WARBLER

Yellow shoulder patch
Two white wing bars

Throat Solid Bright Yellow

YELLOW-BREASTED CHAT*

(1) *Bright yellow throat and white belly.*
(2) *White "spectacles."*

Olive-green above. Long tail. Usually well concealed in leafy trees or thick tangles. Belongs to Warbler family.
FEMALE: Similar but duller.
VOICE: Loud whistles, caws, croaks, all mixed up.
NESTS: Northeastern South Dakota to southern New Hampshire and south to Gulf.
WINTERS: Central America.

Rump Yellow

MAGNOLIA WARBLER*

(1) *Yellow underparts heavily black-striped.*
(2) *Yellow rump. White patches on wings and white bar on tail.*

White line above black mask. Upperparts gray and black.
FEMALE: Lighter striping and mask.
VOICE: Warbling *weeta-weeta-weetee*, rising or falling on last note.
NESTS: Northern Canada to northeastern Minnesota, east to Massachusetts, and in mountains to Virginia.
WINTERS: Central America.

YELLOW-RUMPED WARBLER*

(1) *Yellow crown spot, rump, and sides of breast.*
(2) *Black mask, surmounted by short white line.*

White chin. Underparts white with heavy black stripes. Two white wing bars. Above bluish slate-gray, streaked black. White outer tail tips. Magnolia Warbler easily distinguished from Yellow-rumped Warbler by yellow instead of white underparts.
FEMALE: Duller and more brownish above.
VOICE: Clear warble of about eight notes.
NESTS: Labrador to Alaska, south to northern part of Great Lakes States, and east to Maine.
WINTERS: Frequently in Northeast, mostly southern United States to Central America.

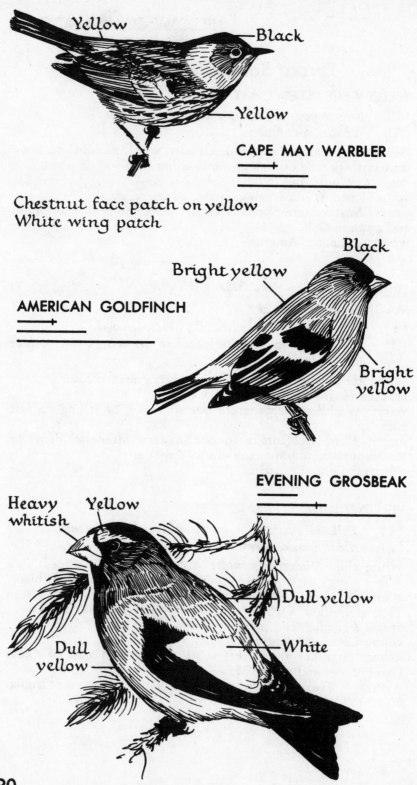

Yellow

Black

Yellow

CAPE MAY WARBLER

Chestnut face patch on yellow
White wing patch

Bright yellow

Black

AMERICAN GOLDFINCH

Bright
yellow

EVENING GROSBEAK

Heavy
whitish

Yellow

Dull yellow

White

Dull
yellow

Rump Yellow

CAPE MAY WARBLER

(1) *Black cap. Chestnut patch on yellow face.*
(2) *Yellow below, heavily striped.*

White wing patch. Yellow rump.
FEMALE: Lighter-striped below, no chestnut cheek patch, yellowish rump. Yellow spot on side of head. Olive above, streaked with black.
VOICE: Hurried, wiry, and irregular.
NESTS: Central Canada to northern edge of Great Lakes States east to southern Maine.
WINTERS: West Indies.

Back and Underparts Yellow or Yellowish

AMERICAN GOLDFINCH*

(1) *Striking yellow body.*
(2) *Black forehead, wings, and tail.*

Wing feathers white-tipped. Winter males resemble summer females.
FEMALE: Olive-yellow; wing bars, no black forehead patch.
VOICE: (1) Canary-like call, with rising inflection. Also in undulating flight a musical *per chickery.* (2) Long, varied, sweet warble.
NESTS OR RESIDENT: Nebraska and Minnesota to Nova Scotia and south to Gulf States.

EVENING GROSBEAK*

(1) *Big, stout whitish bill.*
(2) *Big white patch on black wings.*

Yellow stripe across forehead and above eye. Dull yellow above and below.
FEMALE: Silvery gray. Wings and tail similar to male.
VOICE: (1) Shrill call resembling that of the House Sparrow. (2) Short, uneven warble.
NESTS: Narrow belt from northern New Brunswick to northeastern Alberta, south to northeastern Minnesota in West and Massachusetts in East.
WINTERS: Irregularly throughout area.

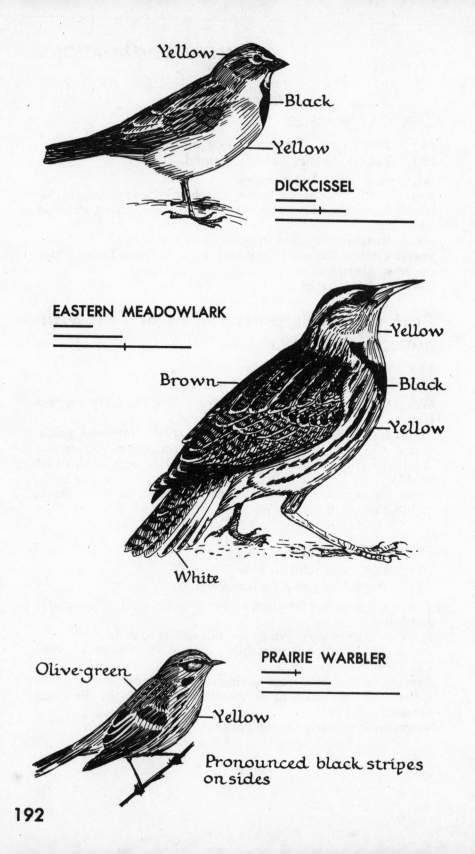

Yellow

Black

Yellow

DICKCISSEL

EASTERN MEADOWLARK

Yellow

Black

Yellow

Brown

White

PRAIRIE WARBLER

Olive-green

Yellow

Pronounced black stripes on sides

192

Underparts Yellow with Black V or Patch

DICKCISSEL

(1) *Yellow breast.*
(2) *Black bib.*

Brownish-striped upperparts; chestnut on shoulder. Yellow stripe above eye.
FEMALE: Much lighter throughout, no bib.
VOICE: A repetition of *dick-ciss-ciss-ciss*.
NESTS: Mostly western or plains. Canadian border states and provinces, south to Texas, and east to South Carolina. Often wanders to east coast.
WINTERS: Mexico to northern South America.

EASTERN MEADOWLARK*

(1) *Broad black V on brilliant yellow underparts.*
(2) *Outer feathers of short tail flash white in flight.*

Long slender bill. Upperparts brown-striped. Usually seen in open fields. Walks, does not hop.
FEMALE: Similar but smaller and duller.
VOICE: The loud beautiful-toned song of this large, conspicuous bird, with its one very common *spring is here*, makes it easily identifiable.
NESTS: Southeastern Canada to North Dakota, south to Arkansas, and east to North Carolina.
WINTERS: Mostly southern United States. Partly resident in Northeast.
NOTE: The Western Meadowlark, generally similar in appearance, has a very different song, of richer lower-pitched, whistled notes. It occurs in the Great Plains or western part of the area treated, but is spreading eastward.

Underparts Yellow, Streaked or Spotted

PRAIRIE WARBLER

(1) *Bright yellow below, with heavy black stripes on sides. Black line through eye and black line under eye.*
(2) *Yellow stripe above eye.*

Olive-green above. Reddish-mottled in middle of back. Two inconspicuous wing bars. Wags tail (an important field mark).
FEMALE: Similar but duller.
VOICE: Thin, distinct *zee-zee-zee-zee-zee-zee-zee-zee*, going up the scale.
NESTS: Southeastern South Dakota east through northern Great Lakes region to southern New Hampshire and south to Gulf.
WINTERS: West Indies.

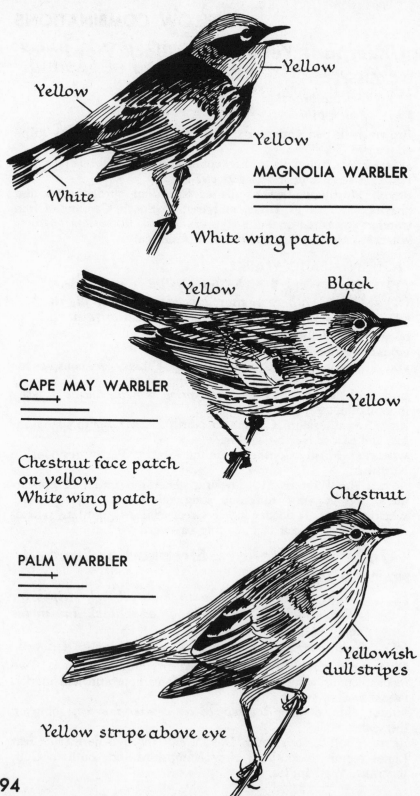

Yellow

Yellow

Yellow

White

MAGNOLIA WARBLER

White wing patch

Yellow

Black

CAPE MAY WARBLER

Yellow

Chestnut face patch
on yellow
White wing patch

Chestnut

PALM WARBLER

Yellowish
dull stripes

Yellow stripe above eye

Underparts Yellow, Streaked or Spotted

MAGNOLIA WARBLER*

(1)   *Yellow underparts heavily black-striped.*
(2)   *Yellow rump. White patches on wings and white bar on tail.*

White line above black mask. Upperparts gray and black.
FEMALE: Lighter striping and mask.
VOICE: Warbling *weeta-weeta-weetee*, rising or falling on last note.
NESTS: Northern Canada to northeastern Minnesota, east to Massachusetts, and in mountains to Virginia.
WINTERS: Central America.

CAPE MAY WARBLER

(1)   *Black cap. Chestnut patch on yellow face.*
(2)   *Yellow below, heavily striped.*

White wing patch. Yellow rump.
FEMALE: Lighter-striped below, no chestnut cheek patch, yellowish rump. Yellow spot on side of head. Olive above, streaked with black.
VOICE: Hurried, wiry, and irregular.
NESTS: Central Canada to northern edge of Great Lakes States east to southern Maine.
WINTERS: West Indies.

PALM WARBLER

(1)   *Chestnut cap. Yellow stripe over eye, dark stripe through eye.*
(2)   *Constantly flicks tail up and down.*

Underparts yellowish, faintly striped. Undertail coverts bright yellow. Back dull olive-gray. Rump yellowish. Usually found on or near ground.
SEXES: Similar.
VOICE: Series of weak *thi-thi-thi-thi*'s.
NESTS: Southern Newfoundland to Mackenzie, south to northeastern Minnesota in West and Maine in East.
WINTERS: Southern States south into West Indies and Central America.

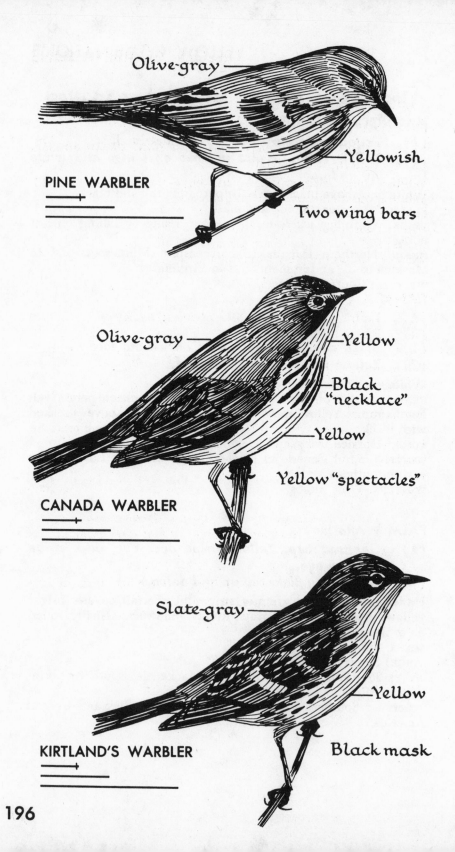

Olive-gray

Yellowish

PINE WARBLER

Two wing bars

Olive-gray

Yellow

Black "necklace"

Yellow

Yellow "spectacles"

CANADA WARBLER

Slate-gray

Yellow

KIRTLAND'S WARBLER

Black mask

Underparts Yellow, Streaked or Spotted

PINE WARBLER
(1) *Yellow throat and breast with faint dusky streaks.*
(2) *Two light wing bars.*
Whitish belly. Upperparts plain olive-gray without streaks. White spot on ends of outer tail feathers.
FEMALE: Duller.
VOICE: Loose, slow, musical trill.
NESTS: Pine forests, southern Canada to Gulf.
WINTERS: Southern New England south.

CANADA WARBLER
(1) *Yellow below with black-striped "necklace."*
(2) *Black forehead.*
Solid olive-gray above. No wing bars. Yellow "spectacles." White under tail coverts.
FEMALE: Similar but duller.
VOICE: Series of eight to fifteen loud, clear, high-pitched, emphatic notes, constantly varying.
NESTS: Northern Ontario to Alberta, south to Minnesota in West, to Maine in East, and in mountains to Georgia.
WINTERS: South America.

KIRTLAND'S WARBLER
(1) *Yellow underparts with black streaks along sides.*
(2) *Upperparts dark slate-gray streaked with black.*
Dark mask on face. Jerks tail.
FEMALE: Generally lighter.
VOICE: Liquid bubbling, resembling somewhat that of the Northern Waterthrush.
NESTS: Central Michigan, in jack-pine areas only.
WINTERS: Bahamas.

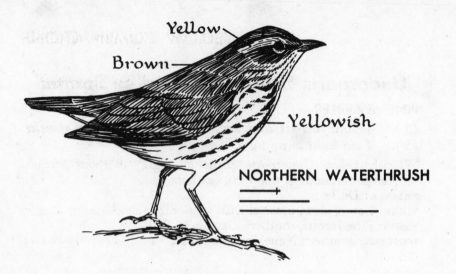

Yellow

Brown

Yellowish

NORTHERN WATERTHRUSH

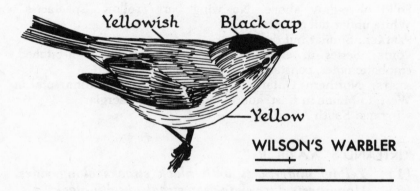

Yellowish

Black cap

Yellow

WILSON'S WARBLER

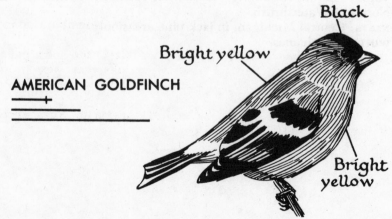

Black

Bright yellow

AMERICAN GOLDFINCH

Bright yellow

Underparts Yellow, Streaked or Spotted

NORTHERN WATERTHRUSH

(1) *Yellowish below, heavily streaked, including middle of throat.*

(2) *Conspicuous yellowish eye stripe. Brown above.*

Constantly teeters. Usually found near water.

SEXES: Alike.

VOICE: Ten or twelve liquid, ringing notes, accelerating at end and dropping in pitch.

NESTS: Northern Canada to northern Great Lakes region and east to Rhode Island.

WINTERS: West Indies, Central and South America.

Underparts Clear Bright Yellow

Conspicuous Black on Head

WILSON'S WARBLER*

(1) *Head and underparts pure yellow.*

(2) *Black cap.*

Olive-green above. No wing bars. Beady black eye.

FEMALE: Black cap less sharply defined.

VOICE: High, thin, chattery, dropping at end.

NESTS: Labrador to Alaska, south to northern Minnesota in West and Maine in East.

WINTERS: Central America.

AMERICAN GOLDFINCH*

(1) *Striking yellow body.*

(2) *Black forehead, wings, and tail.*

Wing feathers white-tipped. Winter males resemble summer females.

FEMALE: Olive-yellow; wing bars, no black forehead patch.

VOICE: (1) Canary-like call, with rising inflection. Also in undulating flight a musical *per chickery*. (2) Long, varied, sweet warble.

NESTS OR RESIDENT: Nebraska and Minnesota to Nova Scotia and south to Gulf States.

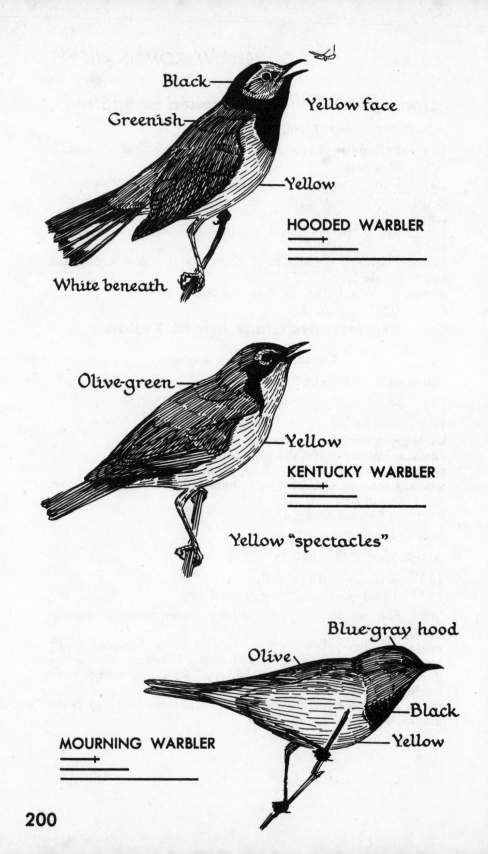

Black —

Greenish —

Yellow face

Yellow

HOODED WARBLER

White beneath

Olive-green —

Yellow

KENTUCKY WARBLER

Yellow "spectacles"

Blue-gray hood

Olive

Black

Yellow

MOURNING WARBLER

Underparts Clear Bright Yellow

Conspicuous Black on Head

HOODED WARBLER*

(1)   *Bright yellow face within black hood.*
(2)   *Belly yellow.*

Upperparts greenish. Tail feathers white below.
FEMALE: No black hood.
VOICE: Sprightly whistle: *hip, hip, horray.*
NESTS: Central Iowa to Rhode Island and south to Gulf.
WINTERS: West Indies and Central America.

KENTUCKY WARBLER*

(1)   *Underparts clear yellow, with black irregular patch below eye.*
(2)   *Yellow eye "spectacles."*

Upperparts olive-green. Top of head blackish. Distinguished from Common Yellowthroat, whose black mask entirely covers eye and forehead.
FEMALE: Black areas dusky; generally duller.
VOICE: A rapid loud *tury-tury-tury-tury.*
NESTS: Southeastern Nebraska to southwestern Connecticut and south to Gulf.
WINTERS: Mexico to northern South America.

Dark Hoodlike Head

MOURNING WARBLER

(1)   *Blue-gray hood, blue-gray throat becoming black at edge of yellow.*
(2)   *Yellow underparts.*

Upperparts olive. Usually found in thickets near ground.
FEMALE: Hood light gray. No black on throat.
VOICE: Variable but usually loud, musical *cheery-cheery-chorry-chorry.*
NESTS: Central Canada to northeastern North Dakota, east to southern Maine, and in mountains to Virginia.
WINTERS: Central and South America.

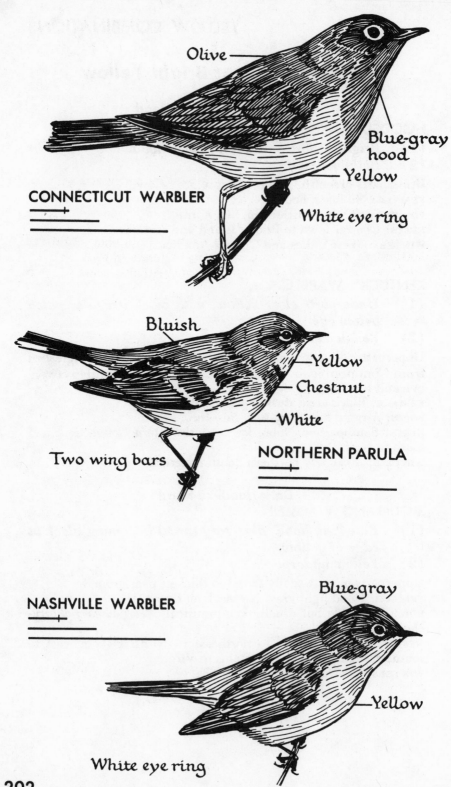

Olive

Blue-gray
hood

Yellow

White eye ring

CONNECTICUT WARBLER

Bluish

Yellow

Chestnut

White

Two wing bars

NORTHERN PARULA

NASHVILLE WARBLER

Blue-gray

Yellow

White eye ring

202

Underparts Clear Bright Yellow

Dark Hoodlike Head

CONNECTICUT WARBLER

(1) *Blue-gray hood.*
(2) *Underparts yellow.*

White eye ring. Upperparts olive. Mostly in northern evergreen bogs of Minnesota and Michigan.
FEMALE: Duller.
VOICE: *beecher, beecher, beecher, beecher, beech.*
NESTS: Northwestern Quebec to British Columbia, south to northern Minnesota in West and central Ontario in East.
WINTERS: South America, migrating along Atlantic coast.

Conspicuous Eye Ring

NORTHERN PARULA

(1) *Bluish above.*
(2) *Yellow throat and breast divided by dark chestnut chest band.*

White wing bars. Greenish patch middle of back. White belly. White patch near tips of outer tail feathers.
FEMALE: Similar but duller.
VOICE: Buzzing, rising trill ending in sharp lower *tup,* or buzzy notes ending in rising trill.
NESTS: Southern Canada to Gulf.
WINTERS: Mostly West Indies, also Central America and eastern Mexico.

NASHVILLE WARBLER

(1) *Blue-gray head with light chestnut patch, usually concealed, on top. White eye ring.*
(2) *Yellow below.*

No wing bars. Olive-green above.
FEMALE: Resembles male but duller.
VOICE: Musical two-part *see-bit, see-bit-see-bit, see-bit,* followed by trilled, fading notes.
NESTS: Nova Scotia to southern Manitoba, south to southeastern Minnesota in West and western Maryland in East.
WINTERS: Mexico and northern Central America.

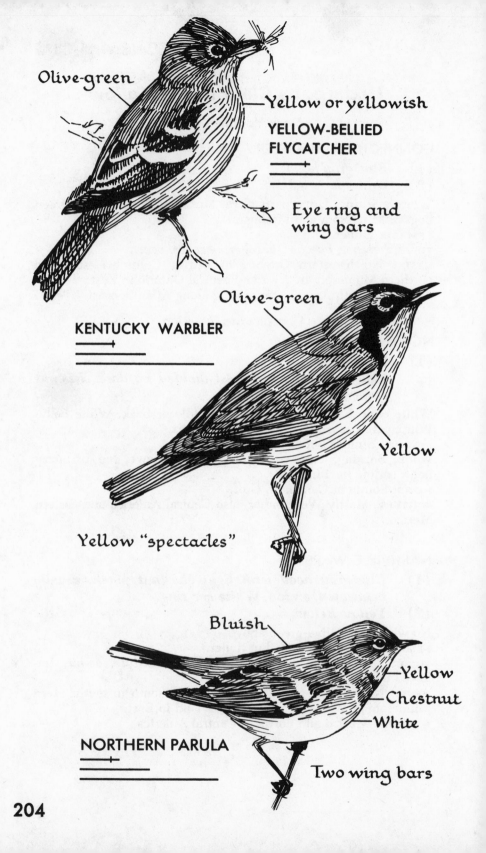

Olive-green

Yellow or yellowish

YELLOW-BELLIED FLYCATCHER

Eye ring and wing bars

Olive-green

KENTUCKY WARBLER

Yellow

Yellow "spectacles"

Bluish

Yellow

Chestnut

White

NORTHERN PARULA

Two wing bars

Underparts Clear Bright Yellow

Conspicuous Eye Ring

YELLOW-BELLIED FLYCATCHER

(1) *Uniform yellowish below, throat to belly. Olive-green above.*

(2) *Eye ring and two wing bars. Lower mandible yellow.*

Flycatchers perch on exposed twigs and catch insects on the wing.

SEXES: Alike.

VOICE: Plaintive, soft *pur weee;* also *killick.*

NESTS: Newfoundland to northern British Columbia, south to North Dakota, and east on border to mountains and Pennsylvania and New York.

WINTERS: Mexico and Central America.

KENTUCKY WARBLER*

(1) *Underparts clear yellow, with black irregular patch below eye.*

(2) *Yellow eye "spectacles."*

Upperparts olive-green. Top of head blackish. Distinguished from Common Yellowthroat, whose black mask entirely covers eye and forehead.

FEMALE: Black areas dusky; generally duller.

VOICE: A rapid loud *tury-tury-tury-tury.*

NESTS: Southeastern Nebraska to southwestern Connecticut and south to Gulf.

WINTERS: Mexico to northern South America.

Underparts Yellow, Upperparts Blue

NORTHERN PARULA

(1) *Bluish above.*

(2) *Yellow throat and breast divided by dark chestnut chest band.*

White wing bars. Greenish patch middle of back. White belly. White patch near tips of outer tail feathers.

FEMALE: Similar but duller.

VOICE: Buzzing, rising trill ending in sharp lower *tup,* or buzzy notes ending in rising trill.

NESTS: Southern Canada to Gulf.

WINTERS: Mostly West Indies, also Central America and eastern Mexico.

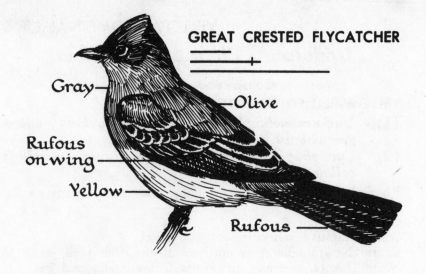

GREAT CRESTED FLYCATCHER

Gray

Olive

Rufous on wing

Yellow

Rufous

Red

Red

YELLOW-BELLIED SAPSUCKER

Belly yellowish
White stripe on wing

Olive-gray

Yellow-green

Yellowish

BELL'S VIREO

White "spectacles"
Faint wing bars

Belly Yellow, Crested Head

GREAT CRESTED FLYCATCHER*

(1)   *Conspicuous rufous tail and side of wing.*
(2)   *Belly yellow.*

Throat gray. Back and head olive. Head with crest. Two wing bars, and wing feathers white-edged.

FEMALE: Underparts grayish. Crown and back gray, washed with yellow on shoulder.

VOICE: Loud, clear *wheeep*, rising at end with seemingly scolding notes. Also loud, harsh, burred *kur, kur, kur, kur, kur.*

NESTS: Central Canada to Gulf.

WINTERS: Florida, Mexico, and Central America.

Belly Yellow, Nape and Throat Red

YELLOW-BELLIED SAPSUCKER*

(1)   *Bright red crown and throat.*
(2)   *Long white wing stripe.*

Yellowish below, light-spotted on sides. White stripe under and over black mask, which goes through eye. Back, wings, and tail black, white-spotted. Drills holes in trees for sap. Usually these Sapsucker holes are of little or no damage to trees unless heavily concentrated on one limb.

FEMALE: Has white throat.

VOICE: (1) A loud *ayow ayow* like mewing of a cat. (2) High-pitched slurred squeal.

NESTS: Labrador to British Columbia, south to eastern Missouri, east to northwestern Connecticut, and in mountains to Virginia.

WINTERS: Southern New England south.

Yellowish Tinge, Mostly Sides, on White or Whitish Underparts

Eye Ring and Wing Bars

BELL'S VIREO

(1)   *White eye ring forms "spectacles."*
(2)   *Faint wing bars.*

Top of head olive-gray. Yellow-green back. Throat white. Belly and sides yellowish. Distinguished from White-eyed Vireo, which has yellow "spectacles," and from Solitary Vireo, which has bluish head and pure-white throat and belly.

SEXES: Alike.

VOICE: Low three-syllabled phrases at short intervals, first phrase rising and second falling at end.

NESTS: Southeastern South Dakota to northeastern Illinois, south to central Texas, and east to Gulf and Tennessee.

WINTERS: Mainly in Mexico.

207

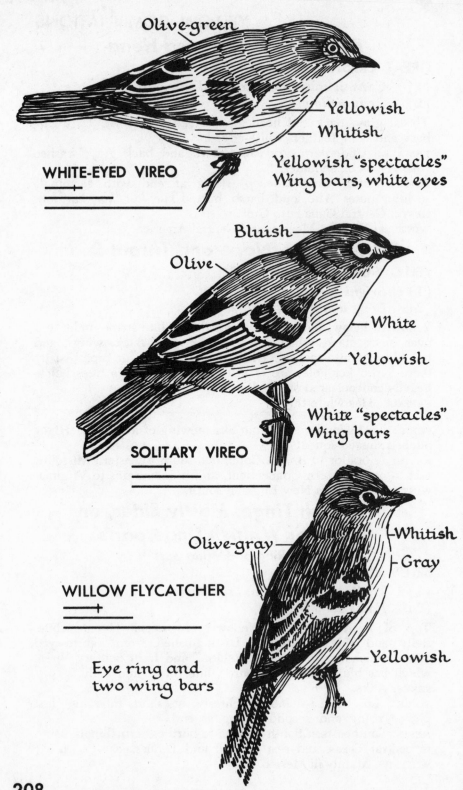

Olive-green

Yellowish

Whitish

WHITE-EYED VIREO

Yellowish "spectacles"
Wing bars, white eyes

Bluish

Olive

White

Yellowish

SOLITARY VIREO

White "spectacles"
Wing bars

Whitish

Gray

Olive-gray

WILLOW FLYCATCHER

Yellowish

Eye ring and
two wing bars

Yellowish Tinge, Mostly Sides, on White or Whitish Underparts

Eye Ring and Wing Bars

WHITE-EYED VIREO*

(1) *Yellowish eye ring forms "spectacles."*
(2) *Two wing bars and white eyes.*

Whitish throat. Yellowish sides. Olive-green above. Immature has dark eye.
SEXES: Alike.
VOICE: Variable, commonly *chip-per-weo-chick,* ending like crack of whip.
NESTS: Southern Nebraska east to southern Connecticut and south to Gulf.
WINTERS: North to South Carolina.

SOLITARY VIREO

(1) *Blue-gray head, white eye ring in "spectacle" form.*
(2) *Wings darker, white-edged, and two wing bars. Back and rump olive.*

Pure-white throat and belly. Yellowish sides. Tail white-edged.
SEXES: Similar.
VOICE: Variable, sweet, high, clear, slow, often in four-note phrases with a pause in between: *teeay-taweeta,* etc.
NESTS: Newfoundland to British Columbia, south through Great Lakes States to northern New Jersey, and in mountains to northern Georgia.
WINTERS: South Carolina to Gulf States and Central America.

WILLOW FLYCATCHER

(1) *Eye ring rather indistinct and two wing bars, some wing feathers white-edged. Olive-gray back, whitish chin, olive-gray throat, yellowish belly.*
(2) *Voice.*

In field distinguishable from Least Flycatcher only by voice. Usually in low thickets or damp places.
SEXES: Alike.
VOICE: A hoarse, burry *we-be-o* or *fitz-bew.*
NESTS: Newfoundland to Alaska, south to northeastern Oklahoma, and east to eastern New York and New Jersey and south to Maryland.
WINTERS: Central and South America.

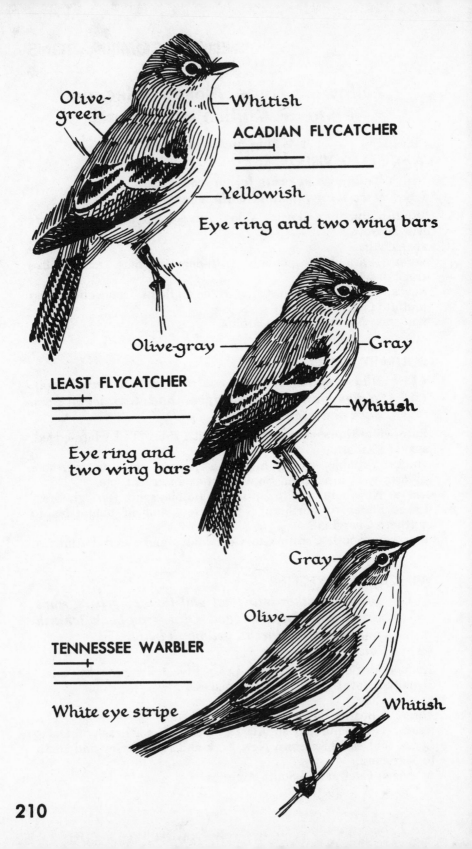

Olive-
green

Whitish

ACADIAN FLYCATCHER

Yellowish

Eye ring and two wing bars

Olive-gray

Gray

LEAST FLYCATCHER

Whitish

Eye ring and
two wing bars

Gray

Olive

TENNESSEE WARBLER

Whitish

White eye stripe

Yellowish Tinge, Mostly Sides, on White or Whitish Underparts

Eye Ring and Wing Bars

ACADIAN FLYCATCHER

(1) *Eye ring and wing bars.*
(2) *Throat whitish.*

Remaining underparts whitish to yellowish. Olive-green above. Wing feathers white-edged. Similar to Least Flycatcher and Willow Flycatcher, distinguishable by its habitat in southern part of area and by its voice. Usually in rich woodland.
SEXES: Alike.
VOICE: A sharp, explosive *we-see!* or *spit-chee!* Also a thin *peet.*
NESTS: South Dakota to Connecticut and south to Gulf. Mostly southern, rare in Northeast.
WINTERS: Central America and northern South America.

LEAST FLYCATCHER*

(1) *Eye ring, two wing bars. Some wing feathers white-edged.*
(2) *Voice.*

Olive-gray above, light below, slightly yellowish. In field distinguishable from Willow Flycatcher only by voice.
SEXES: Alike.
VOICE: Constantly repeated *kerik kerik kerik.*
NESTS: Northern Ontario to Alaska, south to northeastern Kansas in West and northwestern Georgia in East.
WINTERS: Mexico and Central America.

Eye Stripe

TENNESSEE WARBLER

(1) *White stripe above and black stripe through eye. Whitish underparts. Gray head, back olive-green.*
(2) *No wing bars.*

Resembles Vireos but more slender and active, and with slender pointed bill.
FEMALE: Similar markings. Crown olive-green, underparts yellowish-tinged .
VOICE: Variable, very loud short *zit-zit-zit,* etc., lower at end.
NESTS: Labrador to Yukon, south to northern Minnesota in West and southern Maine in East.
WINTERS: South and Central America.

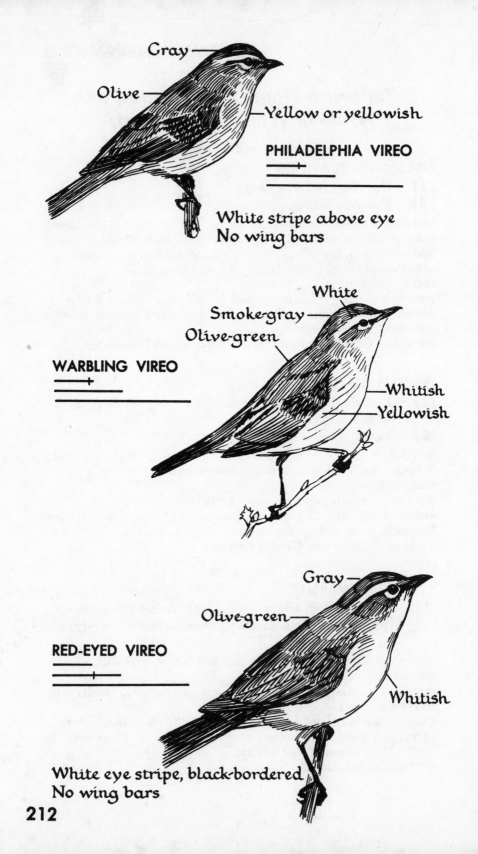

Gray

Olive

Yellow or yellowish

PHILADELPHIA VIREO

White stripe above eye
No wing bars

White

Smoke-gray
Olive-green

WARBLING VIREO

Whitish
Yellowish

Gray

Olive-green

RED-EYED VIREO

Whitish

White eye stripe, black-bordered
No wing bars

Yellowish Tinge, Mostly Sides, on White or Whitish Underparts

Eye Stripe

PHILADELPHIA VIREO

(1) *White stripe above eye.*
(2) *Underparts light yellowish to white. No wing bars.*

Gray head, olive back. Dark spot in front of eye. Yellowish underparts distinguish it from Red-eyed Vireo and Warbling Vireo.

SEXES: Similar.
VOICE: Similar to that of the Red-eyed Vireo, but higher-pitched, weaker, and more deliberate.
NESTS: Central Canada south to North Dakota in West and central Maine in East.
WINTERS: Central and South America.

WARBLING VIREO*

(1) *White eye stripe but no wing bars.*
(2) *Whitish breast, slightly yellowish on sides.*

Top of head and back of neck smoke-gray. Back olive-green.
SEXES: Alike.
VOICE: (1) Wheezy, questioning *whee.* (2) Rather brilliant short warble; resembles somewhat the song of the Purple Finch.
NESTS: Central Canada to Gulf. Rare in coastal plain from New Jersey to Virginia.
WINTERS: Central America.

RED-EYED VIREO*

(1) *White stripe above eye bordered on top by black and below by black stripe through eye.*
(2) *Gray cap.*

Reddish eye at close range. No wing bars. Olive-green above; whitish below, slightly yellow on sides. Found in woods, parks, and suburbs, usually in treetops.
SEXES: Alike.
VOICE: Monotonous, endless, unmusical repetition of generally two- or three-note phrases with definite pause between phrases. Often nicknamed "Preacher Bird."
NESTS: Central Canada to Gulf.
WINTERS: South America.

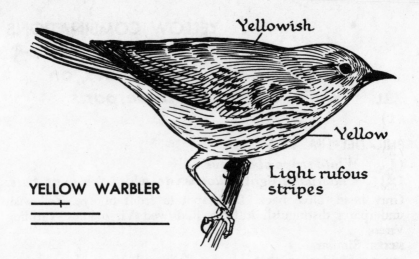

Yellowish

Yellow

Light rufous
stripes

YELLOW WARBLER

Yellow All Over

YELLOW WARBLER*

(1) *Generally bright yellow, with light rufous striping below.*

(2) *Back yellowish.*

No wing bars.

FEMALE: Duller. Little or no breast streaking.   — —

VOICE: (1) A short *chip*. (2) Very high, thin musical *tee tee teedle eedl ee* with variations.

NESTS: Labrador to Alaska, south to northern Arkansas in West and South Carolina in East.

WINTERS: West Indies, Central and South America.

PART II

Woodpeckers

Red — Small

White

DOWNY WOODPECKER

Spots on white

Red patch

White back

Heavy bill

White

HAIRY WOODPECKER

Red

Red

No spots on outer tail feathers

YELLOW-BELLIED SAPSUCKER

Belly yellowish
White stripes on wing

DOWNY WOODPECKER*
(1) *White back.*
(2) *Red spot back of head.*

Small bill. White spots on wings. Outer tail feathers white, spotted with black. Resembles Hairy Woodpecker but much smaller and with very small bill.
FEMALE: No red on head.
VOICE: (1) A light *keek keek*. (2) A musical succession of clear-cut high notes going down the scale.
RESIDENT: Alaska and Canada and south to Gulf.

HAIRY WOODPECKER*
(1) *Red spot on top of head, black crown. Black eye patch on white.*
(2) *White back, black wings and tail.*

Wings spotted white. Tail white-edged. White below. Distinguished from Downy Woodpecker by much larger size and large bill.
FEMALE: No red on head.
VOICE: (1) A rather loud, high *keek keek*. (2) A long, slurred high rattle, running together and descending at end.
RESIDENT: Alaska and Canada and south to Gulf.

YELLOW-BELLIED SAPSUCKER*
(1) *Bright red crown and throat.*
(2) *Long white wing stripe.*

Yellowish below, light-spotted on sides. White stripe under and over black mask, which goes through eye. Back, wings, and tail black, white-spotted. Drills holes in trees for sap. Usually these Sapsucker holes are of little or no damage to trees unless heavily concentrated on one limb.
FEMALE: Has white throat.

VOICE: (1) A loud *ayow ayow* like mewing of a cat. (2) High-pitched slurred squeal.
NESTS: Labrador to British Columbia, south to eastern Missouri, east to northwestern Connecticut, and in mountains to Virginia.
WINTERS: Southern New England south.

Red

Black

White

White

White

RED-HEADED WOODPECKER

Red

Gray

RED-BELLIED WOODPECKER

Black and white

Reddish tinge

Yellow

Black

BLACK-BACKED
WOODPECKER

RED-HEADED WOODPECKER*
(1) *Entire head red.*
(2) *Back and wings black.*

Large white patch on wing and rump. Underparts white.
SEXES: Alike.
VOICE: A loud *querr* or *queeah.*
NESTS: Southern Canada to Gulf. Rare east of Delaware and Hudson rivers.
WINTERS: Southern New England south.

RED-BELLIED WOODPECKER
(1) *Black upperparts heavily cross-barred with narrow white bars.*
(2) *Red crown.*

Tail black-barred in center. Throat and breast gray. Belly whitish with light reddish tinge.
FEMALE: Similar, except red patch on head smaller.
VOICE: (1) Harsh, loud *krrk krrk krrk,* rolling the *r*'s. (2) Loud, rattling *kack kack kack kack,* all on same pitch.
RESIDENT: Southeastern Minnesota through southwestern Ontario to western New York and south to Gulf. Occasionally New Jersey, Delaware, and Maryland.

BLACK-BACKED WOODPECKER
(1) *Head and back solid black.*
(2) *Yellow cap.*

Throat and outer sides of tail white. Sides barred black and white. Broad white stripe below ear and eye. Flight feathers white-spotted.
FEMALE: Lacks yellow crown.
VOICE: Sharp, shrill *chirk chirk;* also loud single call: *click-click.*
RESIDENT OR NESTS: Labrador to Alaska, south to northern fringe of border states to Maine and in mountains from northern New York to New Hampshire.
WINTERS: As far south as New Jersey.
NOTE: Three-toed Woodpecker (rare) is similar to above but back is barred.

Yellow

● THREE-TOED
● WOODPECKER
● .●
───────────── ┼

Black
and
white

Red

Black

Brown

Yellow in flight

White rump

NORTHERN FLICKER
─────────────────
─────────────────
─────────────── ┼

Underside of wings
and tail yellow

THREE-TOED WOODPECKER

(1) *Upperparts black. Back barred black and white.*
(2) *Yellow cap.*

Throat and belly white. Sides black-barred on white. Narrow white stripe behind eye.
FEMALE: Crown not yellow; usually streaked black and white.
VOICE: A sharp *chirk;* a loud *queep;* a long squeal.
RESIDENT: From northern Canada to northern fringe of border states; occasionally in winter as far south as Massachusetts.

NORTHERN FLICKER*

(1) *Black crescent and "mustache" on throat. Red crescent back of head.*
(2) *White rump, prominent in flight. Underside of wings and tail yellow.*

Long Woodpecker bill. Upperparts brown, cross-striped. Underparts with heavy black spots on whitish.
FEMALE: No "mustache."
VOICE: (1) A long succession of semi-musical, fast, far-reaching *kick's*. (2) A sort of squealing succession of *hickup's*. (3) An explosive, piercing *clear clear clear*. (4) A squeaky *eureka eureka eureka*.
NESTS: Alaska and Canada to southern Virginia and in mountains to North Carolina.
WINTERS: In limited numbers to northern limit of range and south to Gulf.

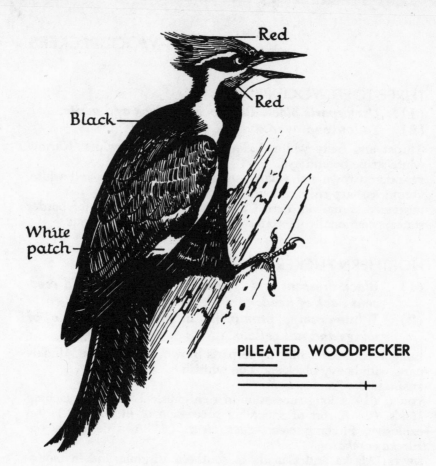

Red

Red

Black

White
patch

PILEATED WOODPECKER

PILEATED WOODPECKER
(1) *Brilliant red crest.*
(2) *Mainly black, long white neck patch and wing patch.*

Very large sharp bill. Red streak behind bill.
FEMALE: No red streak behind bill. Front of crown grayish brown.
VOICE: Loud, deliberate, one-pitched *kuk-kuk-kukkuk-kuk-kuk*, similar to that of the Flicker but deeper-pitched. Often located by heavy chopping sound as it pecks huge oblong holes in decaying trees.
RESIDENT: Forested regions, southern Canada to Gulf.

PART III

Soaring, Skimming Insect Hunters

in Flight

Dusky gray

CHIMNEY SWIFT

Body sooty black

Brown

BANK SWALLOW

Dark breast band

Brown

Dusky

NORTHERN
ROUGH-WINGED SWALLOW

228

SOARING, SKIMMING INSECT HUNTERS IN FLIGHT

Day Fliers

CHIMNEY SWIFT*

(1) *"A cigar with wings."*
(2) *Sooty black except for dusky grayish throat.*

Stubby short tail. No markings. Narrow wings form crescent in flight and are held stiff. Rapid wingbeat in flying. Never perches out of doors.
FEMALE: Similar.
VOICE: Loud, rapid "chippering."
NESTS: Southern Canada to Gulf States. Usually in chimneys.
WINTERS: South America.

BANK SWALLOW*

(1) *Dark band across breast. Rest of underparts white.*
(2) *Back brown.*

Commonly seen in large flocks on telephone wires.
SEXES: Alike.
VOICE: A soft twitter.
NESTS: Labrador to Alaska, south to Arkansas in West and Virginia in East. In holes in sand banks.
WINTERS: South America.

NORTHERN ROUGH-WINGED SWALLOW*

(1) *Throat and breast dusky brown, belly whitish.*
(2) *Notched tail.*

Back light brown. No distinct band across breast as in Bank Swallow. Commonly seen in large flocks on telephone wires.
SEXES: Alike.
VOICE: Rough and burry *trit*, or *trit-trit*, often repetitious.
NESTS: Southern Canada to Gulf States. In holes in sand banks.
WINTERS: Southern States south into Central America.

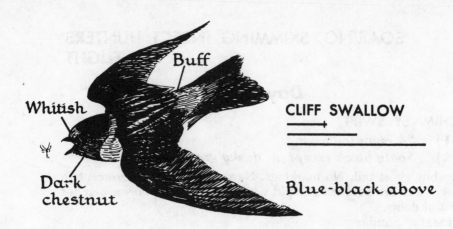

Buff

Whitish

CLIFF SWALLOW

Dark
chestnut

Blue-black above

TREE SWALLOW

Pure white below

Back steely blue

BARN SWALLOW

White spots

Blue-black above

Chestnut

Buffy

Chestnut

Day Fliers

CLIFF SWALLOW*
(1) *Dark throat patch blending into buff and whitish belly.*
(2) *Forehead whitish.*

Blackish brown above. Buff rump. Tail almost square. Commonly seen in large flocks on telephone wires.
SEXES: Alike.
VOICE: (1) Alarm note: loud, down-sloping *eeyo*. (2) Call: a husky, squeaky *wee*, *wit*, or *wit-wit*.
NESTS: Southern Canada to Texas in West and Virginia in East. In gourdlike mud nests outside barns or on bridges or cliffs.
WINTERS: South America.

TREE SWALLOW*
(1) *Pure-white underparts.*
(2) *Steely blue back.*

Tail slightly forked. (Immatures are brown above.) Commonly seen in large flocks on telephone wires.
FEMALE: Usually duller.
VOICE: Clear musical whistle in two-note, sometimes three-note, phrases, often long-continued.
NESTS: Labrador to Alaska, south to northeastern Kansas in West and Maryland in East. Usually in tree cavities or birdhouses.
WINTERS: From Gulf north to Washington, occasionally to Massachusetts.

BARN SWALLOW*
(1) *Tail very deeply forked (swallow-tailed).*
(2) *Forehead and throat chestnut. Underparts buffy.*

Upperparts blue-black. White spots on each tail feather. Commonly seen in large flocks on telephone wires.
FEMALE: Lighter underparts and forehead.
VOICE: Low musical chattering trill in medley of notes.
NESTS: Labrador to Alaska and south to Gulf. Usually inside barns.
WINTERS: Central America to central Chile and Argentina.

PURPLE MARTIN

Solid blue-black

White "window"

COMMON NIGHTHAWK

White bar

White

Black and gray barred

White

White

WHIP-POOR-WILL

Mottled gray and brown

SOARING, SKIMMING INSECT HUNTERS IN FLIGHT

Day Fliers

PURPLE MARTIN*

(1) *Blue-black above and below.*
(2) *Very wide wings at base.*

Notched tail. Catches insects on the wing.
FEMALE: Gray below, top of head and nape speckled gray and whitish. Immature males resembling females often breed.
VOICE: Sweet melodious whistle.
NESTS: Southern Canada to Gulf. In birdhouses or other cavities.
WINTERS: South America.

Night or Dusk Fliers

COMMON NIGHTHAWK*

(1) *White throat and wing patches and white tail band.*
(2) *Mottled gray above, barred below.*

Wings long, slim. Flies at dusk or daybreak, catching insects while in flight over open places.
FEMALE: Throat patch less conspicuous and no white band on tail.
VOICE: Loud sharp *peent* while flying. Often while dive-bombing a loud booming noise caused by air rushing through wings.
NESTS: Northern Canada and Alaska to Gulf States. In open country on bare rock or ground. Sometimes on rooftops.
WINTERS: South America.

WHIP-POOR-WILL*

(1) *Dark throat with white chest band.*
(2) *Breast mottled buffy.*

Tail barred with large patches of white on ends of outer tail feathers. Short stubby bill. Mottled brownish back roughly barred resembles bark of tree. Nocturnal. During day sits on ground, rocks, or branch of tree.
FEMALE: Similar, but tail spots buffy and smaller.
VOICE: Strong, repeated *whip-poor-will;* heard at night.
NESTS: Central Canada to Gulf States.
WINTERS: Mostly Gulf States and eastern Mexico.

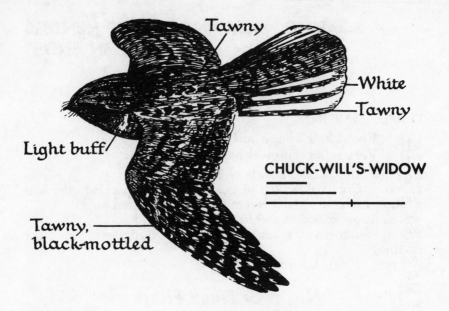

Tawny

White

Tawny

Light buff

CHUCK-WILL'S-WIDOW

Tawny,
black-mottled

Night or Dusk Fliers

CHUCK-WILL'S-WIDOW

(1)   *Tawny-streaked and spotted with black.*
(2)   *Outer tail feathers tawny.*

Band on throat buffy. Much larger than Whip-poor-will, whose throat band and outer tail feathers are white. Usually found in woodlands.

FEMALE: Similar.

VOICE: Repetitious, resembling name: *chuck will's widow.*

NESTS: Eastern Kansas to southern New Jersey and south to Gulf.

WINTERS: Louisiana and Florida south.

Color Pattern Guide

I. By Color Combinations

BLACK

Head

Head all black	2–5
Cap, black	4–11
Head striped black	
Black and buff	10–11
Black and white	12–13
Eye mask black	12–19
Patch below eye bl.	20–21

Upperparts

Bars or spots bl.	32–35
Black with white on wing, and rump white below	34–35
Solid black	
Whitish below	36–39
Buffy below	38–39

Throat or Breast

Bl. U or V on bib	20–23
Breast spot black	22–25
Throat and cap bl.	24–27
Throat black	26–31

Body (Entire)

Striped bl. and w.	40–41
Bl. above and below	40–45
All black	46–61

BLUE

With Wing Bars	62–65	**Crest Pronounced**	68–69
No Wing Bars	64–67		

NOTE: Abbreviations for black (bl.), brown (br.), white (w.), yellow (y.), etc., have been used to avoid two-line entries and thus to simplify and speed up the use of this key.

* Birds commonly found in and near populated areas are starred in the text.

BROWN, RUFOUS, *or* CHESTNUT

Head

    Cap chestnut or br.   70–75
    Head br., body bl.   74–75

Upperparts Solid Br. or Rufous

    Underpts. spotted
      brown   76–83
    Underpts. whitish
      or pure white   82–85

Upperparts Brown-Striped

    Underpts. clear   86–95
    Underpts. striped   96–103

Underparts

    Solid chestnut or
      brown   102–107

Sides

    Chestnut or
      rufous   106–107

Body (Entire)

    Mottled dusky
      brown   108–111
    Light brownish-
      gray   110–111
    Mottled russet
      (long bill)   112–113

Tail Chestnut or Rufous   114–115

Tiny Brown Birds

    Barred wings and
      tail (tail usually
      cocked)   116–119

GRAY, OLIVE-GRAY, *or* OLIVE-GREEN

Wing Bars

    With eye ring   120–125
    Without eye ring   126–127

No Bars or Ring   128–131

Eye Stripe or Mask

    Eye stripe white   130–135
    Eye stripe yellow   134–137
    Stripe or mask bl.   136–141

GREEN   140–141

ORANGE   142–147

RED

Head (Red Markings)

Woodpeckers	146–153
Others	154–157

Shoulder
156–157

Underparts

Breast or throat red   156–159

Body (Entire)

Mostly red	158–163
All red	162–163

WHITE MARKINGS *Important in Identification*

Rump or Back
White   162–169

Tail

Outer feathers w.	168–175
Tip of tail white	176–177

Body

Mostly white   176–177

YELLOW *or* YELLOWISH ORANGE

Head

Cap y. or orange	178–183
Face yellow	182–183
Head all yellowish	
Body black	184–185
Underpts. y.	184–185

Throat

Throat and face y.	184–185
(with bl. mask and bib)	
Throat all yellow	186–189

Upperparts Yellow

Rump yellow	188–191
Underpts. y.	190–191

Underparts Yellow

Yellow with bl. V	192–193
Streaks or spots	192–199
Clear yellow	198–205
Yellow (blue above)	204–205
Belly only, yellow	206–207

YELLOW *or* YELLOWISH ORANGE *(cont.)*

Sides Yellowish, Underparts White

Body All Yellow 214–215

Eye ring and
   wing bars   206–211
Eye stripe   210–213

II. Woodpeckers 218–225

III. Soaring, Skimming Insect Hunters in Flight
228–235

IV. Ground Birds (Chicken-like) 238–249

V. Owls

With Ear Tufts 252–255   *Without Ear Tufts* 254–261

VI. Hawks, Eagles, Vultures, Crows, and Raven
265–321

NOTE: Special keys to the birds in Part VI appear on pages 267–270 (perched) and 295–297 (in flight).

PART IV

Ground Birds (Chicken-like)

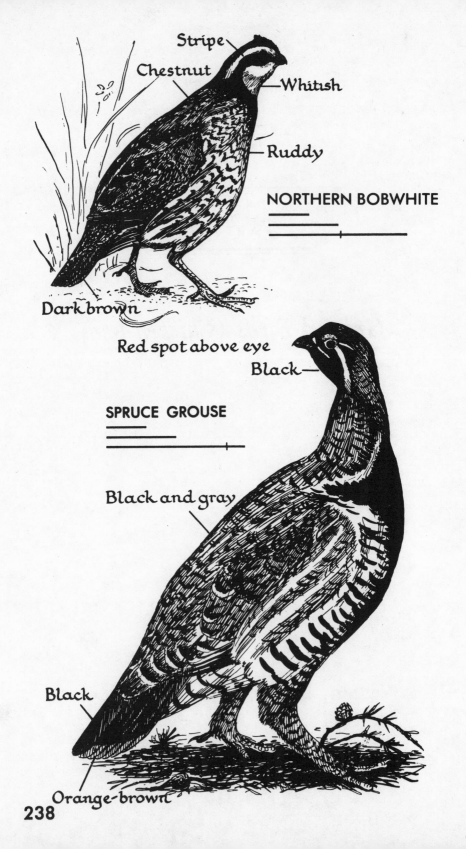

Stripe

Chestnut

Whitish

Ruddy

NORTHERN BOBWHITE

Dark brown

Red spot above eye

Black

SPRUCE GROUSE

Black and gray

Black

Orange-brown

GROUND BIRDS (Chicken-like)

NORTHERN BOBWHITE*
(1) *Ruddy, brown plump bird with conspicuous whitish throat and stripe over eye.*
(2) *Round dark-brown tail.*
Short rounded wings.
FEMALE: Has buffy face.
VOICE: Loud, musical *bob-whoit*.
RESIDENT: Southern Ontario to eastern South Dakota and south to Gulf. Found in farm land and other fairly open areas.

SPRUCE GROUSE
(1) *Chin and throat solid black bordered with white.*
(2) *Tail black with orange-brown tips.*
Upperparts wavy black and gray bars. Red spot above eye. Lower belly black, heavily barred with white.
FEMALE: Duller and lighter. Without red spot above eye.
   A drumming noise is made by male beating wings during mating season.
RESIDENT: Heavy woods. Canadian border north, but almost exterminated because of its trustful disposition in the presence of man.

RUFFED GROUSE

Reddish brown

Whitish buff
Mottled brown

Black
White   Black ruff

GROUND BIRDS (Chicken-like)

RUFFED GROUSE

(1) *Head slightly crested, neck ruff on shoulders usually black.*

(2) *Round, fan-shaped tail having broad, almost black band with light tip.*

Upperparts mottled and striped reddish brown. Underparts whitish buff, mottled brown, chin whitish.

FEMALE: Similar but duller, with shorter tail.

VOICE: Subdued *whit-whit*. Male has loud booming noise, or drumming made by wings, in mating season.

RESIDENT: In forests, Canada and Alaska, south to central Arkansas in West and Virginia in East.

WILLOW PTARMIGAN

Male (winter)

Male (summer)

Summer~ Upper parts, brownish rufous barred
          Underparts, wings, tip of tail white
Winter ~ Entirely white

GROUND BIRDS (Chicken-like)

WILLOW PTARMIGAN

(1) *In summer, upperparts brownish rufous, closely barred.*

(2) *Underparts, including wings, white, tip of tail white. In winter, entirely white.*

FEMALE: Tawny brown, heavily spotted and barred in summer. In winter, white like male.

NESTS: Northern Labrador to northern Yukon, south to northwestern British Columbia, and east to northern shore of St. Lawrence.

NOTE: Rock Ptarmigan, the rarer of the two Ptarmigans, is found in hilly, rocky places in the Far North. It may be distinguished from the Willow Ptarmigan by a black line through the eye in winter plumage.

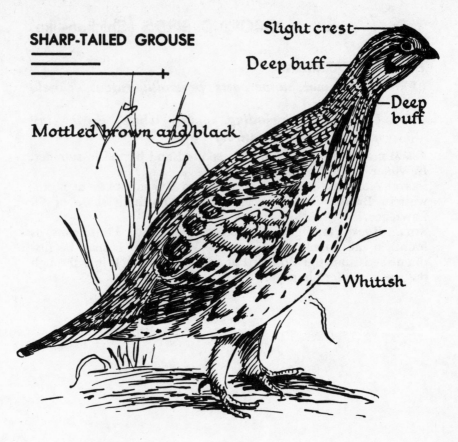

SHARP-TAILED GROUSE

Slight crest

Deep buff

Deep buff

Mottled brown and black

Whitish

SHARP-TAILED GROUSE

(1) *Neck and head dark buff.*

(2) *Long sharp tail.*

Upperparts heavily mottled brown and black. Buffy-whitish throat, white belly.

FEMALE: Similar, but with shorter tail. A loud booming is made by male in mating season. When frightened, a sharp cackling.

RESIDENT: Central Quebec to Alaska, south to Nebraska, and east into northern Michigan, moving as far south as northwestern Iowa in winter.

Light buffy
darkly barred —

Blackish

Light
buffy,
heavily
barred

GROUND BIRDS (Chicken-like)

GREATER PRAIRIE CHICKEN

(1) *Upperparts and lower parts heavily barred.*
(2) *Short, blackish rounded tail.*

A large hen-like bird. Male, in dancing, inflates orange-colored air sacs and raises neck feathers over head.

VOICE: A loud booming or cooing sound.

RESIDENT: Western prairies from western Canada to Texas.

NOTE: Lesser Prairie Chicken is similar but smaller.

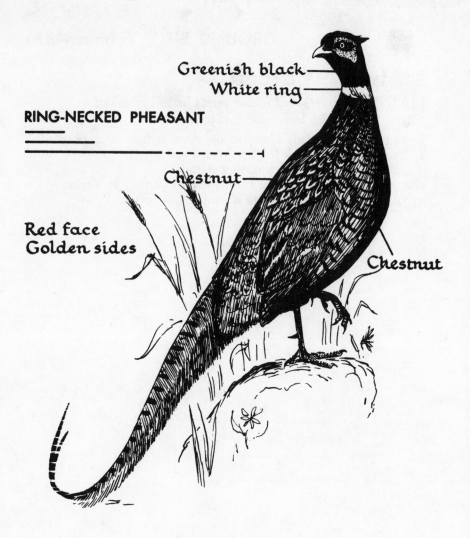

Greenish black

White ring

RING-NECKED PHEASANT

Chestnut

Red face
Golden sides

Chestnut

GROUND BIRDS (Chicken-like)

RING-NECKED PHEASANT*
(1)   *Very long, pointed sweeping tail.*
(2)   *Bright chestnut with dappled appearance.*

Head greenish black, with red patch around eye. Usually white ring on neck. (No long tail in young male.)

FEMALE: No ring. Head mottled brown; tail much shorter but long and pointed.

VOICES: Male: a harsh crow *cack-cack* followed by beating wings. Female: a hen-like cluck to young.

NESTS: In fields throughout area.

RESIDENT: Southern Canada to Texas Panhandle in West and Maryland in East.

PART V

Owls

Whitish and streaked

EASTERN SCREECH-OWL

Red phase – above bright rufous
Gray phase – above gray

Brownish, heavily streaked

SHORT-EARED OWL

Buffy,
streaked

Buffy

Buffy

LONG-EARED OWL

Upper parts – brownish gray

With Ear Tufts

EASTERN SCREECH-OWL*

The only small owl with ear tufts.

In *red phase* upperparts bright rufous. Underparts whitish, heavily mottled and streaked. In *gray phase* gray upperparts, underparts whitish, heavily mottled and streaked.
SEXES: Alike.
VOICE: A long, tremulous wail down the scale. Or a rapidly repeated soft, flutelike note on one pitch.
RESIDENT: Southern Canada to Gulf.

SHORT-EARED OWL

(1) *Ear tufts not conspicuous.*
(2) *Buffy below, streaked. Brownish above, heavily streaked.*

Looks big-headed and neckless. Hunts by day. A flopping flight like a moth. Prefers meadows, open marshes, and grassy sand dunes.
SEXES: Alike.
VOICES: Various; *toot, toot-too,* fifteen to twenty times; a sharp, sneezy bark: *mayhow.*
RESIDENT: Northern Labrador to northern Alaska, south to Missouri in West and to Virginia in East.

LONG-EARED OWL

(1) *Ear tufts long and set close together.*
(2) *Buffy cheeks.*

Underparts buffy, heavily down-streaked. Upperparts a brownish gray, minutely mottled and streaked.
SEXES: Alike.
VOICE: Various; a whining cat-like cry; a low twittering; a puppy-like barking; a mournful soft *hoo hoo hoo.*
NESTS OR RESIDENT: Canadian border to Virginia.

Mottled brown

GREAT HORNED OWL

White throat, collar
Yellow eyes

Brown

NORTHERN SAW-WHET OWL

White,
brown-streaked

Brownish buff

Light buffy

BURROWING OWL

Long legs

254

With Ear Tufts

GREAT HORNED OWL*

(1) *Only large owl with ear tufts.*
(2) *Conspicuous white throat collar.*

Breast with heavy dark streaks. Back brown, mottled. Belly heavily cross-barred. Yellow eyes.

SEXES: Alike.
VOICE: Deep, sonorous, usually five hoots: *hoo-hoohoo, hoo, hoo*. Rarely, a blood-curdling shriek.
RESIDENT: Northern limit of trees to Straits of Magellan!

Without Ear Tufts

NORTHERN SAW-WHET OWL

(1) *White below, with heavy brown striping.*
(2) *No ear tufts and face streaked with dark brown.*

Brown above with white spots. Found in woodlands.

SEXES: Alike.
VOICE: Many variations—a mellow whistle: *too, too, too*, etc., endlessly; a metallic whistle, resembling saw filing, etc.
NESTS: Alaska and Canada to Ohio and east to Maryland.
WINTERS: South to Gulf.

BURROWING OWL

(1) *Upperparts light-brownish buff, with large white spots on back and fine spots on head.*
(2) *Long spindly legs. Underparts barred buffy.*

Lives in holes and often seen on ground or fence posts. Formerly a common resident of prairie-dog towns.

SEXES: Alike.
VOICE: Various; commonly a soft *hoot-oo hoot-oo*.
NESTS: Southwestern Canada south through western edge of Great Plains area into Mexico.
WINTERS: Southern portion of nesting area south into Central America.

Chocolate brown

BOREAL OWL

Brown-streaked

NORTHERN HAWK-OWL

Mottled dark brown

Brown and white

Without Ear Tufts

BOREAL OWL

(1) *Upperparts chocolate brown spotted white. Underparts white-striped lengthwise with chocolate brown.*

(2) *Facial disk grayish, washed with brown.*

Forehead and top of head heavily dotted with small white spots on brown. Tail short and barred.

SEXES: Alike.

VOICE: A low liquid note resembling dripping water.

NESTS: Alaska and northern Canada.

WINTERS: Occasionally to border states and northern New England.

NORTHERN HAWK-OWL

(1) *Dusky appearance; underparts narrowly striped brown and white.*

(2) *Light-gray face surrounded by black.*

Upperparts dark brown, back mottled. Top of head black, finely mottled with white; tail long and barred.

SEXES: Alike.

VOICE: Various; generally musical: (1) A trilling whistle. (2) A low rattle, rising to a loud cry. (3) A melodious *wheop oop oop oop*.

NESTS: Newfoundland to northern Alaska south to northern Michigan and central Ontario.

WINTERS: South to southern Canada and northern United States. Casual as far south as New Jersey.

Tawny, yellowish
dusky, marbled—

COMMON
BARN-OWL

Underparts whitish
Face-heart-shaped,
whitish to yellowish

Brown-mottled—

BARRED OWL

Eyes brown

Brown-
streaked

Without Ear Tufts

COMMON BARN-OWL*

(1) *Underparts whitish. Upperparts tawny yellowish, marbled with dusky.*

(2) *Face heart-shaped, white to yellowish brown.*

SEXES: Alike.

VOICES: Various—an eerie, frightful hiss; a weird scream; a series of *click, click*'s; a feeble, querulous *aek, aek;* etc.

NESTS: Canadian border to Gulf. Usually in old buildings, steeples, barns, or abandoned wells or mines.

RESIDENT: Commonest mostly in southern part of area.

BARRED OWL

(1) *Brown back spotted with white. Eyes brown.*

(2) *Big, puffy, round head. No ear tufts.*

Barred crosswise on throat and streaked lengthwise on belly.

SEXES: Alike.

VOICE: Emphatic, usually eight hoots: *hoo-hoo, ho-hoo, hoo, hoo, ho, hooo-aw.* Often put in human language: *Who cooks for you? Who cooks for you all?* Often sounds like dog barking.

RESIDENT: Northern Canada to Gulf. In forests or wooded swamps.

Mottled brown
on white

Light brown barring
on white

SNOWY OWL

Generally white appearance

GREAT GRAY OWL

Brown mottled
with white

Dusky brown
appearance

Black

Grayish
brown
streaked

Without Ear Tufts

SNOWY OWL
(1) *Very white appearance.*
(2) *Back mottled light brown on white; underparts barred light brown on white.*
FEMALE: Much darker than male. Fore neck and median breast white, remainder heavily barred with dark slate color.
VOICE: (1) A deep barking growl. (2) An intense whistle. (3) A hoarse *who-who*.
NESTS: Northern Greenland to northern Alaska and south to northern Canada.
WINTERS: Irregular winter migrant to northern United States, south as far as central Texas and east to South Carolina.

GREAT GRAY OWL
(1) *Dusky brown appearance. Face round, flat, finely ringed in gray and brown. Black area under chin.*
(2) *Underparts grayish, heavily streaked with brown.*
Legs heavily feathered and barred. Upperparts dark brown, mottled with white. Long tail.
SEXES: Alike.
VOICE: (1) Deep *woo-oo-oo-oo*, usually regularly spaced. (2) A frequent whistle, varying in volume.
NESTS: Forests, Alaska to northern Ontario and northern Minnesota.
WINTERS: South to northern border states; rarely, Ohio to New Jersey.

PART VI

Hawks, Eagles,
Vultures, Crows, and Raven

Hawks, Eagles, Vultures, Crows, and Raven

INTRODUCTION

IDENTIFYING birds in this group is not easy; they present special problems not encountered in observing the other land birds.

(1) The immature plumages of some hawks and eagles persist for up to as many as three or four years. Consequently, it is not uncommon to see many more immature than adult birds.

(2) Usually the immature plumage is strikingly different from the adult.

(3) Identifying the female through association with the male is not usually practicable.

(4) Often the only time you see hawks, eagles, and vultures is in flight.

(5) Usually birds in this category are seen at a considerable distance.

Consequently, we have, first of all, so classified hawks by color and pattern that you should be able to find the group to which it belongs even if you get only one good view. Secondly, we have separate sections for hawks in flight and for hawks perched. Thirdly, we have illustrated all typical patterns, whether male, female, adult, or immature, with drawings.

As those experienced in identifying hawks rely a great deal on the manner of flight, this characteristic is described in each case.

In a large number of cases the markings on the underbody are the major clue to identification—whether, for example, they run across the body or lengthwise.

Most of the birds in this section, with the exception of

the tidewater Fish Crow, the arctic Gyrfalcon, and the southerly Black Vulture, may occur, at some season, almost anywhere in the area covered.

Even after all this, do not be disturbed if you remain uncertain as to the identity of some hawks you see. The most experienced bird students have the same difficulty.

The page number immediately following each bird name in the key to the perched birds refers to the page on which the bird may be seen in flight.

Key to Hawks, Eagles, Vultures, Crows, and Raven (PERCHED)

	LENGTH (INCHES)	PAGE
JET BLACK THROUGHOUT (3 birds)		
Fish crow p. 299	17	271
American Crow p. 299	20	271
Common Raven p. 300	26	272
UPPERPARTS BLACK OR BLACKISH BROWN (7)		
Rough-legged Hawk,		
Black Phase p. 300	22	273
Gyrfalcon, Black Phase	22	273
Osprey p. 316	23	274
Black Vulture p. 301	24	274
Turkey Vulture p. 301	30	275
Golden Eagle, Adult p. 302	30	275
Bald Eagle, Immature p. 303	32	276
UPPERPARTS STEEL-BLUE OR BLUISH GRAY (6)		
Merlin,		
Adult Male p. 307	11	277
Sharp-shinned Hawk,		
Adult Male p. 304	12	277
Cooper's Hawk,		
Adult Male p. 304	17	278
Northern Harrier,		
Adult Male p. 314	18	278
Peregrine Falcon,		
Adult Male p. 306	19	279
Northern Goshawk,		
Adult Male p. 313	22	279

UPPERPARTS CHESTNUT-CROSS-BARRED (2)
Underbody Light-Buff-Spotted (1)

American Kestrel,
Adult Male   p. 313   9   280

Underbody Streaked Lengthwise (1)

American Kestrel, Adult Female
and Immature   p. 306   9–10   280

UPPERPARTS BROWN, GENERALLY MOTTLED (16)
Underbody Buffy-Barred Crosswise (2)

Broad-winged Hawk, Adult
p. 305   16   281
Red-shouldered Hawk,
Adult   p. 305   20   281

Underbody Streaked Lengthwise (9)

Merlin, Adult Female
and Immature   p. 307   11   282
Sharp-shinned Hawk,
Immature   p. 308   12   282
Broad-winged Hawk,
Immature   p. 309   16   283
Cooper's Hawk, Immature p. 308 17   283
Peregrine Falcon,
Immature   p. 310   19   284
Red-shouldered Hawk,
Immature   p. 309   20   284
Northern Harrier, Adult Female
p. 311   21   285
Northern Goshawk,
Immature   p. 310   22   285
Gyrfalcon, Immature   23   286

Breast Only Streaked Lengthwise, Belly Black or Blackish (2)

Rough-legged Hawk, Adult p. 311 22   286

268

Breast Only Streaked Lengthwise,
Belly Black or Blackish (cont.)

       Rough-legged Hawk,
          Immature   p. 312   22   287

Underbody Bright Brown, Unstreaked,
Except for Narrow Chest Band (1)

       Northern Harrier, Immature
          p. 312   18–21   287

Breast and Belly White, Top
of Tail Red (1)

       Red-tailed Hawk, Adult p. 315 22   288

Breast and Belly Whitish,
Top of Tail Gray (1)

       Red-tailed Hawk, Immature
          p. 315   22   288

WHITE RUMP (3)
Upperparts Bluish Gray, Underparts
Light Gray (1)

       Northern Harrier,
          Adult Male p. 314   18   289

Upperparts Brown, Underparts
Light Buff, Heavily Streaked (1)

       Northern Harrier,
          Adult Female p. 311   21   289

Upperparts Brown, Underparts Bright Unstreaked
Buff with Narrow Streaked Neck Band (1)

       Northern Harrier,
          Immature p. 312   18–21   290

WHITE AREA BASE OF TAIL (3)
Breast Only Streaked Lengthwise, Belly Blackish (2)

Rough-legged Hawk,
    Adult p. 311   22   291

Rough-legged Hawk,
    Immature p. 312   22   291

Body Black (1)

Rough-legged Hawk,
    Black Phase p. 300   22   292

WHITE HEAD, NECK, AND TAIL (1)

Bald Eagle, Adult p. 320   32   293

MAINLY WHITE (1)

Gyrfalcon, White Phase,
    Mature p. 321   22   294
    (There is also a grayish-white
    phase, not illustrated)

Jet Black Throughout

FISH CROW

Solid black

AMERICAN CROW

Solid black

Jet Black Throughout

COMMON RAVEN

Solid black

Upperparts Black or Blackish Brown

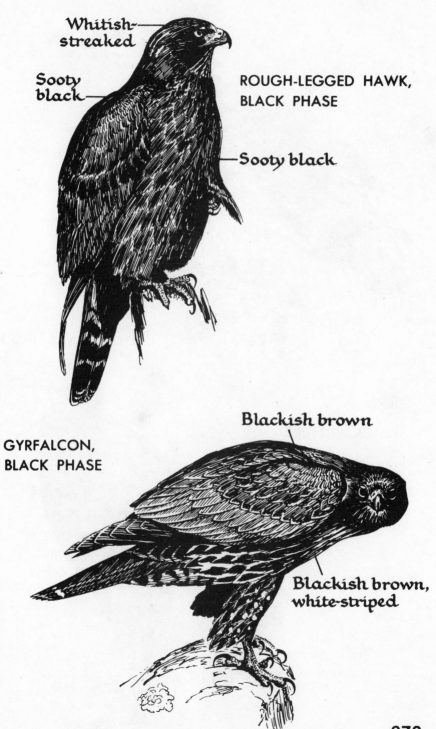

Whitish-streaked

Sooty black

ROUGH-LEGGED HAWK,
BLACK PHASE

Sooty black

GYRFALCON,
BLACK PHASE

Blackish brown

Blackish brown,
white-striped

273

Upperparts Black or Blackish Brown

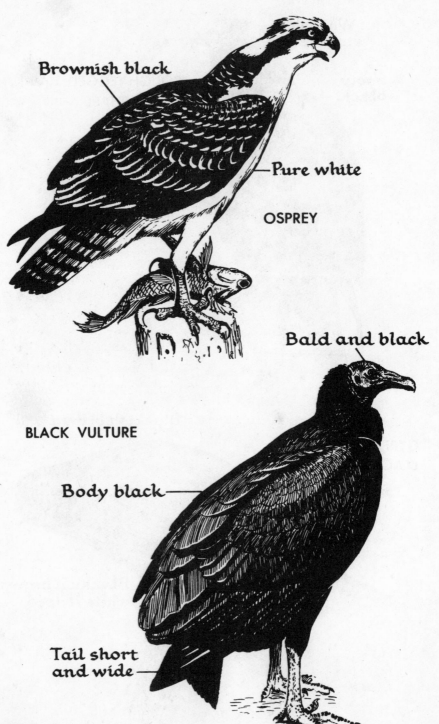

Brownish black

Pure white

OSPREY

Bald and black

BLACK VULTURE

Body black

Tail short
and wide

Upperparts Black or Blackish Brown

Bald and red

TURKEY VULTURE

Body
rusty black

Golden

GOLDEN EAGLE, ADULT

Body blackish
brown

Upperparts Black or Blackish Brown

Body dull black

BALD EAGLE, IMMATURE

MERLIN, ADULT MALE

Upper parts steel-blue

Whitish

Heavily dark-streaked on buff

Black

SHARP-SHINNED HAWK, ADULT MALE

Blue-gray

Rusty-barred crosswise on white

Long tail

White

Squarish

Upperparts Steel-Blue or Bluish Gray

Blackish ——————

Blue-gray ——————

COOPER'S HAWK,
ADULT MALE

Rusty-barred crosswise

NORTHERN HARRIER, ADULT MALE

Bluish gray ——————

Smoke-gray

Light buff barring on white

White

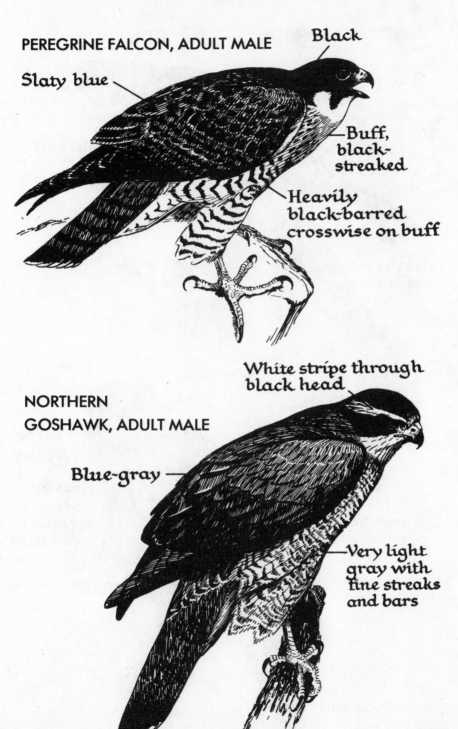

PEREGRINE FALCON, ADULT MALE

Black

Slaty blue

Buff, black-streaked

Heavily black-barred crosswise on buff

White stripe through black head

NORTHERN GOSHAWK, ADULT MALE

Blue-gray

Very light gray with fine streaks and bars

Upperparts Chestnut-Cross-Barred
Underbody Light-Buff-Spotted

AMERICAN KESTREL, ADULT MALE — Blue

Bright-chestnut-barred

Light buff

Wing shoulders blue

Whitish

Bright chestnut

Underbody Streaked Lengthwise

AMERICAN KESTREL,
ADULT FEMALE
AND IMMATURE

Throat white

Heavily buff-streaked on whitish

Dark-chestnut-barred

White

Dark chestnut

280

Upperparts Brown, Generally Mottled
Underbody Buffy-Barred Crosswise

Dark brown

BROAD-WINGED HAWK, ADULT

Brownish-buff-barred on white

Broad white bands

Streaked buff and brown
White streaks

RED-SHOULDERED HAWK, ADULT

Dark reddish brown mottled with white

Bright reddish buff

Shoulders chestnut

Light buff

Narrow white bands

Upperparts Brown, Generally Mottled
Underbody Streaked Lengthwise

Dark brown

MERLIN,
ADULT FEMALE
AND IMMATURE

Buffy,
heavily streaked
with dark brown

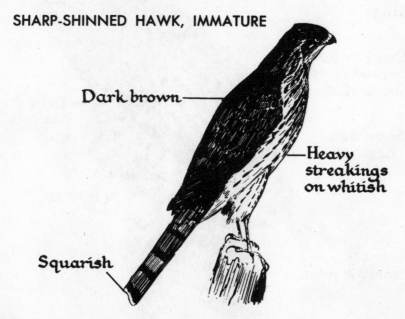

SHARP-SHINNED HAWK, IMMATURE

Dark brown

Heavy
streakings
on whitish

Squarish

Upperparts Brown, Generally Mottled
Underbody Streaked Lengthwise

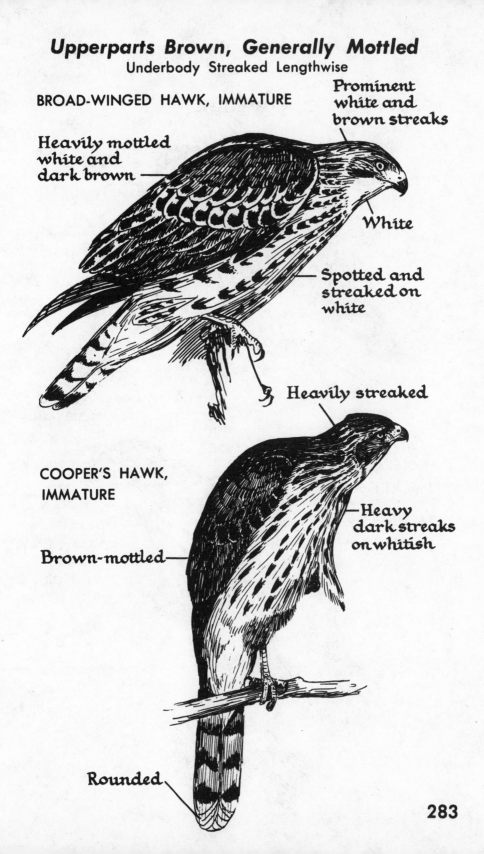

BROAD-WINGED HAWK, IMMATURE

Prominent white and brown streaks

Heavily mottled white and dark brown

White

Spotted and streaked on white

Heavily streaked

COOPER'S HAWK, IMMATURE

Heavy dark streaks on whitish

Brown-mottled

Rounded

Upperparts Brown, Generally Mottled
Underbody Streaked Lengthwise

PEREGRINE FALCON, IMMATURE

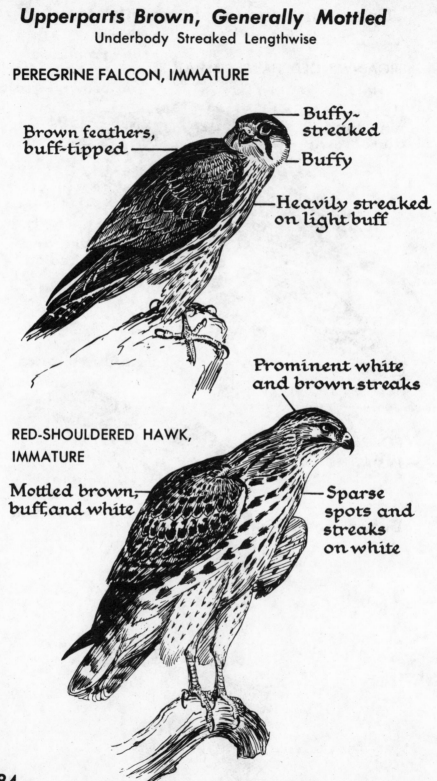

Brown feathers, buff-tipped

Buffy-streaked

Buffy

Heavily streaked on light buff

Prominent white and brown streaks

RED-SHOULDERED HAWK, IMMATURE

Mottled brown, buff, and white

Sparse spots and streaks on white

Upperparts Brown, Generally Mottled
Underbody Streaked Lengthwise

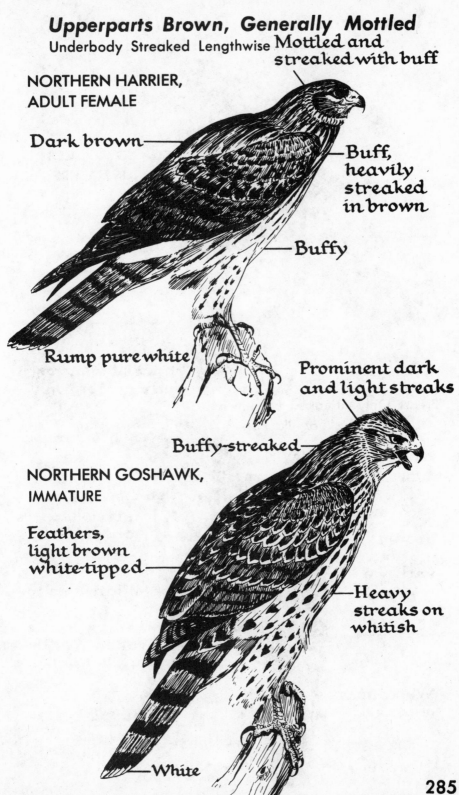

Mottled and streaked with buff

NORTHERN HARRIER, ADULT FEMALE

Dark brown

Buff, heavily streaked in brown

Buffy

Rump pure white

Prominent dark and light streaks

Buffy-streaked

NORTHERN GOSHAWK, IMMATURE

Feathers, light brown white-tipped

Heavy streaks on whitish

White

Upperparts Brown, Generally Mottled
Underbody Streaked Lengthwise

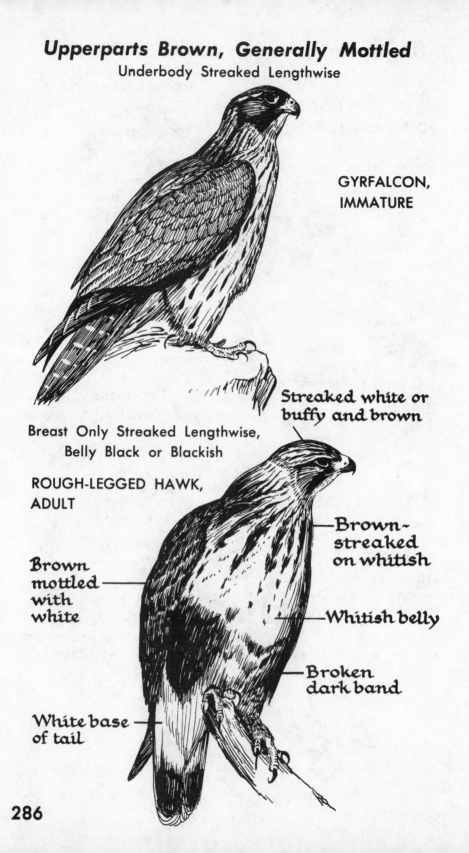

GYRFALCON,
IMMATURE

Streaked white or
buffy and brown

Breast Only Streaked Lengthwise,
Belly Black or Blackish

ROUGH-LEGGED HAWK,
ADULT

Brown-
streaked
on whitish

Brown
mottled
with
white

Whitish belly

Broken
dark band

White base
of tail

Upperparts Brown, Generally Mottled

Breast Only Streaked Lengthwise, Belly Black or Blackish

ROUGH-LEGGED HAWK, IMMATURE,

Feathers,
dark brown,
buff-edged

Buff,
brown-
streaked

Buffy,
heavily streaked

Blackish brown

White

Underbody Bright Brown, Unstreaked,
Except for Narrow Chest Band

NORTHERN HARRIER,
IMMATURE

Mottled and
streaked with
light buff

Dark brown
streaked and
mottled
with buff

Dark-
streaked
band

Clear brown,
unstreaked

Pure white rump

Upperparts Brown, Generally Mottled
Breast and Belly White, Top of Tail Red

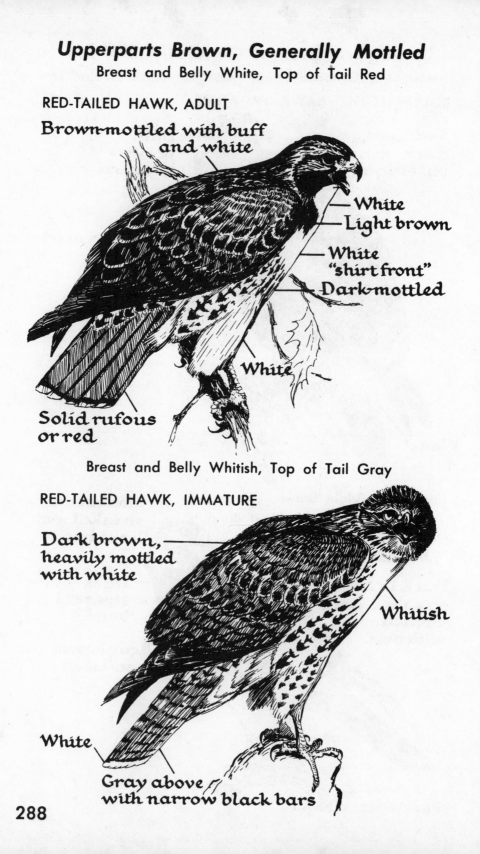

RED-TAILED HAWK, ADULT

Brown-mottled with buff and white

White
Light brown

White "shirt front"
Dark-mottled

White

Solid rufous or red

Breast and Belly Whitish, Top of Tail Gray

RED-TAILED HAWK, IMMATURE

Dark brown, heavily mottled with white

Whitish

White

Gray above with narrow black bars

White Rump

Upperparts Bluish Gray, Underparts Light Gray

NORTHERN HARRIER, ADULT MALE

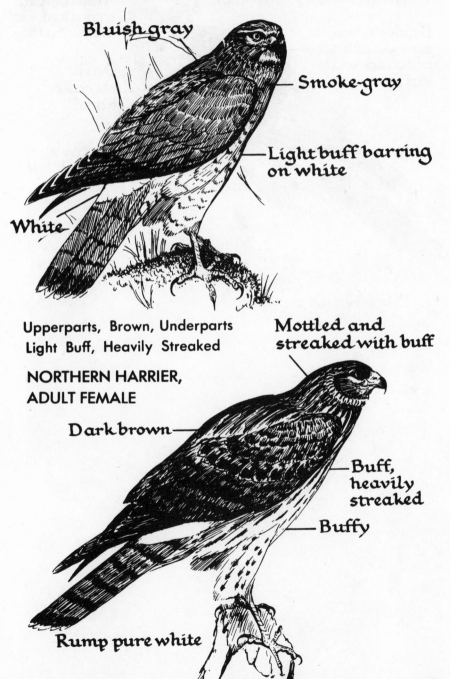

Bluish gray

Smoke-gray

Light buff barring on white

White

Upperparts, Brown, Underparts Light Buff, Heavily Streaked

NORTHERN HARRIER, ADULT FEMALE

Mottled and streaked with buff

Dark brown

Buff, heavily streaked

Buffy

Rump pure white

White Rump

Upperparts Brown, Underparts Bright Unstreaked Buff with Narrow Streaked Neck Band

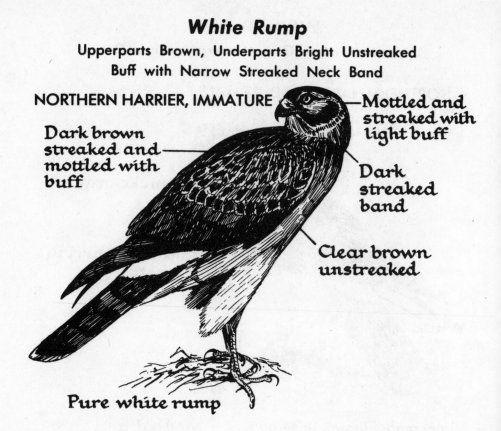

NORTHERN HARRIER, IMMATURE

Mottled and streaked with light buff

Dark streaked band

Dark brown streaked and mottled with buff

Clear brown unstreaked

Pure white rump

White Area Base of Tail
Breast Only Streaked Lengthwise, Belly Blackish

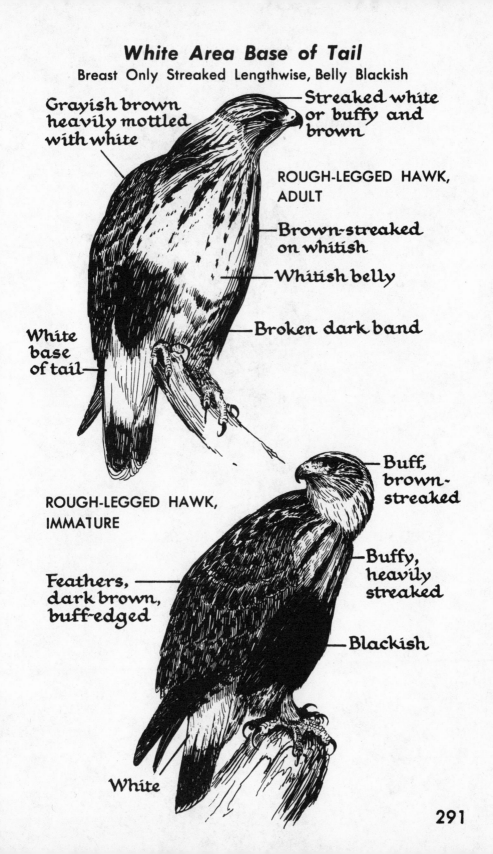

Grayish brown heavily mottled with white

Streaked white or buffy and brown

ROUGH-LEGGED HAWK, ADULT

Brown-streaked on whitish

Whitish belly

Broken dark band

White base of tail

ROUGH-LEGGED HAWK, IMMATURE

Buff, brown-streaked

Buffy, heavily streaked

Feathers, dark brown, buff-edged

Blackish

White

White Area Base of Tail
Body Black

Whitish-streaked—

Sooty black—

—Sooty black

ROUGH-LEGGED HAWK, BLACK PHASE

White Head, Neck, and Tail

White

Brownish
black

White

BALD EAGLE, ADULT

Body generally pure white with light brown markings

GYRFALCON,
WHITE PHASE

Key to Hawks, Eagles, Vultures, Crows, and Raven

AS SEEN *IN FLIGHT* FROM BELOW

PAGE

JET BLACK THROUGHOUT (3 birds)

Fish Crow	299
American Crow	299
Common Raven	300

MOSTLY BLACK OR BLACKISH BROWN (7)

Rough-legged Hawk, Black Phase	300
Black Vulture	301
Turkey Vulture	301
Golden Eagle, Adult	302
Golden Eagle, Immature	302
Bald Eagle, Adult	303
Bald Eagle, Immature	303

UNDERBODY BARRED RUSTY OR DUSKY CROSSWISE (5)

Sharp-shinned Hawk, Adult	304
Cooper's Hawk, Adult	304
Broad-winged Hawk, Adult	305
Red-shouldered Hawk, Adult	305
Peregrine Falcon, Adult	306

UNDERBODY RUSTY- OR DUSKY-STREAKED LENGTHWISE (10)

American Kestrel, Adult Female and Immature	306
Merlin, Adult Male	307
Merlin, Adult Female and Immature	307
Sharp-shinned Hawk, Immature	308
Cooper's Hawk, Immature	308

UNDERBODY RUSTY- OR DUSKY-STREAKED LENGTHWISE (cont.)

Broad-winged Hawk, Immature   309

Red-shouldered Hawk, Immature   309

Peregrine Falcon, Immature   310

Northern Goshawk, Immature   310

Northern Harrier, Adult Female   311

BREAST BROWN-STREAKED LENGTHWISE, SOLID OR BROKEN DARK BAND ACROSS BELLY (2)

Rough-legged Hawk, Adult   311

Rough-legged Hawk, Immature   312

SOLID BROWN, UNSTREAKED EXCEPT FOR NARROW BREAST BAND (1)

Northern Harrier, Immature   312

UNDERBODY BUFF AND WHITE WITH SMALL BLACK SPOTS (1)

American Kestrel, Adult Male   313

UNDERBODY LIGHT GRAY, FINELY STREAKED AND BARRED (1)

Northern Goshawk, Adult   313

CONSPICUOUS WHITE MARKINGS (17)
White Undertail Coverts (2)

Sharp-shinned Hawk (see pages 304 and 308)

Cooper's Hawk (see pages 304 and 308)

White Prominent on Underbody and Wings (4)

Northern Harrier, Adult Male   314

Red-tailed Hawk, Immature   315

Red-tailed Hawk, Adult   315

Osprey   316

CONSPICUOUS WHITE MARKINGS (cont.)

White Mainly under Wings (8)

Broad-winged Hawk, Immature	316
Broad-winged Hawk, Adult	317
Red-shouldered Hawk, Immature	317
Rough-legged Hawk, Adult	318
Rough-legged Hawk, Immature	318
Rough-legged Hawk, Black Phase	319
Black Vulture	319
Golden Eagle, Immature	320

White Head, Neck, and Tail (1)

Bald Eagle, Adult	320

All White (1)

Gyrfalcon, White Phase	321

White Rump (1)

Although invisible from below, this white rump is conspicuous in the low-flying Northern Harriers from almost any angle (see pages 311, 312, and 314).

Note

FOR the sake of clarity of detail in silhouette and in feather pattern on the underparts of the hawks, eagles, vultures, crows, and raven, all the flight patterns have been drawn to the same size. In each case, however, the average wingspread is given in feet and inches, and below the name of each hawk in flight is a line showing *relative* wingspread. For further indication of size, note that these same birds in the perched section are drawn to scale on each page of drawings, thus providing proper comparisons.

Hawks, Eagles, Vultures, Crows, and Raven

As seen *in flight* from below
(WINGSPREAD IN FEET)

Jet Black Throughout

FISH CROW 2½ ft.   p. 271

Lives near tidewater. Most easily distinguished from American Crow by smaller size and by voice, which is a short *ock, ock* instead of a drawn-out *caw*. Food: fish, crustaceans, birds' eggs, etc.

AMERICAN CROW 3ft.   p. 271

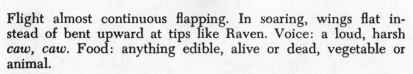

Flight almost continuous flapping. In soaring, wings flat instead of bent upward at tips like Raven. Voice: a loud, harsh *caw, caw*. Food: anything edible, alive or dead, vegetable or animal.

NOTE: Page number of the same bird *perched* follows "wingspread."

299

Jet Black Throughout

COMMON RAVEN   4 ft.   p. 272

In flight, alternates flapping and soaring, when wing tips bend upward. Voice: various; often a harsh croak. Food: anything edible, alive or dead.

Mostly Black or Blackish Brown

ROUGH-LEGGED HAWK, BLACK PHASE   4½ ft.   p. 273

White patch

Upperparts black. Sluggish flight, often perching, flying from tree to tree; also hovers or soars. Food: mostly harmful rodents or insects.

Mostly Black or Blackish Brown

BLACK VULTURE   4¾ ft.   p. 274

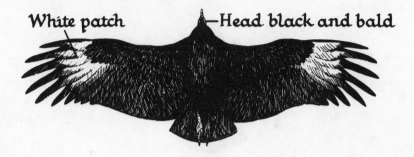

White patch —— ——Head black and bald

Easily identified, even at a distance, by habit of few short flaps and sailing. Food: carrion.

TURKEY VULTURE   6 ft.   p. 275

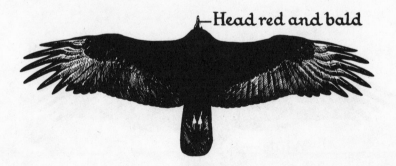

——Head red and bald

Almost always seen soaring with wings nearly motionless. Wings two-toned, lighter in rear. Food: carrion.

NOTE: The rare black phase of the Gyrfalcon of arctic regions is illustrated on page 273, in the *perched* section. It is sooty black above and below, with streaked belly.

Mostly Black or Blackish Brown

GOLDEN EAGLE, ADULT 6–7 ft.   p. 275

Top of head and neck golden. Soars with little flapping. In hunting, often flies low, ready to pounce on prey—mostly rabbits, a few larger animals, and carrion.

GOLDEN EAGLE, IMMATURE 6–7 ft.

White patch on wing

White

Little or no gold on top of head and neck. Will flap to gain altitude, but usually seen soaring at great heights.

Mostly Black or Blackish Brown

BALD EAGLE, ADULT   6–7 ft.   p. 293

Flaps and sails to gain altitude, then soars in great circles high in the air. Food: fish, which it catches on surface of water, not diving like Osprey, or seizes from Osprey, which when chased drops fish.

BALD EAGLE, IMMATURE   6–7 ft.   p. 276

First two years entirely blackish, then underwing becomes grayish.

Underbody Barred Rusty
or Dusky Crosswise

SHARP-SHINNED HAWK, ADULT   2 ft.   p. 277

Rusty-barred

White under tail

Wing wide, short, and blunt

Squarish

Blue-gray above. Sometimes circles high in the air but usually flies low at great speed to overtake and catch birds. Also eats rodents and insects. Female larger than male.

COOPER'S HAWK, ADULT   2¾ ft.   p. 278

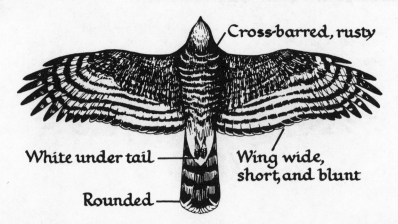

Cross-barred, rusty

White under tail

Wing wide, short, and blunt

Rounded

Bluish-gray above. Replica of smaller Sharp-shinned Hawk. Flight rapid, often through undergrowth to surprise and overtake small birds. Also eats chickens, pigeons, and small mammals. Female larger than male.

Underbody Barred Rusty
or Dusky Crosswise

BROAD-WINGED HAWK, ADULT   3 ft.   p. 281

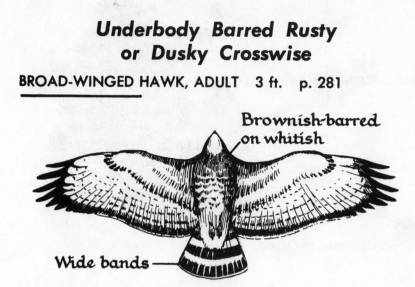

Brownish-barred
on whitish

Wide bands

Upperparts mottled brown, streaked with white. Often seen soaring. Flight sluggish, from perch to perch, usually in wooded areas. Food: largely injurious rodents and insects.

RED-SHOULDERED HAWK, ADULT   3 ft.   p. 281

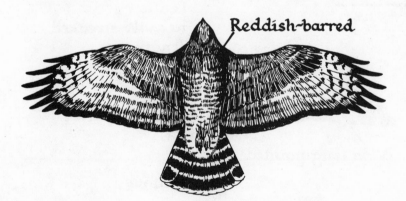

Reddish-barred

Upperparts brown, mottled with buff and white. Soars often. In hunting, flies low and rapidly at treetop level or lower if over marshland. Food: mostly rodents, also frogs, reptiles, and insects.

Underbody Barred Rusty
or Dusky Crosswise

PEREGRINE FALCON, ADULT
3¾ ft.   p. 279

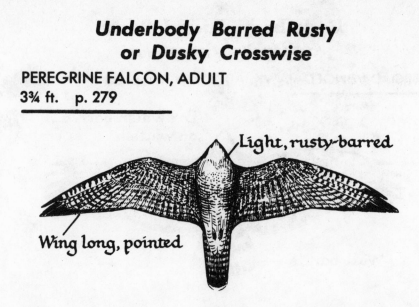

Light, rusty-barred

Wing long, pointed

Head and cheeks black, remainder of upperparts black or bluish black lightly mottled. Perches often. Hunts birds at great speed, attacking from behind in the air.

Underbody Rusty- or
Dusky-Streaked Lengthwise

AMERICAN KESTREL, ADULT FEMALE AND IMMATURE
1¾ ft.   p. 280

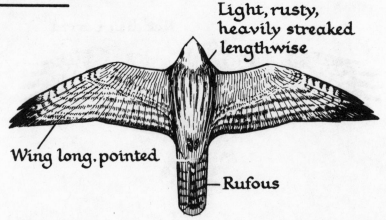

Light, rusty,
heavily streaked
lengthwise

Wing long, pointed

Rufous

Upperparts chestnut-barred. Commonly seen in open areas, on telephone wires or poles, from which it flies down for rodents, insects, etc. Often hovers with beating wings.

306

Underbody Rusty- or
Dusky-Streaked Lengthwise

MERLIN, ADULT MALE   2 ft.   p. 277

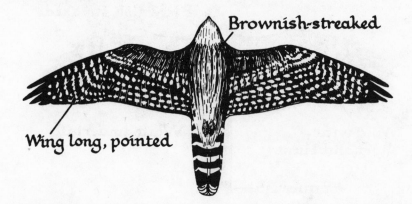

Brownish-streaked

Wing long, pointed

Upperparts slaty blue. Perches on posts or low limbs and catches birds in quick dash, often through undergrowth. Also eats rodents and insects.

MERLIN, ADULT FEMALE AND IMMATURE
2 ft.   p. 282

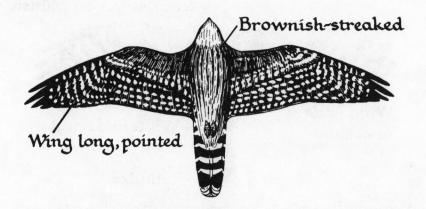

Brownish-streaked

Wing long, pointed

Upperparts dark brown. Habits as above.

Underbody Rusty- or Dusky-Streaked Lengthwise

SHARP-SHINNED HAWK, IMMATURE 2 ft. p. 282

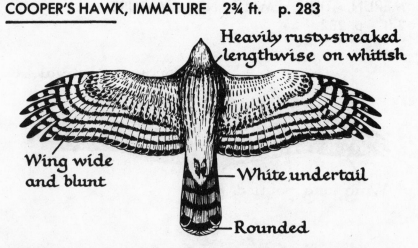

Brownish-streaked

Wing wide, short, and blunt

White undertail

Squarish

Upperparts brown, slightly mottled with black. Sometimes circles high in the air but usually flies low at great speed to overtake and catch birds. Also eats rodents and insects. Female larger than male.

COOPER'S HAWK, IMMATURE 2¾ ft. p. 283

Heavily rusty-streaked lengthwise on whitish

Wing wide and blunt

White undertail

Rounded

Upperparts brown, mottled, head streaked. Flight rapid, often through undergrowth to surprise and overtake small birds. Also eats chickens, pigeons, and small mammals. Female larger than male.

Underbody Rusty- or
Dusky-Streaked Lengthwise

BROAD-WINGED HAWK, IMMATURE 3 ft. p. 283

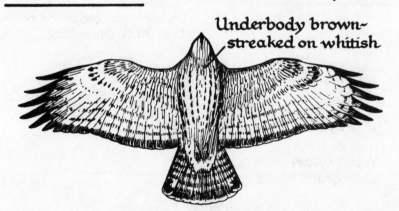

Brownish-streaked
on whitish

Wing wide
and blunt

Upperparts brown, heavily mottled with white. Often seen soaring. Flight sluggish, from perch to perch, usually in wooded areas. Food: largely injurious rodents and insects.

RED-SHOULDERED HAWK, IMMATURE 3½ ft. p. 284

Underbody brown-
streaked on whitish

Upperparts brown, heavily mottled with white and buff. Soars often. In hunting, flies low and rapidly at treetop level or lower if over marshland. Food: mostly rodents, also frogs, reptiles, and insects.

Underbody Rusty- or
Dusky-Streaked Lengthwise

PEREGRINE FALCON, IMMATURE
3¾ ft.   p. 284

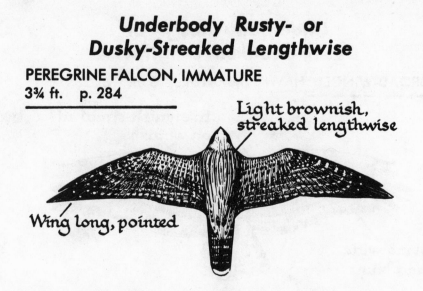

Light brownish, streaked lengthwise

Wing long, pointed

Upperparts dark brown, edged with buff. Head buffy-streaked. Blackish face mark. Perches often. Hunts birds at great speed, attacking from behind in the air.

NORTHERN GOSHAWK, IMMATURE   3½ ft.   p. 285

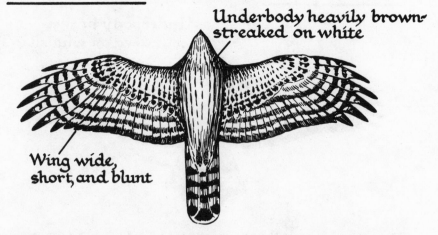

Underbody heavily brown-streaked on white

Wing wide, short, and blunt

Upperparts brown, mottled. Head buffy, black-streaked. In flight, flaps and sails. Attacks prey, bird or mammal, in swift drive from cover. Food: lemmings, ptarmigan, game birds and other animals, and chickens if in settled country.

Underbody Rusty- or Dusky-Streaked Lengthwise

NORTHERN HARRIER, ADULT FEMALE 4 ft. p. 289

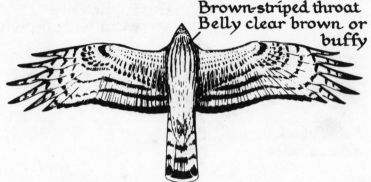

Brown-striped throat
Belly clear brown or
buffy

White rump. Remainder of upperparts mottled dark brown and streaked with buff. Flies very low over open marshes and fields, feeding largely on meadow mice and rats, also frogs, small snakes, and occasionally birds.

Breast Brown-Streaked Lengthwise, Solid or Broken Dark Band across Belly

ROUGH-LEGGED HAWK, ADULT 4½ ft. p. 286

Heavy brown streakings
on whitish underbody

Top of head and neck buffy to white, heavily streaked; remainder dark brown, lightly mottled with white. Base of tail white. Flight sluggish, mostly at dusk, low over marshy or open land, often perching at low elevation. Both soars and hovers. Food: largely destructive rodents.

Breast Brown-Streaked Lengthwise, Solid or Broken Dark Band across Belly

ROUGH-LEGGED HAWK, IMMATURE   4½ ft.   p. 287

Buffy, heavily streaked with brown

Solid black band across belly

Top of head and neck buff with thin dark streaks above and heavy streaks below. Remainder of upperparts brown, mottled with buff. White area at base of tail. Habits and food as above.

Solid Brown, Unstreaked Except for Narrow Breast Band

NORTHERN HARRIER, IMMATURE   3⅓—4 ft.   p. 290

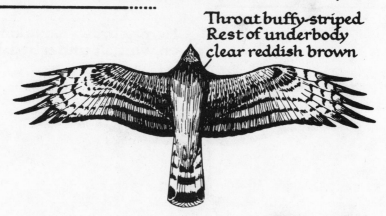

Throat buffy-striped
Rest of underbody clear reddish brown

Base of tail white, remainder of upperparts dark brown, mottled and streaked with buff. Flies very low, feeding largely on meadow mice and rats, also frogs, small snakes, and occasionally birds.

Underbody Buff and White
with Small Black Spots

AMERICAN KESTREL, ADULT MALE 1¾ ft. p. 280

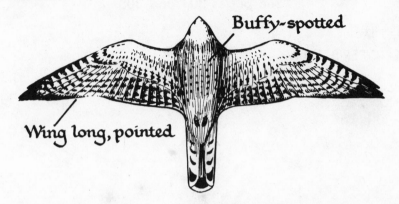

Buffy-spotted

Wing long, pointed

Top of head and wing shoulders blue. Back chestnut-barred. Tail chestnut, black-tipped. Commonly seen on telephone wires or poles, from which it flies down for rodents, insects, etc. Often hovers with beating wings.

Underbody Light Gray, Finely Streaked
and Barred

NORTHERN GOSHAWK, ADULT 3½ ft. p. 279

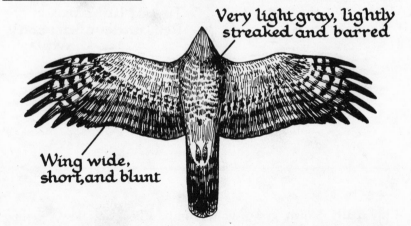

Very light gray, lightly streaked and barred

Wing wide, short, and blunt

Top of head black, cut by white line above eye. Remainder of upperparts blue-gray. In flight, flaps and sails. Attacks prey, bird or mammal, in swift drive from cover. Food: lemmings, ptarmigan, game birds and other animals, and chickens if in settled country.

Conspicuous White Markings

White Undertail Coverts

SHARP-SHINNED HAWK
      See pages 304 and 308

COOPER'S HAWK
      See pages 304 and 308

White Prominent on Underbody and Wings
NORTHERN HARRIER, ADULT MALE 3½ ft. p. 278

Throat light gray
Remainder underbody
whitish

Upperparts bluish gray, white rump. Flies very low, feeding largely on meadow mice and rats, also frogs, small snakes, and occasionally birds.

NOTE: As white often is the most conspicuous feature on many hawks, eagles, and the Black Vulture, several drawings are repeated in this "white markings" section for ease of reference.

Conspicuous White Markings

White Prominent on Underbody and Wings

RED-TAILED HAWK, IMMATURE 4½ ft. p. 288

Gray, finely barred above and below —

Upperparts brown, heavily mottled with white. Top of tail gray, narrowly barred. In flight, often soars. Frequently perches on elevated spots. Food: mostly injurious rodents, a few birds.

RED-TAILED HAWK, ADULT 4½ ft. p. 288

White "shirt front"

Grayish below, — red above

Upperparts brown, mottled with buff and white. Flight and food as in Immature above. Red upperside of tail seen as hawk veers in soaring.

315

Conspicuous White Markings

White Prominent on Underbody and Wings

OSPREY   5 ft.   p. 274

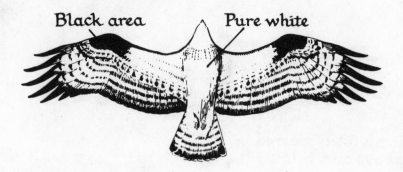

Black area   Pure white

Upperparts mostly black. Black patch through white head. Follows shores of large bodies of water, catching fish by diving from air.

White Mainly under Wings

BROAD-WINGED HAWK, IMMATURE   3 ft.   p. 283

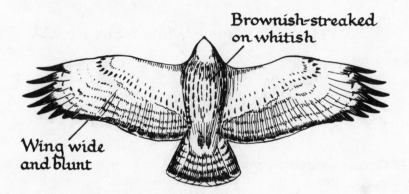

Brownish-streaked on whitish

Wing wide and blunt

Upperparts brown, head streaked with white, back mottled, tail with broad white bands. Flight sluggish, from perch to perch, usually in wooded areas. Food: largely injurious rodents and insects.

Conspicuous White Markings

White Mainly under Wings

BROAD-WINGED HAWK, ADULT   3 ft.   p. 281

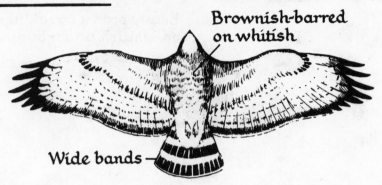

Brownish-barred on whitish

Wide bands

Upperparts mottled brown, streaked with white. Often seen soaring. Flight sluggish, from perch to perch, usually in wooded areas. Food: largely injurious rodents and insects.

RED-SHOULDERED HAWK, IMMATURE   3½ ft.   p. 284

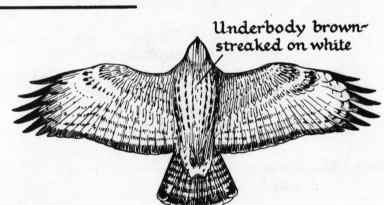

Underbody brown-streaked on white

Upperparts brown, head streaked with white, back mottled with buff and white. Soars often. In hunting, flies low and rapidly at treetop level or lower if over marshland. Food: mostly rodents, also frogs, reptiles, and insects.

317

Conspicuous White Markings

White Mainly under Wings

ROUGH-LEGGED HAWK, ADULT   4½ ft.   p. 286

Heavy brown streakings on whitish underbody

Top of head and neck light buffy to white, heavily streaked; remainder dark brown, lightly mottled with white. Base of tail white. Flight sluggish, mostly at dusk, low over marshy land, often perching at low elevation. Both soars and hovers. Food: largely destructive rodents.

ROUGH-LEGGED HAWK, IMMATURE   4½ ft.   p. 287

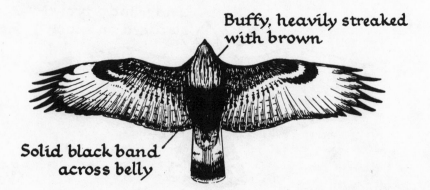

Buffy, heavily streaked with brown

Solid black band across belly

Top of head and neck buff with thin dark streaks above and heavy streaks below. Remainder of upperparts brown, mottled with buff. White area at base of tail. Habits and food same as Mature.

Conspicuous White Markings

White Mainly under Wings

ROUGH-LEGGED HAWK, BLACK PHASE   4½ ft.   p. 273

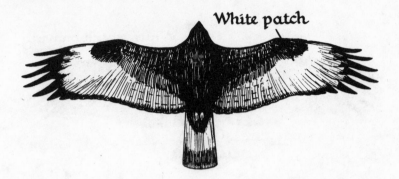

White patch

Upperparts black. Sluggish flight, often perching, flying from tree to tree; also hovers or soars. Food: mostly harmful rodents or insects.

BLACK VULTURE   4¾ ft.   p. 274

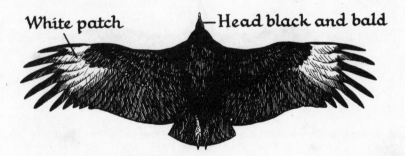

White patch

Head black and bald

Upperparts black except for white area near wing tips. Easily identified even at a distance by habit of few short flaps and sailing. Food: carrion.

Conspicuous White Markings

White Mainly under Wings

GOLDEN EAGLE, IMMATURE 6–7 ft.

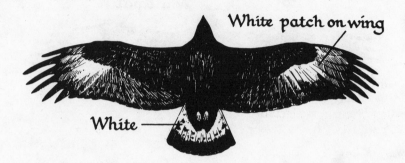

White patch on wing

White

Upperparts blackish brown. Little or no gold on top of head and neck. Will flap to gain altitude, but usually seen soaring at great heights.

White Head, Neck, and Tail

BALD EAGLE, ADULT 6–7 ft. p. 293

Flaps and sails to gain altitude, then soars in great circles high in the air. Food: fish, which it catches on surface of water, not diving like Osprey, or seizes from Osprey, which when chased drops fish.

Conspicuous White Markings

All White

GYRFALCON, WHITE PHASE   4 ft.   p. 294

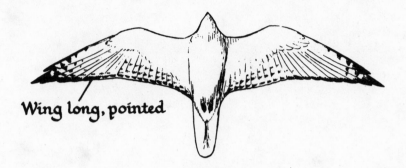

Wing long, pointed

Upperparts white, mottled with light brown. Food: lemmings, other mammals, and land and water birds. Arctic regions, very rarely farther south.

White Rump

Although not visible from below, this white rump is usually conspicuous in the low-flying Northern Harriers from almost any angle. See pages 311, 312, and 314.

Classification of Birds

by Scientific Names

AND

Index

Classification of Birds by Scientific Names

In the 1983 edition of the *American Ornithologists' Union Check-List*, birds in this guide are classified and arranged as follows:

Falconiformes
   Cathartidae: American Vultures
   Accipitridae: Kites, Eagles, Hawks, & allies
   Falconidae: Caracaras & Falcons
Galliformes
   Phasianidae: Partridges, Grouse, Turkeys & Quail
Charadriiformes
   Scolopacidae: Sandpipers, Phalaropes & allies
Columbiformes
   Columbidae: Pigeons & Doves
Cuculiformes
   Cuculidae: Cuckoos, Roadrunners & Anis
Strigiformes:
   Tytonidae: Barn-owls
   Strigidae: Typical Owls
Caprimulgiformes
   Caprimulgidae: Goatsuckers
Apodiformes
   Apodidae: Swifts
   Trochilidae: Hummingbirds
Coraciiformes
   Alcedinidae: Kingfishers
Piciformes
   Picidae: Woodpeckers & allies
Passeriformes
   Tyrannidae: Tyrant Flycatchers
   Alaudidae: Larks
   Hirundinidae: Swallows
   Corvidae: Jays, Magpies & Crows
   Paridae: Titmice
   Sittidae: Nuthatches
   Certhiidae: Creepers
   Troglodytidae: Wrens
   Muscicapidae: Muscicapids
      Sylviinae: Old World Warblers, Kinglets & Gnatcatchers
      Turdinae: Solitaires, Thrushes & allies
   Mimidae: Mockingbirds, Thrashers & allies
   Motacillidae: Wagtails & Pipits
   Bombycillidae: Waxwings

Laniidae: Shrikes
Sturnidae: Starlings & allies
Vireonidae: Vireos
Emberizidae: Emberizids
   Parulinae: Wood-warblers
   Thraupinae: Tanagers
  Cardinalinae: Cardinals, Grosbeaks & allies
  Emberizinae: Emberizines (Sparrows, Juncos, & Buntings)
  Icterinae: Icterines (Meadowlarks, Blackbirds & Orioles)
Fringillidae: Fringilline & Cardueline Finches & allies
Passeridae: Weavers

As stated in the introduction, these classifications are based largely on complicated anatomical characteristics. For example, a standard text on Birds of New York defines the perching birds, Passeres, as follows:

"Oil gland nude; skull aegithognathous; atlas perforated by the odontoid process; I carotid, left; coeca present, small; muscle formula A X Y; no biceps slip or expansor secondariorum" (Beddard). First toe is directed backward and is on a level with the front toe, that is, perfectly incumbent; none of the other toes are ever changed in position; the sternum usually has a forked manubrium and a single pair of notches on the rear; the aftershaft is very weak and downy; the flexor hallucis is wholly independent of the flexor communis; the syrinx is well developed with numerous intrinsic muscles to regulate the voice; the formula of the toe joints is 2-3-4-5; primaries are 9 or 10 in number; the tail usually of 12 rectrices. In reproductive nature they are all psilopaedic and altricial in nature, the young being born weak, helpless and nearly naked, and brooded and cared for by the parents for a long time in the nest.

Those interested in advanced study in ornithology will follow such classifications. However, it should be emphasized that one can spend a lifetime identifying and enjoying birds without any need for this scientific nomenclature and classification, as, thanks to the painstaking work of ornithologists, popular names in the United States are almost universally agreed upon.

The classification and identification of birds has now arrived at a point where even the professionals, when a skin comes into a museum, rely almost entirely on the external characteristics just as the amateur does. Hundreds of thousands of bird skins in museums in the United States are almost automatically identified and classified and put in their proper trays by experts who recognize the bird by size, color, markings, etc. Only after the expert has made his identification, say of a Song Sparrow, does he tuck the skin away in a tray labeled *Melospiza melodia!* (Subspecies have not been included in this guide.)

Index

Blackbird, Red-winged, 43, 157
   Rusty, 47
   Yellow-headed, 45, 185
Bluebird, Eastern, 67, 105
Blue Jay, 69
Bobolink, 41, 165
Bobwhite, Northern, 239
Bunting, Indigo, 67
   Lark, 43
   Snow, 93, 177

Cardinal, Northern, 161
Catbird, Gray, 11, 131
Chat, Yellow-breasted, 189
Chickadee, Black-capped, 7, 25
   Boreal, 31, 71, 93
   Carolina, 7, 25
Chicken, Greater Prairie, 247
   Lesser Prairie, 247 n
Chuck-will's-widow, 111, 235
Cowbird, Brown-headed, 43, 75
Creeper, Brown, 89
Crossbill, Red, 159
   White-winged, 159
Crow, American, 55, 271, 299
   Fish, 53, 271, 299
Cuckoo, Black-billed, 85
   Yellow-billed, 85

Dickcissel, 21, 31, 193
Dove, Mourning, 111, 175

Eagle, Bald, 276, 293, 303, 320
   Golden, 275, 302, 320

Falcon, Peregrine, 279, 284, 306, 310
Finch, House, 157, 161
   Purple, 155
Flicker, Northern, 23, 151, 169, 223

Flycatcher, Acadian, 125, 211
   Great Crested, 115, 207
   Least, 125, 211
   Olive-sided, 131
   Yellow-bellied, 123, 205
   Willow, 125, 209

Gnatcatcher, Blue-gray, 65, 169
Goldfinch, American, 9, 191, 199
Goshawk, Northern, 279, 285, 310, 313
Grackle, Boat-tailed, 51
   Common, 49
Grosbeak, Blue, 65
   Evening, 191
   Pine, 163
   Rose-breasted, 3, 159, 165
Grouse, Ruffed, 241
   Sharp-tailed, 245
   Spruce, 239
Gyrfalcon, 273, 286, 294, 321

Hawk, American Kestrel, 280, 306, 313
   Broad-winged, 281, 283, 305, 309, 316, 317
   Cooper's, 278, 283, 304, 308, 314
   Merlin, 277, 282, 307
   Northern Goshawk, 279, 285, 310, 313
   Northern Harrier, 278, 285, 287, 289, 290, 311, 312, 314, 321
   Osprey, 274, 316
   Peregrine Falcon, 279, 284, 306, 310
   Red-shouldered, 281, 284, 305, 309, 317
   Red-tailed, 288, 315

Hawk (cont.):
    Rough-legged, 286, 287, 291, 311, 312, 318
    Rough-legged Black phase, 273, 292, 300, 319
    Sharp-shinned, 277, 282, 304, 308, 314
Hummingbird, Ruby-throated, 141, 157

Jay, Blue, 69
    Gray, 141
Junco, Dark-eyed, 129, 169

Kingbird, Eastern, 39, 177
Kingfisher, Belted, 69
Kinglet, Golden-crowned, 131, 143, 179
    Ruby-crowned, 121, 155

Lark, Horned, 17, 95, 185
Longspur, Lapland (Spring), 27, 173
    Lapland (Winter), 103

Martin, Purple, 47, 233
Meadowlark, Eastern, 21, 173, 193
    Western, 21 n, 173 n, 193 n
Mockingbird, Northern, 127, 173

Nighthawk, Common, 109, 233
Nuthatch, Brown-headed, 73
    Red-breasted, 5, 65, 103, 137
    White-breasted, 11

Oriole, Northern, 3, 145, 147
    Orchard, 3, 105
Osprey, 274, 316
Ovenbird, 77, 145, 181
Owl, Barred, 259
    Boreal, 257
    Burrowing, 255
    Common Barn, 259
    Eastern Screech, 253
    Great Gray, 261
    Great Horned, 255
    Hawk, 257
    Long-eared, 253
    Northern Saw-whet, 255
    Short-eared, 253
    Snowy, 261

Pewee, Eastern Wood, 127
Pheasant, Ring-necked, 249
Phoebe, Eastern, 127, 129
Pipit, Water, 79, 171
Prairie Chicken, Greater, 247
    Lesser, 247 n
Ptarmigan, Rock, 243 n
    Willow, 243

Raven, Common, 57, 272, 300
Redpoll, Common, 155
    Hoary, 155 n
Redstart, American, 37, 143
Robin, American, 107

Sapsucker, Yellow-bellied, 35, 149, 207, 219
Shrike, Loggerhead, 19, 139, 167, 175
    Northern, 19, 139, 167, 175
Siskin, Pine, 97
Sparrow, Chipping, 73, 87
    American Tree, 25, 73, 89, 95
    Field, 75, 87
    Fox, 99, 115
    Grasshopper, 91
    Henslow's, 101
    House, 31, 89, 93
    Lark, 23, 95, 171
    Lincoln's, 101
    Savannah, 103
    Seaside, 97
    Sharp-tailed, 101
    Song, 23, 99
    Swamp, 75, 87
    Vesper, 99, 171
    White-crowned, 13, 91
    White-throated, 13, 91
Starling, European, 49
Swallow, Bank, 83, 229
    Barn, 39, 231
    Cliff, 37, 231
    Northern Rough-winged, 83, 229
    Tree, 37, 231
Swift, Chimney, 47, 229

Tanager, Scarlet, 161
    Summer, 163
Thrasher, Brown, 81
Thrush, Gray-cheeked, 81
    Hermit, 79, 115
    Swainson's, 83
    Wood, 79
Titmouse, Tufted, 129
Towhee, Rufous-sided, 5, 107

Veery, 81
Vireo, Bell's, 121, 207
    Philadelphia, 133, 213
    Red-eyed, 135, 213
    Solitary, 121, 209
    Warbling, 133, 213
    White-eyed, 123, 209
    Yellow-throated, 123, 187
Vulture, Black, 59, 274, 301, 319
    Turkey, 61, 275, 301

Warbler, Bay-breasted, 17, 105
    Black-and-white, 41
    Blackburnian, 145
    Blackpoll, 9, 41
    Black-throated Blue, 29, 67
    Black-throated Green, 27,
        141, 183
    Blue-winged, 63, 137
    Canada, 197
    Cape May, 9, 191, 195
    Cerulean, 63
    Chestnut-sided, 107, 179
    Common Yellowthroat, 15,
        187
    Connecticut, 203
    Golden-winged, 15, 29, 179
    Hooded, 27, 183, 201
    Kentucky, 21, 201, 205
    Kirtland's, 197
    Magnolia, 13, 189, 195

Mourning, 29, 201
Nashville, 203
Northern Parula, 63, 203,
    205
Palm, 71, 97, 137, 195
Pine, 197
Prairie, 135, 193
Prothonotary, 143, 185
Redstart, American, 37, 143
Tennessee, 133, 211
Wilson's, 7, 199
Worm-eating, 11
Yellow, 215
Yellow-rumped, 17, 181, 189
Yellow-throated, 5, 15, 135,
    187
Waterthrush, Louisiana, 77
    Northern, 77, 199
Waxwing, Cedar, 19, 71, 139
Whip-poor-will, 109, 233
Woodcock, American, 113
Woodpecker, Black-backed, 39,
    183, 221
    Downy, 33, 147, 163, 219
    Hairy, 33, 147, 167, 219
    Northern Flicker, 23, 151,
        169, 223
    Pileated, 45, 153, 225
    Red-bellied, 35, 149, 221
    Red-headed, 35, 149, 165,
        221
    Three-toed, 33, 181, 223
    Yellow-bellied Sapsucker,
        35, 149, 207, 219
Wren, Bewick's, 119
    Carolina, 119
    House, 119
    Marsh, 117
    Sedge, 117
    Winter, 117

Yellowthroat, Common, 15, 187